MAKING YOUR POINT

MAKING YOUR POINT
A Guide to College Writing

LARAINE E. FLEMMING

Pittsburgh Informal Studies Program

Elizabeth Sommers, Research Consultant

HOUGHTON MIFFLIN COMPANY   BOSTON

DALLAS   GENEVA, ILLINOIS

LAWRENCEVILLE, NEW JERSEY   PALO ALTO

ACKNOWLEDGMENTS

Book and Cover design: Daniel Earl Thaxton
Cover photograph: James Scherer
Photograph, Chapter 1: © David S. Strickler/Monkmeyer Press Photo
Photographs, Chapter 2: © Karin Rosenthal/Stock, Boston
                        © Suzanne E. Wu 1978/Jeroboam
Photographs, Chapter 3: © George W. Gardner
                        © Wide World Photos
Photograph, Chapter 4: © Peter Marlow/Magnum
Photograph, Chapter 5: © UPI/The Bettmann Archive
Photograph, Chapter 6: © David S. Strickler/The Picture Cube
Photograph, Chapter 7: © Roger Lubin/Jeroboam
Photograph, Chapter 8: © Bernard Wolf/Omni-Photo Communications
Photograph, Chapter 9: © Gilles Peress/Magnum
Rupert Brooke, "The Great Lover": From *The Collected Poems of Rupert Brooke* (New York: Dodd, Mead & Company, Inc., 1980). Used by permission of the publisher.

Copyright page continued on page 359.

Printed in the U.S.A.

Library of Congress Catalog Card Number: 85-80770

ISBN: 0-395-35514-1

ABCDEFGHIJ-MP-898765

CONTENTS

PREFACE   ix

CHAPTER 1   THE ROLE OF THE WRITER'S NOTEBOOK   1
Free Writing   2
Collecting Ideas   4
Analyzing the Writing Process   6
Suggestions for Your Writer's Notebook   13

CHAPTER 2   DISCOVERING A CONTROLLING IDEA   16
Narrowing a Topic and Discovering a Thesis   17
  Focused Free Writing   21
  Discovery Questions   23
  Defining a Problem   26
  Combining Methods   27
Deciding on a Tentative Thesis   30
Writing Assignment: Exploring Discovery Strategies   32
Writing Assignment: Telling Stories with a Point   32
Suggestions for Your Writer's Notebook   35
Combining Sentences   40

CHAPTER 3   DEVELOPING THE CONTROLLING IDEA   48
Drafting the Thesis Paragraph   48
  The Role of the Reader   50
  Becoming Your Own Reader   51
Drafting the Supporting Paragraphs   53
  The First Draft   56
  Analyzing the First Draft   58
  The Second Draft   62

Analyzing the Second Draft   65
Final Editing   68
Writing Assignment: Challenging a Traditional Viewpoint   72
Suggestions for Your Writer's Notebook   73
Combining Sentences   76

CHAPTER 4   FIVE USEFUL PATTERNS OF DEVELOPMENT   86

Providing Illustrations   86
Tracing Chronological Order   90
Explaining Cause and Effect   94
Comparing and Contrasting   97
Using Classification   101
Writing Assignment: Tracing Historical Development   108
Suggestions for Your Writer's Notebook   112
Combining Sentences   117

CHAPTER 5   PARAGRAPHING AND THE PARAGRAPH   124

The Importance of Paragraphing   124
The Topic Sentence   130
    The Function of the Topic Sentence   131
    The Placement of the Topic Sentence   132
The Importance of Supporting Sentences   135
The Unity of Paragraphs   138
Writing Assignment: The Summary   144
Suggestions for Your Writer's Notebook   148
Combining Sentences   152

CHAPTER 6   WRITING A COHERENT ESSAY   160

Using Repetition and Reference   160
    Within Paragraphs   160
    Between Paragraphs   162
Limiting Inferences   167
    Within Paragraphs   167
    Placing Information Properly   168
    Between Paragraphs   170
Transitional Markers and Transitional Sentences   173
    Within Paragraphs   173
    Between Paragraphs   176

The Principle of Parallel Form   180
Writing Assignment: Writing a Synthesis   187
Suggestions for Your Writer's Notebook   198
Combining Sentences   203

CHAPTER 7   THE WRITER'S VOICE   210
A Range of Voices   210
The Appropriate Academic Voice   220
Writing Assignment: Composing an Evaluation   228
Suggestions for Your Writer's Notebook   232
Combining Sentences   235

CHAPTER 8   WRITING TO PERSUADE   242
Developing a Debatable Thesis   242
Building an Argument   244
Analyzing Your Argument   246
Anticipating the Opposition   249
The First Draft   250
   Analyzing the First Draft   251
The Second Draft   255
The Final Draft   257
Writing Assignment: Writing a Persuasive Essay   260
Suggestions for Your Writer's Notebook   263
Combining Sentences   265

CHAPTER 9   RESEARCH AND WRITING   272
The Function of the Exploratory Essay   273
The Card Catalog   275
   Making Note Cards   277
   Surveying Sources   278
Indexes for Periodicals   279
Indexes for Newspapers   283
Additional Library Sources   285
Taking Notes   286
Making Use of the Research   289
Paraphrasing and Quoting   293

Documentation   297
    How to Document   297
    What to Document   299
Revising the Research Paper   300
A Model Research Paper   301
Writing Assignment: Writing a Biography   312
Suggestions for Your Writer's Notebook   315
Combining Sentences   317

POINTERS FOR FINAL EDITING   323

Sentence Fragments   323
Fused or Run-On Sentences   326
Pronoun Case Forms   330
Pronoun Reference   333
Pronoun Agreement   335
Dangling and Misplaced Modifiers   337
Essential and Nonessential Adjective Clauses   339
Appositives   341
The Apostrophe   342
Subject-Verb Agreement   344
Wordiness   346
Word Choice   348

GLOSSARY OF GRAMMATICAL TERMS   352
INDEX   361

PREFACE

Making Your Point presents a practical, step-by-step approach to writing essays. Focussing on writing with a thesis, the text explains and illustrates strategies for discovering and narrowing a topic, stating a thesis, and developing and revising a paper. With skills and experience in expository writing, students move to writing persuasive essays and then to a research paper.

Traditional in both content and terminology, *Making Your Point* still incorporates current composition theory. That theory stresses how important it is for instructors to emphasize the exploratory nature of composing, wherein writing and revision go hand in hand. But many students have difficulty with this concept of composition. They cling to the illusion of that first and perfect draft, to the notion that a writer sits down and, in a single moment of inspiration, produces a finished paper. What students need, in order to have faith in the creative power of drafting and revision, is to see this process at work in others. For this reason, *Making Your Point* follows several students through successive drafts of essays that begin as little more than random jottings or skeletal outlines but still become final, finished papers. Given concrete illustrations of how other writers discover what they want to say through the process of writing and rewriting, students will have the confidence to begin drafting, even when they are not sure of what they want to say in every individual paragraph.

But, if I have been influenced by current composition theory, with its emphasis on writing as exploration and discovery, I have also tried to modify that theory to make it practical for an academic setting where students must live with the constant pressure of due dates and deadlines. In *Making Your Point*, students learn very specific strategies for finding a topic, developing a thesis statement, and revising a draft, without losing themselves in an endless series of drafts that do not result in a final paper.

All explanations and models in the text are followed by opportunities for students to write. Immediately following, for example, the examination of a first draft, students write one of their own. In addition, each chapter ends with a carefully selected writing assignment. These final assignments have all been tested with a variety of students, who have found them to be both original and stimulating. Step by step, each of these assignments offers students advice for beginning, organizing, and revising their papers. In short, *Making Your Point* gives students numerous chances to write, and the explanation of how to write never takes precedence over the act of writing itself.

Making Your Point, however, does not ignore the need for writing that takes place outside the constraints of an academic setting. On the contrary, this text assumes that students must have a time and a place to indulge in the kind of rambling, unfocused, and fragmentary writing that they must limit when faced with an academic deadline. For this reason, there are over fifty suggestions for organizing and maintaining a Writer's Notebook, where students can explore the resources of language through the writing of poetry, fairy tales, dialogues, and sketches.

The Writer's Notebook is introduced in Chapter 1, where students are encouraged to use their notebooks for the kind of private experimentation and play that will ultimately fuel their more public efforts. Divided into three sections, the chapter explains the goal of free writing, stresses the importance of an idea file, and shows students how to begin analyzing their own individual writing process.

Chapter 2 describes the purpose of the expository essay and identifies it as the mainstay of academic writing. In this chapter students learn how to use free writing, problem solving, and discovery questions to generate, as quickly as possible, a tentative thesis statement that will initiate their first exploratory drafts. Chapter 2 also offers the first of eighteen sentence-combining exercises. Because research suggests that sentence combining, to be effective, must be a continuing part of any writing course, each chapter ends with exercises for combining and writing sentences that show increasing levels of syntactic complexity. As an additional benefit, the exercises have been designed to give students practice with some essential rules of punctuation, and these rules are further elaborated in the "Pointers for Final Editing" at the end of the text.

Chapter 3 continues the analysis of the drafting process begun in Chapter 2, and at this point students learn how to think of themselves in that very complicated dual role of writer and reader. The focus here is on how to shape that initial jumble of words into a logical piece of prose that can be read and understood by someone other than the writer. Again, student models serve to illustrate the recursive nature of this process.

Chapters 4, 5, and 6 concentrate on less difficult but still necessary points of revision. In Chapter 4, students learn about five methods for developing and organizing essays: providing illustrations, chronological order, comparison and contrast, cause and effect, and classification. Chapter 5 focuses on the paragraph, illustrating the communicative power and efficiency of topic sentences. Chapter 6 outlines ways in which students can help their readers by making coherent connections between sentences and paragraphs.

Given the academic setting that this text addresses, Chapter 7 places limits on the voices students can employ in college compositions, and it avoids what I consider a mistake of many other writing texts, where students are treated as youthful journalists who need to develop a spirited and personal style that will engage their readers' attention. Although I have tried hard not to encourage the pompous and pretentious prose Ken Macrorie in *Telling Writing* calls "Engfish," I have tried to make students more aware of the conventions that govern academic prose, where a breezy or chatty tone, no matter how personally genuine, is seldom desirable.

Chapter 8 introduces the persuasive essay by defining its purpose and comparing its requirements to those of the expository essay. Here too the focus is on the drafting process, and students see how one student progresses from a very skeletal outline to a final paper.

In Chapter 9 my intention is to show students that writing with research is an extension of what they have already learned. Thus students are encouraged to use the persuasive essay written for Chapter 8 as an exploratory or working paper that provides the stimulus for further research. Students learn to find sources and to compare their position with that of the experts, noting similarities and differences that support or undermine their initial statements. Presented as a further development of persuasive writing, the composition of a research paper becomes an act of discovery rather than an exercise in documentation—which is what many students erroneously perceive it to be.

This book is the product of many years spent teaching composition. During that time, I have read thousands of student papers and tried hard to formulate advice that would help my students improve as writers. Their success has given me the confidence to write this book. However, as I say to my students, I offer advice or guidelines for effective writing; I do not offer any hard and fast rules. As the writer, researcher, and critic, E.D. Hirsch has pointed out in *The Philosophy of Composition*, "Probably no single maxim of composition holds for all cases." I believe that, and I hope this text embodies that flexibility of theory and practice.

I would like to thank the following reviewers for their helpful comments on previous drafts of this text:

☐ Kristine F. Anderson, Southern Technical Institute
☐ Domenick Caruso, Kingsborough Community College
☐ Helen Bridge, Chabot College
☐ Alma G. Bryant, University of South Florida
☐ Marlene Griffith, Laney College
☐ Susan Helgeson, The Ohio State University
☐ James S. Mullican, Indiana State University
☐ Joan L. Piorkowski, College of St. Thomas
☐ William H. Pixton, Oklahoma State University
☐ Sandra Roy, University of South Carolina at Aiken
☐ David E. Schwalm, University of Texas at El Paso
☐ Judith Stanford, Merrimack College
☐ M. Beverly Swan, University of Rhode Island
☐ A. M. Tibbetts, University of Illinois

CHAPTER 1

The Role of the
Writer's Notebook

For the most part, the chapters in this book concentrate on explaining what you have to do to produce the clear and concise essays that will meet the written requirements of your courses. This text emphasizes writing to the point, without rambling or digressing. Throughout, it recognizes the constraints of an academic setting, where you have a limited amount of time to use writing for experiment, exploration, and play.

Yet to explore fully the resources of language, you need, at some point, to indulge in just the kind of rambling, unfocused, and seemingly unproductive word play that you have to restrict when faced with an academic deadline. For this purpose, you need a writer's notebook. This is the place where you can explore ideas without worrying whether that exploration will lead to a finished paper. It is the place where you can collect words that strike your fancy—even if you do not immediately use them. It is the place to say the unthinkable without worrying about a critical evaluation. Although at times you may want to share your entries with someone else, you do not have to.

Over time, however, you will find that keeping a writer's notebook is more practical and more productive than you might think at first. It can, in fact, influence your more public and more finished papers. If you make consistent use of your notebook, you will sit down one day to fulfill an assignment and discover that you have begun to feel more confident about your ability to translate thought into language. You will discover that your style has grown more fluid, that your word choice has become more vivid and expressive. The principle here is simple: Writing creates writers. The more you use writing to explore the resources of language, the more those resources will be at your disposal, for whatever purpose you choose.

The following pages offer some general suggestions for starting and organizing your writer's notebook. For the most part, the notebook is your responsibility. But the suggestions given here, and the further suggestions at the end of individual chapters, will help you realize the importance of keeping a writer's notebook.

Free
Writing

Leave one section of the notebook just for free writing—at least ten minutes every day. This is not writing that you plan or organize in any way. Simply sit down and write whatever comes into your head without editing or correcting a thing. Here is an example from one student's notebook:

Laura Kruper

It is time to free write again. I have almost come to the conclusion that I do not like writing. The reason is that I don't get much out of it. I don't get very much satisfaction writing. You could even say that I hate it. When I get a good grade on a paper, I feel satisfaction. But I don't think that the purpose of writing is just to get good grades. However, a good grade on a paper shows that the writing is basically good. Writing is a good skill to have, but as a doctor, why would I need it? I'll just have to write prescriptions, and nobody can read those anyway. What I'd like to know is this: If you are not an English teacher or a professional writer, why do you need to know how to write anyway? I think I am going to call Strunk and White, Skunk and White. That title really expresses my feelings about that book. I can't write for fifteen minutes. I don't have anything left to say. My hand is really unique. The palm is small yet the fingers are long and thin. My nails are flat and curved. There are so many wrinkles on my palm. I love the way some people use their hands. They are so graceful, they move so beautifully. You

can tell a lot about people just from their hands. My sister
calls it body language. My sister used to bite her nails right
down to the nub. She did it all the time. There's a woman in
my class who is always biting her nails. It makes me crazy
just to watch her. I like trees, I like to look at them.
Depending on the seasons, they make me think different
things. When they are fading and brown, I start getting
depressed and cold, like winter had already arrived. But in
spring when everything starts to bloom. I feel the same way,
like I was coming to life. But when the trees are naked again,
I start feeling a sense of loss, a little scared like oh no, it's
happening again and I didn't want it to. Winter I mean. I
don't ski and I hate the winter. I wonder if everybody is so
affected by their surroundings. Like they say, people go crazy
during the full moon. I wonder if that's true. My mother said
that's where the word "lunatic" came from because "luna"
means moon in Italian. Maybe you could control behavior by
controlling the seasons. This doesn't make any sense at all.
It's just stupid nonsense.

In fact, Laura's entry is not nonsense at all. For that one entry raises
some interesting questions, questions that might be pursued in a formal
essay.

1. Just how much hard evidence is there for the idea that the moon
   affects human behavior?
2. What are some of the different ways in which people use their hands
   to express themselves?
3. What is body language and how can you use it?
4. What role does writing play in the professional world outside of school?

Admittedly, free writing does produce a lot of useless material. But
that is not all it produces. Over time you will notice that certain ideas,
phrases, or images appear again and again. These are clues to your
"personal subject matter," to the kind of topics you might pursue in more
polished prose. Sometimes, when you try consciously to think about what
you want to write, nothing comes to mind. This is very often the time
to free write and let your imagination tell you where your interests truly
lie.

Initially, for many students, free writing seems an odd or even silly activity. But with time, that attitude usually changes noticeably. As one student expressed it,

> Paul Martin
> These pages serve as an outlet for feelings that are hard to explain, for ideas that seem crazy at first but take on meaning over time. Things I couldn't write about if I knew I was going to be graded.

Eventually most students discover that free writing offers even more than the intellectual freedom Paul describes. It also gives them a form of confidence. For they discover that they have much more to say than they ever realized. In addition, they experience the pleasure of writing without the pressure of wondering whether their grammar is correct or their word choice appropriate.

Collecting Ideas

Another suggestion is to use one section of your notebook for the more conscious collection of ideas. Here is the place for quotations, fragments of conversation, memories, dreams—for anything that interests you.

I have always liked the term the writer Henry James used for the initial ideas of his stories: "germs." James collected brief observations that somehow begged for further development. These "germs" can take any form, from single words to phrases, sentences, and paragraphs. Here are some samples.

> Pat Fresa
> A man and a woman at dinner. They are all dressed up. They stare around the room and at one another. Is this marriage?

> Marcy Federbusch
> A dog, listening with his nose. (Paul Horgan, Approaches to Writing, p. 95)

> Joe Kelley
> Museums and libraries. Why do I hate them so? I like to read. I like to look at pictures but libraries make me go to

sleep and museums bore me. Five minutes inside one, and I
can't wait to get out.

You can also use this section to collect interesting words, sentences,
or quotes from your reading. This is precisely what the following student
has done after reading Toni Morrison's book *Sula*.

Marcy Federbusch

"But my lonely is mine. Now your lonely is somebody else's.
Made by somebody else and handed to you. Ain't that
something? A secondhand lonely." (<u>Sula</u>, p. 90)

A "secondhand lonely." That's being lonely because you
follow other people's direction rather than you're own. Sula's
friend Nell does that. She doesn't make her own lonely. I'd
rather make my own than get it secondhand. It's better that
way. Who wants to be lonely for somebody else?

This student has done more than just record the words of another writer.
She has also responded to them. Actually, such responses are probably
the most important part of this particular section. Through responding
to what you read, hear, or see, you begin to develop your own unique
perspective or point of view on the world you inhabit.

Therefore, whenever you find an idea that interests or excites you, do
not just record it. Interpret it as well. You can begin by simply paraphrasing,
or restating in your own words, what you have heard or read. This is
one of the best ways to discover whether you have really understood what
you have recorded.

You can also respond by gathering the thoughts or associations triggered
by what you have written down. Jotting down your associations can lead
you in interesting directions. You may, for example, jot down several
examples that challenge what you have written. Or, on the other hand,
you may immediately think of several examples that affirm it, as this
student did in response to a quotation she copied down from F. Scott
Fitzgerald.

Glenda Williams

"The test of a first-rate intelligence is the ability to hold two
opposed ideas in the mind at the same time, and still retain
the ability to function." (F. Scott Fitzgerald, <u>The Crack Up</u>)

Fitzgerald means that you can think two things at the

same time, two things that contradict one another, and you
accept them both. To him that's a good mind. Like loving and
hating somebody at the same time or knowing that
something is both good and bad without trying to make it
just one or the other. I know people like that. They just
aren't all one or the other.

You can also use this section to imitate other writers. When you find
a sentence or passage that you think is particularly effective, for example,
copy it down with different content but similar form.

Basil Williams

"But most of all this little man, barely a hundred pounds and
sadly unfitted for outdoor life, mastered the forest, noting all
things that occurred therein." (James A. Michener,
Chesapeake)
   But most impressive the fat midget, hardly three and one-
half feet tall and physically inadequate for major-league
soccer, mastered the sport, remembering all intricate
strategies for the game play.

Analyzing the Writing Process

Keep one whole section of your notebook just to analyze your own
personal writing habits. Each time you finish a paper, try to discover
something new about your own particular writing process. Ask yourself
which part or parts of that process were easy for you and which parts
were difficult. Was it easy, for example, to discover an idea to write about
but hard to put that idea into words that your readers could clearly
understand?

Use your notebook to compare your papers and to record similarities
and differences between them. Try to answer such questions as "Why
did my first writing assignment need only two drafts while my second
needed six?" What you might discover is that increased drafts are a sign
of your improvement as a writer. As you tackle more complicated ideas,
you probably will need more time and more revision to communicate
your thoughts. But if you do not use your notebook for this kind of
reflection, you could easily interpret an increased number of drafts as a

sign of failure. Part of your notebook should be a record of your growth as a writer, an analysis of where you are succeeding and where you are still weak, at least for the time being.

Along the same lines, use your notebook to keep track of your instructor's comments on your essays. What do they tell you about your writing? What areas do you need to concentrate on? Analyzing critical comments in your notebook can keep you from focusing on the grade and ignoring your reader's attempt to show you how and where you can improve.

You may be one of those many people who feel anxiety whenever they sit down to write. Then use your notebook to discover what causes that anxiety and to explore strategies for handling it. As Laura Kruper once wrote, "My writing is me. When I put words on paper, I put myself on the line to be judged, and if someone doesn't like it, I feel rejected." For Laura, writing a paper became much easier when she realized that her paper could not be equated with her own personal intelligence or sensitivity. Rather, it had to be viewed as the result of her struggle to bring what was inside outside—a complicated battle that all writers fight. For Laura, this realization came about through finding and collecting comments famous writers had made about the difficult process of communication. For example,

> "You don't know what it is to stay a whole day with your head
> in your hands trying to squeeze your unfortunate brain so as to
> find a word." (Gustav Flaubert)

By reading what other writers had written about the struggle to write and thinking about her own struggles, Laura began to see her writing in a different light:

```
When I write, I try to communicate what I think about a
subject. If I fail, it's not that my ideas aren't good, but that
language is so tricky. Putting thoughts into words is hard
work.
```

For Laura, her writer's notebook was crucial in relieving her anxiety about writing.

To help you become more aware of your own writing process, I have included in this chapter a writer's questionnaire. Its purpose is to make you consider in detail your particular set of writing habits and attitudes. After you are finished with your own questionnaire, turn to page 10 and read the one completed by a student whose answers reflect much of what current research has revealed about the habits and strategies of successful writers. Pay attention to those places where your answers differ from hers. Such differences do not mean you should automatically change your own writing habits, particularly if they have been successful. But, if your methods are *not* effective, you might consider trying other strategies of composing.

WRITER'S QUESTIONNAIRE

1. What kinds of people make good writers? Describe what you believe are the basic characteristics of a good writer.

   _____

   _____

   _____

   _____

2. Describe in detail your personal system for writing. Where do you write best? For how long do you write without a break? Do you write best in long sessions or short snatches of time? Do you need specific deadlines?

   _____

   _____

   _____

   _____

3. Imagine yourself in this situation: You are preparing to write a paper for class. You have already jotted down a few ideas, but clearly not enough to complete the assignment. Should you wait until you have all your ideas ready before you write anything? Or should you just start writing in the hope that one idea will produce another?

   _____

   _____

   _____

   _____

4. Check off what you believe to be your problem areas.
   a. I have no talent. I am just not a writer.

b. I have ideas but I can't find the words to express them.

c. I can't organize my thoughts.

d. I can never come up with enough ideas to fulfill an assignment longer than a paragraph.

e. I hate to write.

f. I postpone writing until the very last minute. Then I get so nervous I can't write.

g. All my sentences are the same.

h. Describe any other problem you have that is not listed here.

5. What do you do when you are writing and suddenly discover you have nothing more to say? Your mind has gone blank.

_____

_____

_____

_____

6. When the ideas for your papers are not assigned to you by your instructor, what strategies do you use to discover one?

_____

_____

_____

7. How many drafts do you need before you have a paper that is acceptable to both you and your instructor? Is it safe to assume that your last draft is your best?

_____

_____

_____

_____

8. When you write, whom do you imagine yourself writing for?

_____

_____

_____

_____

9. When you become a really good writer, you won't have to revise so much. True or False?

   _____

   _____

   _____

   _____

10. Describe the kind of writing you like to do best.

   _____

   _____

   _____

   _____

STUDENT RESPONSE (BY MEGAN DONNELLY)

1. What kinds of people make good writers? Describe what you believe are the basic characteristics of a good writer. When I think of a good writer, I usually think of someone who pays attention to detail and can really describe things. But more importantly a good writer is someone who has his own original point of view. They don't just say the expected or the traditional. They try and find their own special point of view. I think too that good writers have a lot of patience and discipline. They don't mind writing and rewriting, over and over again.

2. Describe in detail your personal system for writing. When I write for school, I usually wait until after dinner. I go up to my study and look at the assignment. If an idea comes to me right away, I just outline some of my thoughts, making a real simple list. Usually, whatever I've written, I leave until the next day. Then I go back and see if I still like it or not. Most of the time, I don't. Just a couple of sentences still sound right, and I use them to begin another draft. I keep on doing this until I get a paper I like, even after I have left it alone for a day. I also always give myself deadlines no matter how long I have for the assignment. Even if I have a month, I still give myself a deadline for everything, from first draft to last.

3. Should you wait until you have all your ideas ready before you

start writing? Or should you just start writing in the hope
that one idea will produce another? If I waited until I had all
my ideas, I'd wait forever sometimes. Even when I just have
nothing more than the topic, I start writing. Start writing and
maybe as you get into your first ideas, you'll see new ones
branch off from the original. I force ideas to "pop up" in mind.

4. Check off what you believe to be your problem areas.

   a. I have no talent. I am just not a writer.

   b. I have ideas but I can't find the words to express them.

   c. I can't organize my thoughts.

   d. I can never come up with enough ideas to fulfill an
      assignment longer than a paragraph.

   e. I hate to write.

   f. I postpone writing until the very last minute. Then I get so
      nervous I can't write.

   (g.) All my sentences are alike. They sound boring.

   h. Describe any other problem you have that is not listed
      here.

5. What do you do when you are writing and suddenly discover
   you have nothing more to say? Your mind has gone blank.
   When I draw a blank, I just stop. I don't keep on beating my
   head against a stone wall. It took me a long time to learn to
   do that. I used to keep on trying and trying, getting more and
   more frustrated. But now I take a walk. I copy over my notes.
   I write in my journal or I do anything that will give me some
   kind of break. What I find is that, sooner or later, the ideas I
   need do come, and I don't get so nervous any more if I do go
   blank for a while. One thing I have learned to do is to quit
   while I am ahead. I usually try and stop while I am still hot,
   while the ideas are still coming. Then I just jot down some
   key words to tell me where I left off and I pick up the next
   day. If I stop while I am cold, I dread going back the next day.
   I am already convinced I won't be able to get started.

6. When the ideas for your papers are not assigned by your
   instructor, what strategies do you use to discover one?
   Sometimes the ideas just come to me if I sit and stare out the
   window. Sometimes I just start drafting any old thing about
   the topic. Sometimes I think about a particular problem or
   controversy that could be interesting to write about.

7. <u>How many drafts do you need before you have a paper that is</u> <u>acceptable to both you and your instructor? Is it safe to</u> <u>assume that your last draft is your best?</u> Anywhere from four to five. Sometimes it's my best; sometimes it's my worst. If I get frantic because things are not going right and don't take a break, then my drafts tend to get worse not better.

8. <u>When you write, whom do you imagine yourself writing for?</u> If I am writing for school, I think about what my professors or my classmates would say about what I've said. In particular I try to think about the comments I've gotten on papers before, like "Can you explain or illustrate that point?" And I ask myself if I have explained enough or explained too much. When I write in my journal, though, I just write for me, particularly for me in the future. I want to know twenty years from now what I was like at eighteen, and I don't think my memory is enough. I want to see it in print.

9. <u>When you become a really good writer, you won't have to</u> <u>revise so much. True or False?</u> I think this is definitely false. When I write more, I think more and I get new ideas so I have to revise. Nobody is so good that they can stop thinking, and if you keep thinking, you keep revising. The only time I stop is when I know time is running out, and I can't afford to keep revising and revising. Things can always get better, but you have to be practical.

10. <u>Describe the kind of writing you like to do best.</u> I like to write stories better than essays. For me it is easy to create characters and plots. It's much harder to write essays where you really have to spell out an idea. My instructor keeps telling me that essays can be creative too, and maybe they can. But it is a different kind of creativity, one that doesn't come naturally, at least not to me. When I write a short story, I just see it all in my head. When I write an essay, I don't begin by seeing anything. Piece by piece it comes to me, and it's slow and painstaking. If I had my choice, I would write only stories and descriptions.

Suggestions for
Your Writer's Notebook

SUGGESTION 1

Pick someone or something that has been part of your life since childhood. Write two paragraphs describing how you felt in the past, and how you feel in the present, about this person or object. Use those two paragraphs to define the way in which your feelings about the subject have changed over time. Here is an example by a student.

Paul Snyder

As a child, my favorite food was candy corn, and I never seemed to get enough. Even Halloween couldn't satisfy me. I devised elaborate techniques for eating the stuff. Some I would eat from beginning to end, starting at the triangular tip and ending at the sugary base. Others I would throw casually into the air, letting them land in my wide open mouth.

A few months ago my little brother brought home a trick-or-treat bag half full of candy corn, and I couldn't wait to get at it. But when I did, what a surprise. The stuff tasted like polyurethane, and it had the consistency of old candle wax. It made me feel sick to my stomach. It's just like my father always says, "Things that were great when you were a kid don't always stand the test of time."

SUGGESTION 2

Euphemisms substitute pleasant or polite terms for unpleasant or blunt ones: "underarm" for "armpit," "sanitation engineer" instead of "garbage collector." The word itself comes from the Greek word meaning "to use words of good omen." Make a list of euphemisms you have used or heard. In what kinds of situations do people tend to use euphemisms? When do you find yourself using them?

SUGGESTION 3

If you are one of those people who insists you just can't write, make a list of all the writing you do in one year, in and out of school, including letters, diaries, lists, tax forms, and applications. After you make that list,

look it over and see what number you can insert in the blank in the
following sentence:

"I can't write, but this year I wrote _____ times.

SUGGESTION 4

Try to remember and describe your very first writing experience. What
did you write about? Why did you write and for whom? How did you
feel about what you wrote?

SUGGESTION 5

While you are watching television, look for examples of commercials
that use elderly men and women. When you have at least three or four
examples, write a paragraph describing the image that television conveys
of old age.

SUGGESTION 6

In a wonderful book called *I Never Told Anybody*, the poet Kenneth
Koch tells of teaching men and women in their seventies and eighties
how to write poetry. During the workshops, Koch was impressed by the
many wonderful stories these people had to tell about themselves —
stories that, as the title of his book says, they had never told anybody.

Interview one or two senior citizens. Ask them what they remember
most about their youth, about their relationship with their parents, or
about their courtship and marriage. Spend at least two sessions talking
and taking notes. Then select one incident you find particularly interesting
or moving. Write a one-page paper focused on that incident. To recreate
that moment in writing, use as many specific details as your subject can
remember.

SUGGESTION 7

Imagine the following scene: A well-dressed man and woman are standing
at a bar. After a few minutes they turn and introduce themselves. He
buys her a drink. They talk casually for about five minutes, but suddenly
the situation becomes tense. He tries to take her arm; she pulls it away.
Their voices grow louder. He tries to put his arm around her shoulder,

and she hits him with her pocketbook. At this point, a second man intervenes and hits the first one on the chin. The bartender immediately calls the police. When the police come, all four say it was a misunderstanding. No one meant any harm and no one wants to press any charges.

Write four versions of this incident. Describe how each person (woman, first man, second man, and bartender) would report the incident to the police in order to make it clear that his or her motives were above reproach.

CHAPTER 2

Discovering a Controlling Idea

Expository essays are the mainstay of academic writing. Written to inform, explain, or instruct, they define and develop one controlling idea or thesis. For some assignments, your instructors will provide that controlling idea. For example, you may be asked to "Write a paper describing how the use of computers has dramatically altered the writing process." Here the thesis is given, and you know immediately the intended message of your paper: You want to show your readers how the use of computers has dramatically changed the writing process.

But writing assignments are not always so directed. At times you may be given little more than a topic. For example, you might be instructed to "Write a brief paper on some aspect of white-collar crime." Although this assignment gives you a general topic for your paper—white-collar crime—it says nothing about your thesis. It does not tell you what you should say *about* that topic. It does not define the particular perspective or point of view that you want to explain for your readers.

When you are given an undirected assignment such as this one, you need to develop a tentative or experimental thesis that will focus your search for and selection of information. That first tentative thesis will probably change enormously as you write. Nevertheless, it is a useful focusing device that can save you time and energy.

Faced with an assignment that gives you nothing more than the subject matter, it is easy enough to throw up your hands in despair, convinced that the page in front of you will remain forever blank. But there are, in fact, a number of strategies that can help you narrow a topic and discover your thesis. This chapter introduces several of them.

Narrowing a Topic and Discovering a Thesis

Most of the time, the topics that instructors assign are fairly general. You might be asked, for example, to write an essay concerned with "nutrition," "health care," "sports," or "technology." What your instructors are providing, however, is not the specific topic of your individual paper. Rather, they are suggesting an area to explore or investigate. In effect, they are giving you the widest possible boundaries for your assignment. It is your responsibility as a writer to map out your *particular* piece of intellectual territory.

For example, say you are assigned to write a short paper on "modern architecture" due in one week. Your instructor knows full well that you cannot cover all of the many more specific topics that are included in that one general topic:

- ☐ Building types
- ☐ Architects
- ☐ Building methods
- ☐ Building materials
- ☐ Styles
- ☐ Relationship to surroundings
- ☐ Specific examples of modern architecture

Your instructor does not expect you to discuss all of these different topics in one paper. Rather, he or she expects you to narrow and restrict the more general topic, making it specific enough to be explored within the limits of time and space at your disposal.

To be sure, part of that restricting takes place through the drafting of your essay. For example, you might begin a paper thinking that "the causes of alcoholism" is a perfect topic for a two-page essay and then discover, through your writing, that such a topic is far too large and far too general for the limits of your assignment. As a result, you would place further restrictions on your initial or tentative topic and decide to write about one cause rather than several.

But some of that narrowing process should take place right from the start. It does not matter whether you receive an assigned topic or develop your own. From the very beginning of the writing process, impose some limits on your topic and narrow the scope of your exploration.

Restricting your topic at this stage does not commit you to it no matter what new ideas occur to you. As you begin to explore that topic in search of a thesis, you may well narrow it further. You may change your topic from "sports gear for runners" to "varieties of running shoes." Or you may discover that the topic you initially chose is too *narrow* and decide to expand its scope—from "my cousin's football injury" to "injuries suffered by football players," for example.

For that matter, you may even abandon your first topic altogether as you try to develop it and find you cannot or do not want to take it any further. Narrowing your topic at this point simply provides a focus for your first attempts to discover a thesis. It can be time-consuming and discouraging to spend hours exploring a topic that was much too broad and general for the limitations of your assignment. If you want to avoid wasting time and energy when you write, you should always consider whether you need to make your initial topic more specific.

For example, a student named Joan Amato was asked to write a two-to-three-page paper on any aspect of "health care." The paper was due in one week. In response to that assignment, Joan produced a list of more specific topics. In contrast to the general topic "health care," which loomed large and vague before her, the topics on this list gave her some point of reference.

-- Health insurance

-- HMOs

-- Natural health care

-- Nurse's aides

-- Training for medical personnel

-- Hospitals

-- The quality of health care in America

-- Medical bills

-- Clinics

-- Medicare

Joan now had a number of tentative topics to choose from, but obviously she had to select one. Her next step was to explore those topics from her individual point of view. She asked herself whether she knew more about health insurance or hospitals. She considered which of the topics on her list intrigued or interested her. By asking those questions, Joan realized that she knew much more about hospitals than about any other topic. Using her personal experience and knowledge as a guide, Joan had a tentative topic, "hospitals." She had completed the first preliminary step in the writing process.

As you will see in the next section, that tentative topic changed as she wrote. Nevertheless, it provided an effective starting point for Joan's thinking. That is the major objective of restricting and defining your topic at this stage in the writing process. It gives you an initial point of focus or reference. This is essential, particularly when time is short. Once you have a tentative topic, you can begin your search for an equally tentative thesis. The following sections introduce three methods for making that search both efficient and productive.

The following is a list of topics indicating general areas of exploration for a two-to-three-page paper that is due in two weeks. Under each general area, write down at least three *specific* topics that could be included under that heading. The first one is done for you.

EXERCISE   1

1. Nutrition
    a. nutritional education
    b. nutritional experts
    c. improper nutrition
    d. megadoses of vitamins
    e. nutritional misinformation

2. Music

    _____

    _____

    _____

3. Education

    _____

    _____

    _____

4. The media

_____

_____

_____

5. Social problems

_____

_____

_____

6. The family

_____

_____

_____

7. Unemployment

_____

_____

_____

8. Communication

_____

_____

_____

9. Science

_____

_____

_____

10. Painting

_____

_____

_____

Now examine the list of specific topics you wrote. Circle several topics that you might be able to write about.

FOCUSED FREE WRITING

The method described in this section is already familiar to you; it begins with a more focused form of the free writing that you do in your writer's notebook. You just sit down, think about your topic for a few moments, and start writing. You shouldn't stop until you have nothing more to say. This was the method Joan Amato chose to explore her tentative topic "hospitals."

Joan Amato

Even though you go there to get well, hospitals are terrible places that scare people. No matter how many soap operas might use them as the setting for a romance, nobody I know wants to spend time in the hospital. There's that awful smell like life has been cleaned out by antiseptic. Maybe if hospitals were more homey and not so unfamiliar, people wouldn't be afraid to go there. But they look like space stations. Particularly when you see the doctors and nurses walking around in uniform with those masks on their faces. When my grandmother was told to go to the hospital for tests, she went, but when she got there, she got so scared she didn't stay. She made my cousin take her home. She still hasn't had those tests. I had a friend who used to be a T.V. lady; she told me the really expensive private rooms were like hotels. Maybe that makes a difference. But nobody I know can afford that. When my brother-in-law was in the hospital, I went to visit and I felt sick walking through the halls. I felt short of breath and anxious. When I told him about it, he just laughed, but my brother said he felt the same way. From now on when anybody I know gets sick I am going to call them on the phone and tell them I will do anything to help but I won't visit the hospital. My friends will just have to understand.

Having done this free writing, Joan knew more about her specific topic. Clearly she had a more restricted topic than "hospitals" in mind. She wanted to talk about the "fear of hospitals" that she and others had experienced. But that was still just a topic.

At first glance, Joan did not see that her free writing suggested a thesis for her essay. She believed that what she had written was more appropriate to an informal diary or journal than to an academic essay. What could she tell her readers? "My grandmother got scared when she went to the hospital." But in order to use free writing as a strategy for discovering a thesis, you need to analyze it. You have to know what you are looking for.

When you finish a piece of free writing, it is a good idea to let it alone for an hour or so. Then go back and examine it by posing the following questions:

1. Is there a focus to your writing? Do you come back to one idea more than to any others? Is one idea developed more than others? Is there one sentence you particularly like?
2. If you have concentrated on a personal experience, can you generalize on the basis of that experience? That is, do you know of other people who have had such an experience? Have you seen similar experiences treated in books, plays, or movies?

Using these questions, Joan was able to see more in her free writing than she did at first. Clearly it had a focus. Repeatedly, she returned to her particular fear of hospitals. In effect, she was saying "Even if hospitals are places of healing, I'm still afraid of them!"

But for the most part, instructors in college do not request papers describing your individual experiences. Rather, they are interested in the generalizations you can draw from those experiences. *Generalizations are conclusions about a whole class or group on the basis of a study of its members*. Therefore, when you finish a piece of free writing, you have to think about whether others have shared your experience. First, you can consider whether you have seen the same experience treated in movies or books. You can also talk to other people and try to discover whether you can use your own experience to generalize about the experiences of others. This process is called "decentering"; it emphasizes the writer's need to find a link between the private and the public world.

When Joan thought about her free writing in those terms, she felt free to generalize on the basis of her personal experience. She had already cited other people who felt the same way. In addition, when she talked to her classmates about her reaction to hospitals, she discovered that many of them had had the same experience. Moreover, she had seen a number of television programs that supported her point of view. Although she couldn't overgeneralize and claim that everyone shared her fear—some of her classmates did not—she could make a limited generalization about her own experience. She was ready, then, to write out a *tentative thesis statement. This is the sentence (or sentences) that a writer can use to define the controlling idea of an essay.* It represents the writer's first attempt to formulate, in writing, the message of an essay. Joan's first tentative thesis statement was "Places of help and healing, hospitals still scare many people."

Look through the topics you circled for Exercise 1. Select one and free write on it for at least fifteen minutes. When you are through, take a break. Then go back to see whether you can formulate a tentative thesis statement based on what you have written during those fifteen minutes.

EXERCISE 2

DISCOVERY QUESTIONS

For Joan, free writing on a topic gave her the thesis she needed to get started writing. But if it had not, she could have used discovery questions. With this method, you ask a number of different questions designed to explore different aspects of your topic.

For example, let's say you had decided on "fad diets" as the tentative topic of your paper, but you still did not have a thesis. To discover one, you could ask questions that would focus on the consequences or effects of fad diets. "When people lose weight on fad diets, do they keep it off?" "How many people gain back every pound they lost?" "Have there been reports of people becoming ill because of fad diets that are nutritionally unsound?"

You could also explore your topic through questions emphasizing the perspective of time and change. "In the last year, exactly how many fad diets have been popularized by the media?" "Are those same diets still popular today, or have they been forgotten? "Have fad diets always been part of American culture?" "If I were to look back in magazines published during the nineteenth century, would I find ads for the newest miracle diet?"

Through answering those questions, you could begin to restrict your topic further and discover your tentative thesis. Each of the following thesis statements, for example, is based on an answer to one of the questions cited above.

1. Fad diets can result in a variety of serious disorders ranging from chronic insomnia to heart disease.
2. Within the past year, three different and equally bizarre diets have attracted the public's attention.
3. Studies show that fad diets do not produce long-term weight loss.

Although each individual topic will generate its own set of specific questions, there are five general categories of questions you should keep in mind and have at your disposal.

1. *Questions About Description and Identification.* What are the essential characteristics? What does the topic resemble? If you had to compare the topic to something, what would you choose? Can it be divided into parts or segments? How do the individual parts work together? To what larger group does the topic belong? How is it different from or similar to other members of the larger group to which it belongs? Is the topic better or worse than other members of the larger group to which it belongs? Would everyone describe it the same way, or does it appear different to different groups (men or women, the young or the old)?

2. *Questions About Present and Past Time.* Does the topic change in any way over time? When did it first appear? Does it belong only to this century or to a previous one also? Did it exist for a limited period of time only? If the topic existed in only one particular period, what other events occurred at this time? Is there a relationship? Can the topic be broken down into individual stages or steps?

3. *Questions About Place and Location.* Where does the topic take place or appear? Where is it not present? Under what conditions does it exist? What conditions can endanger it in some way? Who uses it? What do they use it for?

4. *Questions About Source and Origin.* How did the topic come into being? Is there one particular cause or several? Is the origin of the topic known, or is it a mystery? Is one individual responsible for the topic? One particular group?

5. *Questions About Purpose and Effect.* What function does the topic serve? Does it fulfill that function effectively or ineffectively? Does it have value for everyone or only for members of a particular group? Can that value diminish or increase over time? Does the topic have one effect or many? Are all the effects or consequences of equal value? Or is one more important than the others?

Discovery questions like the above are a valuable tool for writing. Not only can they help you further restrict your topic and discover your thesis, but they can also provide you with material for developing it. Once you decide on a tentative thesis, you can look over all the answers you gave to your questions and decide what material you might be able to use in order to explain that thesis. Equally important, discovery questions can help you uncover gaps in your knowledge. For example, you may decide that you are interested in developing a thesis involving the effects of fad diets. Yet your answers to questions concerning the consequences of those diets may well reveal that you need to do some additional research.

Select one of the topics you circled in Exercise 1. Using discovery questions, try to develop one or more tentative thesis statements for this topic.
 Here is an illustration of the procedure you should follow. The topic is "close friendships between teen-age girls."

  1. *Questions About Description and Identification.* What are some of the essential characteristics of such friendships? How would I describe them?

> much emotional intimacy; exclusiveness, more characteristic of females than males; feeling of being "soulmates," best friends; tendency to form private clubs; constant contact; long phone conversations; stream of notes; similarity in dress and behavior; appearance of being like twins; in contrast to males, more sharing of emotions than activities; feelings of "them" against "us"

  2. *Questions About Time.* When do these friendship begin? Do they have a definite starting point?

> begin around the age of thirteen; frequently not of long duration but can last into adulthood

  3. *Questions About Place and Location.* Where do these friendships begin?

> usually develop through school rather than family

  4. *Questions About Source and Origin.* Why do teen-age girls seem to need these close friendships?

> society stresses emotions and feelings in girls, and girls need to share them, to compare feelings; a way of surviving the emotional ups and downs of adolescence

5. *Questions About Purpose and Effect.* What purposes do these friendships serve? Are there any possible ill effects?

> can help develop independence; can also limit individuality, girls can become too nervous about what their friends think

Here are some tentative thesis statements based on the answers to two of the groups of questions.

QUESTION 1: "Close friendships between teen-age girls are characterized by a lot of emotional intimacy and by a need for privacy."

"Teen-age friendships between males are characterized by the sharing of activities while those enjoyed by girls emphasize the sharing of emotions."

QUESTION 5: "The friendships girls share as teen-agers can help them make the first step toward adult independence. They can be a way of loosening a childlike dependence on the family."

"The teen-age friendships many girls form to survive the stresses of adolescence can work against them. In an attempt to please her "best friend," a young girl can forget that she needs to be an independent individual."

Once you have two or three thesis statements, go through the answers to all your questions and look for details that you might use for further explanation. Circle anything you think might be relevant to the thesis statements you have written out. Jot down any other associations that come to mind as you examine your answers.

DEFINING A PROBLEM

Another way to explore your topic is to think about the problems, conflicts, or contradictions that are associated with it in some way. This will be easier to do if you keep in mind a standard definition of the word *problem*: a discrepancy, difference, or contradiction between things as they are and things as they should be.

Imagine, for example, that you had restricted the general topic of "boxing" to the more specific "safety regulations governing boxers." Your next step would be to identify some possible problems associated with that topic. You can do this by asking questions like the following: "What is the purpose of safety regulations for boxers?" "What should these rules accomplish?" One answer would be "They should be preventing boxers from sustaining any serious injury." The desirable state, then, would guarantee the safety of fighters.

Once you can define the desirable state, your next step is to define the existing one with a question like this: "Do the existing safety regulations keep boxers from being seriously injured?" Clearly they do not. In the last few years, there have been several well-publicized examples of boxers seriously or fatally injured. The answers to these two questions reveal a discrepancy, or difference, between things as they are and things as they should be. Given these two answers, it is possible to state the following problem: "At the present time, the safety regulations for boxers are not adequate. They do not protect the athletes from serious injury." That statement of a problem could also function as a tentative thesis statement for your paper.

Thinking about your topic in terms of a problem that needs to be defined or stated is yet another useful way of restricting that topic and framing your tentative thesis statement. This approach to a topic can lead you very quickly to a clear statement of what you hope to demonstrate in your paper.

EXERCISE 4

Using some of the topics you circled in Exercise 1, write out two or three thesis statements that define a problem.

Say you had restricted the general topic "energy" to the more specific "home heating." You would need, first of all, to define some desirable state associated with that topic — for example, "People should be able to heat their homes and stay warm." Then you would need to define the existing state: "For some people, heating their homes is not possible; their bills are just too high." Having defined the desirable state and the existing state with those two sentences, you would have a tentative thesis statement like this: "Because of the high cost of energy, many people cannot afford to heat their homes properly."

COMBINING METHODS

When you are trying to discover a tentative thesis statement, keep in mind that you do not have to rely on just one method. You do not have to use *just* free writing, *just* discovery questions, or *just* defining a problem.

You can use one method or a combination of two. And to arrive at a thesis statement that satisfies you, you may even have to use all three. They are presented individually here merely to simplify the explanations. There is no reason why you have to maintain that artificial separation. Here, in one student's free writing on the topic of relationships between parents and teen-agers, is an example of the effective use of more than one technique. First this student tried free writing.

Glenda Williams

Being a parent when your kid is a teen-ager is an almost impossible task, a task I just can't seem to master. Whatever I do it's wrong. When my son was little, he thought everything I said or did was wonderful, the perfect mother that was me, but now we can't talk without screaming at one another. We can't communicate at all. We can't communicate. He so obviously thinks I am an idiot who has no idea of how the world works. He has all the answers. I have none. On television they talk about communications breaking down between countries well in my house communications have broken down between mother and son, and I can't say I have any idea how to mend them. I don't have any Secretary of State to carry my messages to the other country. Even if I did, I don't think it would do much good. If anybody arrived with my messages, my son would just turn his stereo up louder.

For Glenda, this free writing clearly had focus and direction. She wanted to talk about the communication problems that arise among parents and their teen-agers. Because every parent she knew had the same problem, and because she had seen it treated in countless movies and television programs, Glenda felt she could generalize on the basis of her personal experience. Given this first free writing, she had a tentative thesis statement that could express that generalization: "Parents and their teen-age children have difficulty communicating with one another. They just don't seem to speak the same language."

But she wasn't satisfied with that thesis statement. From her perspective it was too conventional and lacked originality. As she put it, "Everyone knows that. What's the point of saying it all over again?" What Glenda wanted was a fresh point of view. She wanted to find a thesis that might not be so obvious to her readers. If possible, she wanted to tell them something they hadn't heard many times before. To develop what she

thought might be a more interesting thesis statement, she decided to free write again. Only this time she wrote in response to a discovery question: "What causes the communication gap between parents and their teen-agers?"

Glenda Williams

I never really thought about that, about why parents and teen-agers have so much trouble communicating. It just seemed a fact of life, like death and taxes. Everybody I know has the same problem, if they have kids that is. But I do know one thing. The movies my son sees don't help. They all encourage him to think of me as an idiot. I saw a movie the other night called First Born, and Steven had raved about it, the best movie he'd seen all year. Sure the teen-age son was smart, sensitive, and funny. The mother, played by an actress I really like, Dee Wallace, was still a fool. She had absolutely

no common sense. I wouldn't listen to her either. And there
are others when I start to think about it. <u>E.T.</u>, <u>Risky
Business</u>, <u>Christine</u>. It's even on T.V. My younger son likes to
watch something called <u>Silver Spoons</u>, and in it the son,
around fourteen, always has to take the father in hand to
keep him from making a fool of himself. No wonder kids
don't respect their parents or listen to their advice.
Everything they hear tells them it's a waste of time.

From this free writing, Glenda was able to draw the following thesis
statement: "Movies and television contribute a lot to the difficulty parents
and teen-agers have communicating." Her second free writing, inspired
by a discovery question, gave her a thesis statement she really liked.
Because she had not seen numerous references to the idea it expressed,
Glenda considered it more original and more interesting to write about.

Equally important, her second free writing suggested a method of
development for her thesis. In rough form, she now had several specific
illustrations that could explain what she meant. In this case at least, a
combination of two methods was much more productive than reliance
on just one. That is something to think about when you are trying to
formulate a thesis for your own essay.

Look over some of the thesis statements you have produced in response   **EXERCISE 5**
to the previous exercises in this chapter. Select the one that you like *least*
and try a different method of discovery. If you produced that thesis by
asking questions, try thinking about it in terms of a problem statement.
Or use it as the focus for free writing. See whether another method helps
you discover another thesis statement — one that is more satisfying.

Deciding on a
Tentative Thesis

By the time you finish exploring a topic for potential ideas to write
about, you may well have several different possibilities to choose from.
At this point you have to decide on a tentative thesis that will guide your
first draft. When you make that decision, you should keep the following
guidelines in mind:

1.   Start with an idea you think is appropriate to the amount of time
and information available to you. If you have only a few days in which

to write, choose a thesis you are familiar with and are reasonably well informed about. Remember, the purpose of your essay is to give your readers a clear understanding of your thesis. If you cannot give them a clear understanding of your thesis without a month of intensive research, you need to consider another thesis.

Along the same lines, be wary of a thesis statement that commits you to twenty pages rather than two. If you have one week to write your essay, a few moments' thought should tell you which of the following thesis statements would make a good starting point for your first draft.

The causes of alcoholism are psychological, social, and genetic.

Alcoholism has a genetic basis.

2.   Even if the topic has been assigned to you and you are not particularly interested in it, try to develop a thesis that arouses some excitement or interest on your part. Perhaps you are not interested in writing about "building codes." But given your experience as a volunteer in the veterans' hospital, you might well be interested in pursuing the following thesis: "The majority of public buildings in this city are not accessible to the handicapped." Whether you are refining your topic or deciding on a thesis, try to find some link with your own personal interests or experiences. When *you* care about what you write, chances are your readers will, too.

Following the two guidelines described in this section, choose one of the tentative thesis statements you produced in the preceding exercises. It will be the starting point for the essay you are going to develop throughout Chapter 3.

EXERCISE 6

Write two or three paragraphs that outline for the other students in the class your particular reasons for finding one strategy or combination of strategies especially effective or useful. When you are finished, exchange papers with some of the other students in the class. Compare the similarities and differences in the various responses.

Use a story or narrative from your own life to illustrate a thesis statement that defines a moral or principle of human behavior. For example, to show that first impressions are usually false, you might recall an incident in which you assumed one thing only to discover the exact opposite was true.

GETTING STARTED

Think for a few moments about how you believe people should behave if they want to lead a reasonably healthy and happy life. Make a list of those beliefs. The list might look something like this:

1. Honesty may be the best policy most of the time, but, occasionally, it can cause trouble.
2. To be professionally successful, it's important never to mix business and romance.
3. Sometimes getting angry can make a tense situation better, rather than worse.

If it is difficult for you to come up with such a list, try some of the discovery questions listed on pages 24 and 25. Take, for example, the topic "friendship" and ask yourself "How do friends recognize one another?" "What characterizes a potential friendship?" Or, take the topic marriage and ask "What produces or contributes to a bad marriage?" Such questions can provide tentative thesis statements like the following:

> Mutual laughter is probably the first and most essential sign
> of a budding friendship.

When one or both members of a marriage lose their sense
of humor, it's usually time to separate.

GETTING ORGANIZED

Outline your story first, listing the events you want to cover. Then try
to visualize those events one by one. Close your eyes and try to see each
one in your mind. Jot down all the details you can recall. Do not worry
about grammar, order, or spelling. Just get the events of the narrative
from your mind to your paper. You can correct and order them afterwards.
Once you think you have exhausted your imagination, begin putting
those details into story form.

When you have finished the story you want to tell, go back and write
a brief paragraph that introduces the thesis you are trying to illustrate.

The following sample paper may help you get organized.

Guilt   Bill Shannon

When you are really desperate to get good grades, even cheating
seems like a good idea. But in the end, it really isn't worth it.
Cheating, even when you're successful at it, causes more harm
than good.

I remember what I went through when I decided to cheat on my
math final. I woke up at five o'clock in the morning, already
feeling pangs of anxiety in my stomach. But I made a cheat sheet
anyway. I knew the test would be on formulas, so I wrote them all
on my left wrist above my watch.

When I got dressed I put on a long-sleeved pullover to hide my
ink stained arm. I remember my mom asking me why I was
wearing such a heavy sweater in May, and I told her I felt chilled
because I hadn't slept well. I had stayed up too late studying. She
felt sorry for me, and I felt awful. But I still was going through
with my plan.

When I got to the university, everybody asked me if I was
prepared. I said "yes." But I didn't say how I was prepared. After
all, how could I tell them I was going to cheat? My friends would
lose their respect for me.

Five minutes after I arrived in the hall, the teacher handed out a
two-page test, and everyone set to work. I did too. For each
question, I pretended I was looking at my watch to check the time.

Then I would fill in the answer. Every time I did it, I got more
nervous. Somebody was bound to suspect. How could I have been
so stupid as to think I could write the answers on my arm. Kids
did stuff like that and got caught. I was no kid.

But no one noticed or suspected. In the end, I was the first one
to finish the final. When I handed it in, my professor smiled at me
and took the test without even glancing at my arm.

When we got our final grades, I received an "A" in mathematics,
and when I saw my professor, she told me I had gotten the
highest grade on the final. She even congratulated me. At the time,
I was with my friends, and they congratulated me too. Every time
I got another compliment I felt like throwing up.

I have never cheated since. The very idea makes me sick with
guilt. I still think about telling my professor that I cheated on the
final, and it's been almost a year and a half since the whole thing
happened. In the long run, cheating, no matter what the grade,
just isn't worth it.

SUGGESTIONS FOR REVISION

For most people, writing and revision go hand and hand. You may
have to produce two or even three drafts before you are satisfied with
this paper. There is nothing wrong with that. Most people write, revise,
and write again until the finished product meets their expectations.

It is absolutely essential that you let this paper, and any others you
write, rest between drafts. At the moment you feel you have nothing
more to say, stop for a while, for an hour or more. Then go back and
read what you have written. But this time, try to read it as if you had
never seen the paper before. Read it as if you were an intelligent but
skeptical stranger who needed to be convinced. Pay special attention to
the relationship between the controlling idea and the narrative. Does the
story you tell clearly illustrate your principle about human conduct or
relationships?

Remember too that story telling is an art. It relies on the teller's ability
to separate the essential from the inessential. The secret of an effective
narrative, whether spoken or written, is the speaker's ability to select and
eliminate detail. For example, if your paper relates the story of a particularly
disastrous day at school when you failed every final, you do not want to
spend time on minor events like waking up and brushing your teeth.

Suggestions for
Your Writer's Notebook

SUGGESTION 1

There are times when your instructor may not provide even the topic of your essay. In preparation for that day, start making a file of articles that interest or intrigue you in some way. Such a file can prove invaluable when your topic is not assigned and you cannot think of anything to write about.

SUGGESTION 2

According to Mark Twain, "the difference between the almost right word and the right word is really a large matter — 'tis the difference between lightning and the lightning bug." How would you explain that quote? How could you apply it to your own writing?

SUGGESTION 3

In film there is an interesting cinematic device known as "montage." To use it, a director combines a series of scenes that individually have nothing to do with one another but together create an atmosphere or suggest an idea. As a writer, you too can make use of this technique. But in your case it will be a literary montage, and you will create meaning by combining words rather than pictures.

Begin by trying, in general terms, to express your feelings about the world you live in. Do you think that, despite all its ups and downs, life is worth living? Or do you feel that the world has become a dangerous place where destruction and death seem to wait around every corner? Maybe you think that the world is in chaos but that the presence of family and friends makes it bearable. Whatever your position, start leafing through magazines, newspapers, and advertisements to find pieces of prose that you could combine to suggest your impression of the world you inhabit. Listen to songs on the radio and watch the news, jotting down snatches of songs or speeches that would convey your outlook on reality. After you have a fairly large collection of lyrics, headlines, slogans, and quotes, paste them together in a way that suggests your "world view."

The following montage was done by a student named Jeni Snyder. Read it over to discover what Jeni thinks about the world she lives in. Then start gathering material for your own literary montage.

Don't want to believe the world today
Just want to make it go away
Just want to tune it out,
Deaf and dumb
To what it's all about.

A world full of surprises

Cabbage doll chaos

One of the greatest phe-
nomena in the toy industry
since the Hula-Hoop has
shoppers enduring shoving,
trampling, mauling, and long
waits in the cold for a chance
to buy the doll everyone
seems to want this season.

A pregnant woman was
trampled a month ago when
the dolls went on sale.

**A ten-year-old boy was hit
over the head by a man who
grabbed one of two dolls the
youngster was holding.**

All over the world
People dying
People crying
War is hell they say
There's just no other way

Picture this in your mind:

Six hundred or more people waiting from 6 A.M. outside a store to buy a doll! fighting, arguing and trampling one another—for a doll!

When was the last time you saw 600 or more people waiting outside a church or synagogue from 6 A.M. for a service to honor God and give thanks and gratitude with peace and love?

Listen brother, your country needs you
You gotta understand
It's time to go to war
Cause peace is a bore
And life ain't nothing without dying
To keep that country flying.

Attack in Beirut Follows U.S. Raids

Druse gunners blasted the U.S. Marine base at the Beirut airport with rockets and artillery shells last night, killing eight Marines and wounding two.

There's many lost but tell me who has won . . .

SUGGESTION 4

In his poem "The Great Lover," Rupert Brooke tried to communicate some sense of his pleasure and enjoyment in the everyday world. To do that he listed, in very specific and precise form, the things that most pleased him:

THE GREAT LOVER

These I have loved:
White plates and cups, clean-gleaming,
Ringed with blue lines; and feathery, faery dust;
Wet roofs, beneath the lamp-light; the strong crust
Of friendly bread; and many tasting food;
Rainbows; and the blue bitter smoke of wood;
And radiant raindrops couching in cool flowers;
And flowers themselves, that sway through sunny hours,
Dreaming of moths that drink them under the moon . . .

Having read a small portion of Brooke's poem, take a few minutes to imagine your own response to the words "These I have loved." Just concentrate on that phrase for a few minutes and allow your mind to call up a response. Write down whatever comes to mind. Then, once you have a fairly long list of things, eliminate everything that does not deal with ordinary objects and images. Remember, Brooke's poem was a celebration of the simple pleasures. If you feel comfortable doing so, read your list aloud to a friend. It's fun to see what different people enjoy about everyday living. High on one student's list, for example, was the smell of Coast soap and gasoline!

SUGGESTION 5

Certain rooms from our past can evoke powerful emotions because they are filled with memories. Here is one student's description of a cellar basement:

It was always so dark in the cellar, and there was a damp, musty smell in the air. The stairs were steep and they creaked when you walked on them. As a child, I thought their creaking sounded like crying. Because of the darkness it was hard to see, and the one light bulb seemed to be forever going out, particularly when I had to go in the cellar.

Everytime I went down there I heard or thought I heard
rustling, things scattering in the darkness. It was probably
mice, but that's not what I thought at the time.

Now try visualizing yourself as you walk in and out of rooms from
your childhood. Which room emerges with special clarity? Which room
seems to call up the strongest feelings, positive or negative? Is it a room
where you felt very safe and secure or uncomfortable and ill at ease?
Write a description of that room. But don't tell your readers how it made
you feel at the time. Try to create that feeling without expressing it.
When you are finished, read your description aloud to a friend. Have
you successfully created the appropriate atmosphere?

Combining
Sentences

Inevitably, the ability to write well comes down to how you construct your sentences. You can have the cleverest ideas imaginable, but if you do not have control over your sentences, the results will still be disappointing. "Control" over sentences means the ability to employ different kinds of sentence patterns or forms. It means the ability to substitute a sentence like this: "Not only did Sylvester Stallone produce and direct the film, but he also wrote it" for a series of sentences like these: "Sylvester Stallone wrote the film." "He directed it." "He produced it."

Because it is important to have many different sentence patterns at your disposal when you write, Chapter 2 and each of the following chapters ends with exercises devoted to particular sentence patterns.

PATTERN   1

In this sentence pattern, the emphasis is on increasing the number of adverbs and adjectives in a single sentence. Notice the relationship among the following sentences:

> The shark swallowed the swimmer.
> The shark swallowed suddenly.
> The shark was huge.
> The shark was gray.
> The swimmer was helpless.

In this example, the last four sentences use adverbs and adjectives to "modify" the shark, the swimmer, and the swallowing. However, the adverbs and adjectives in those five, separate sentences can be combined into one sentence containing the same amount of modification:

Suddenly, the huge gray shark swallowed the helpless swimmer.

EXERCISE

Combine the following sentences so that the first sentence (the base sentence) contains all of the italicized words and phrases. Although these sentences can be combined in more than one way, you should combine them according to the signals provided. Each caret ∧ shows where to insert a modifier, and you can insert the various modifiers according to the order of presentation. If a modifier requires punctuation, there will be a comma at the end of the sentence. (*Note*: You are to combine according to signals because that is a good way to get some controlled practice with punctuation, not because there is only one acceptable way to complete the exercise.)

1.   ∧ The ∧ impersonator wore a ∧ ∧ dress.
        He was *in a new movie*. [,]
        He impersonated a *female*.
        The dress was *long*.
        The dress was *red*.

_____

_____

2.   ∧ The ∧ ∧ players celebrate their ∧ victory.
        They celebrated *after the game*. [,]
        The players were *happy*.
        The players were *young*.
        The victory was *final*.

_____

_____

3.   ∧ The ∧ ∧ man joined a club ∧ .
        He joined *out of desperation*. [,]
        The man was *lonely*. [,]
        The man was *middle-aged*.
        The club was *for singles*.

_____

_____

4.   ∧ The ∧ ∧ dancer fell ∧ .
        It was *during the performance*. [,]
        The dancer was *lithe*. [,]
        The dancer was *young*.
        The dancer fell *off the stage*.

_____

_____

5.   ∧ The ∧ ∧ fighter entered the ∧ ring.
        He entered *after the first announcement*. [,]
        He was *nervous*. [,]

He was *young*.
The ring was *lighted*.

_____

_____

6.   The ∧ band played the ∧ ∧ songs ∧ .
       The band was *new*.
       The songs were *old*.
       The songs were *rock and roll*.
       The songs were *from the sixties*.

_____

_____

7.   The ∧ ∧ plane landed ∧ ∧ .
       The plane was *damaged*.
       The plane was a *jet*.
       The plane landed *safely*.
       The plane landed *on the ground*.

_____

_____

8.   ∧ The ∧ ∧ woman was arrested ∧ .
       It was *in the drugstore*. [,]
       The woman was *poor*.
       The woman was *old*.
       The arrest was *for shoplifting*.

_____

_____

9.   ∧ The ∧ director fired the ∧ crew ∧ .
       It was *after the shooting*. [,]
       The director was *furious*.
       The crew was *incompetent*.
       The crew consisted *of stunt people*.

_____

_____

10.   ∧ The ∧ couple adopted a ∧ ∧ child.
        It was *after some deliberation*. [,]
        The couple was *middle-aged*.

The child was *homeless*.
The child was *Vietnamese*.

_____

_____

Write five sentences that loosely imitate the sample sentence: "Suddenly,   EXERCISE
the huge gray shark swallowed the helpless swimmer."

1. _____

   _____

2. _____

   _____

3. _____

   _____

4. _____

   _____

5. _____

   _____

PATTERN 2

Pattern 2 concentrates on using coordinate conjunctions (*and, but, or,
nor, for, so, yet*) to combine (1) sentence elements and (2) whole sentences.

Combining Parts of Sentences:
1.   ∧ He ∧ played poker ∧ ∧ .
      They played *on their honeymoon*. [,]
      His wife played poker. [and]
      They both played *gin rummy*. [and]
      They played *all night long*.
  On their honeymoon, he and his wife played poker and gin rummy
all night long.

Combining Whole Sentences:
2.   The students did not like the ∧ methods.
      They were the *new teacher's*.

[, nor]
They did not care for his personality.
The students did not like the new teacher's methods, nor did they
care for his personality.

As in Pattern 1, directions for punctuation appear in brackets. Notice   EXERCISE
that, when the coordinate conjunctions combine whole sentences, they
require a comma: "He had hoped to get the job, *but* he found it unre-
warding." But coordinate conjunctions do not require a comma when
they connect only parts of sentences: "They wanted to win the hearts
and minds of the people."

1.   ∧ The judge made comments ∧ .
        They were *during the trial*. [,]
        They were *about the defendant*.
     [, so]
     The lawyer asked for a mistrial.

     _____

     _____

2.   ∧ Marilyn Monroe was a ∧ superstar.
        This was *without question*. [,]
        She was *glamorous*.
     [, but]
     She was also an insecure ∧ woman.
        She was *unhappy*. [and]

     _____

     _____

3.   ∧ The jury had to find him guilty.
        This was *after two days of disagreement*. [,]
     [, or]
     They had to let him go.

     _____

     _____

4.   The gangsters broke his legs ∧ ∧ .
        They broke *his arms*. [and]
        Then they *left him for dead*. [and]

     _____

     _____

5. The store detective was highly qualified.
   [, but]
   He overreacted to the situation ∧ .
       He *arrested the wrong man.* [and]

   _____

   _____

6. He had nothing to show ∧ .
       This was *for all his work.*
   [, so]
   He decided to leave.

   _____

   _____

7. She got a jail term ∧ ∧ .
       She got *a five-hundred-dollar fine.* [and]
       It was *for drunken driving.*
   [, and]
   She deserved them both.

   _____

   _____

8. ∧ ∧ He lost his appetite.
       He was *in love.*
       It was *for the first time.* [,]
   [, and]
   He *couldn't eat* ∧ .
       It was *for an entire twenty-four hours.*

   _____

   _____

9. She needed money ∧ .
       She needed *help.* [and]
   [, yet]
   She refused offers ∧ .
       The offers were *of both.*

   _____

   _____

10. The President ∧ tries hard.
        His advisors try hard. [and]

[, but]
They have made things worse ∧ .
    Things are *not better.* [,]

_____

_____

  Write five sentences that loosely imitate the two sample sentences.   EXERCISE
One example is provided for each sample sentence.

Sample Sentence:
        On their honeymoon, he and his wife played
        poker and gin rummy all night long.

Example:
        After the game, the player and his coach argued
        about the score.

1. _____

_____

2. _____

_____

3. _____

_____

4. _____

_____

5. _____

_____

Sample Sentence:
        The students did not like the new teacher's methods,
        nor did they care for his personality.

Example:
        The diver jumped into the water, but he never
        came up for air.

1. _____

   _____

2. _____

   _____

3. _____

   _____

4. _____

   _____

5. _____

   _____

CHAPTER 3

Developing the Controlling Idea

When you compose an expository essay, your purpose is to make your readers understand your thesis as clearly as you do. They might not be nodding in agreement after reading your paper, but they should be saying, "Yes, I see what you mean." To achieve that goal, you need more than a thesis statement. You need a *thesis paragraph* that introduces and clarifies that statement for your readers. In addition, you need several supporting paragraphs that anticipate and answer any questions your readers might have about your thesis statement. Step by step, this chapter shows you what to do once you have formulated your tentative thesis statement and are ready to draft your essay.

Drafting the Thesis Paragraph

Once you have a tentative thesis statement, you are ready to draft the thesis paragraph. In academic essays this is usually the first or second paragraph, and it can serve a variety of functions, depending on what you think your reader needs to know about your thesis. Sometimes it clarifies the language of your thesis statement by adding specific examples designed to prevent misinterpretation. Here is an example:

> The best-selling novelist Stephen King is a man who knows the value of horror. Carrie, The Shining, Cujo, and Christine

all became best sellers, earning the author millions of dollars.
All four became best sellers because they contain enough
blood and gore to satisfy even the most avid fans of horror
stories. By the end of every novel the setting is littered with
corpses, and, for King's numerous fans, those corpses are
part of the novels' charm. They are the main reason why he
is a millionaire today.

In this example, the thesis statement announces that King knows the
value of horror. But by itself this statement can suggest more than one
interpretation. It could mean that King knows the value of being scared
as a way of exciting the imagination. Or it could mean that he knows
horror stories earn money. To prevent misinterpretation on the part of
the readers, the author uses the thesis paragraph to provide specific examples
illustrating what he means.

But sometimes your thesis statement needs to be supplemented not
with specific examples but with some background information about your
topic. This was the case in the following example:

Karen Werner

In 1921 John Larson invented the polygraph machine,
better known today as the lie detector. The machine's
purpose was to help police detect criminal testimony.
Witnesses giving testimony would be connected to the
machine and asked numerous questions. As they answered,
the machine would record their pulse, blood pressure, and
heartbeat. Marked changes in any of those things were
supposed to indicate dishonest testimony. However simple
and effective as that all sounds, lie detectors have not made
the great contribution to criminal justice that was once
anticipated. In fact, they are subject to more error than
anyone ever suspected.

What these examples show is that the form and content of thesis
paragraphs can change depending on the demands of your thesis statement.
The essential thing is that you look carefully at your thesis statement and
imagine what your readers will need to know in order to understand
clearly the controlling idea you intend to explain in your paper.

Drafting a thesis paragraph at this stage in your writing does not commit
you to the thesis statement it contains. In fact, the thesis paragraph you

produce now and the one that opens your final paper might well have nothing in common. Writing out a thesis paragraph at this point is a clarification strategy. It forces you to define, in precise terms, the intended message of your paper.

THE ROLE OF THE READER

Drafting the thesis paragraph also forces you to consider consciously the role and responses of your readers. Up to this point in the writing process, you have been thinking primarily in terms of what you want to say. But once you begin thinking about the thesis paragraph, you must take into account your relationship to your reading audience.

From your perspective as a student writer, the relationship you share with your reading audience may seem all too simple and obvious. From your point of view, you don't have "readers"; you have *a* reader, and that reader is your instructor. Your instructor is the one who gives the assignment and grades it. Therefore, if you keep him or her in mind as you write, you will be able to anticipate and answer any questions he or she might have.

However, the relationship shared by student writers and their instructor readers is not so simple as it seems. Of course, you may know a great deal about the personal likes and dislikes of an individual instructor: She teaches composition. She is a Republican. In her spare time she writes poetry and lifts weights. She likes to read the novels of Joyce Carol Oates, and she despises those of Stephen King. She seldom goes to the movies, and if she does, the movies always have subtitles.

But for you, in your role as a student writer, such specific and concrete information can be more misleading than helpful. For when that imagined instructor sits down to read your paper, she does not do it simply — or even primarily — as Ms. X, the Republican and the poet. In her role as your composition instructor, she reads it primarily as Professor X, the representative of a scholarly community who places a high value on writing that is logical, clear, and concise. This means that our imaginary instructor can pick up a paper that perfectly expresses her personal opinion and still give it a low grade if the writer has not explained that thesis logically, clearly, and concisely.

Throughout this text the use of the word *readers* to talk about your audience does not ignore or deny the reality of the academic setting, where you usually write for one person at a time. It merely indicates that your composition instructor does, in fact, represent a larger academic group. By discussing good and bad writing, by making comments on your paper, and by selecting writing samples for you to analyze, your instructor is trying to pass on to you the general criteria that members of the "academic community" apply when they read your paper. When she reads your paper, she reads it with what amounts to double vision. She is both an individual reader and a representative of the readers you will face throughout your academic career.

Grasping this concept of audience can help you avoid a common mistake that many student writers make. They assume that, if their thesis statement expresses an opinion their instructor shares, they do not have to explain it. When the instructor asks for more specific details, their response is something like "But you know what I mean." *But even if they are familiar with the ideas you present, your composition instructors will try to read as though they were not.* They will play the role of intelligent but skeptical readers who have never seen a thesis statement like yours before and who are likely to misinterpret it unless you provide the appropriate guidance. This is their way of testing your ability to communicate with the clarity and directness demanded of academic writers.

As you grow more specialized in one individual discipline or subject, this relationship to your readers may change. You may become able to write as one expert to another, assuming a body of shared knowledge. But at this stage in your academic career, you will probably be more successful if you think of your readers as people who are intelligent enough to understand your thesis but not necessarily well enough informed to explain it themselves.

To properly imagine the role that your particular instructor plays when reading your paper, you need to spend time analyzing his comments. When you get a paper back, read all the comments carefully. See whether you can revise your work in terms of what these comments suggest. If you can not do that, make an appointment to see your instructor. Ask for more explanation and examples, and then go back and carry out the instructions you have been given, even if it means rewriting the whole paper. Comments on your paper are not intended to make you feel bad. They are intended to communicate your reader's expectations of your work. Their purpose is to show you how you can most effectively communicate your thoughts in an academic setting.

BECOMING YOUR OWN READER

The time you spend analyzing your instructor's comments will eventually yield important results. After a while, as you write, you yourself will be able to recognize those places where your instructor might make comments

like "Too vague," "What's the connection here?" and "This is not clear;
I need an example."

As an illustration, consider the thesis paragraph Joan Amato composed
after discovering her thesis statement.

> Joan Amato
>
> Hospitals are places to heal and help the sick. They should
> make people feel safe and secure. But they don't. Mention the
> word "hospital" and people become afraid. They just don't
> want to go, no matter what the consequences.

At first Joan felt this paragraph fulfilled the requirements of a thesis
paragraph. But then her instructor asked her to go back and read some
of the comments he had written on previous papers. After she had done
that, he asked her to read her paragraph again, this time playing the role
of the instructor. Here are her comments.

1. You say hospitals scare people. Do they scare everybody in
the same way? Which "people" are you talking about here. Can you
be more precise?

2. I understand your topic, "fear of hospitals." But I am not
clear about what you want to say in your thesis statement. Are
you just saying that this fear exists? Are you saying it exists and
is silly? Do you want to say it exists and with good reason? Can
you give your thesis statement a more precise direction? Right
now I don't have a clear idea of what you want to tell me about
this fear. It might help if you first explain your thesis in
conversation. Just talk to somebody about it. Then try writing it
out.

In answer to those imagined questions, comments, and suggestions,
Joan rewrote her paragraph:

> Joan Amato
>
> Hospitals are places that help and heal the sick. They
> should make people feel safe and secure. But that is not
> always the effect they have. For some people the word
> "hospital" is terrifying. There are people who, when told they
> need major surgery, refuse it. For them being in the hospital
> is more anxiety-producing than the threat of death. There are

people who won't even visit a sick friend. When they walk
through the hospital doors, not as a patient but as a visitor,
they panic. At first glance these reactions probably seem
childish, even silly. But I believe they have a real basis in
experience.

As you will see in the following pages, this thesis paragraph will undergo
numerous revisions. Nevertheless, at this stage in the writing process, it
is a good paragraph. It clearly defines for both Joan and her readers the
thesis of her essay.

Write a brief paragraph that outlines what you think are your instructor's
expectations for your written work.   EXERCISE   1

Pick one of the thesis statements you developed for the exercises in   EXERCISE   2
Chapter 2. Compose a thesis paragraph that provides any necessary background and clarifies your point of view.

Once you have written that paragraph, try to read it from your instructor's
perspective. Make a list of comments you think your instructor might
have written in response to your paragraph. Turn in the thesis paragraph.

When you get it back, compare your comments with your instructor's.
See how effectively you anticipated his responses. Finally, revise the
paragraph to incorporate his comments and your own.

Drafting the
Supporting Paragraphs

Like the thesis paragraph, the supporting paragraphs must anticipate
the responses of your readers. That means you have to read the thesis
paragraph carefully and try to predict the questions it could raise. Your
supporting paragraphs should provide the answers.

For example, when Joan Amato looked at her revised thesis paragraph
on fear of hospitals, she was convinced that her readers would respond
with the following question: "If you claim that the fear you describe has
a real basis in experience, what experience or experiences do you have
in mind?"

To answer that question, Joan used a technique called brainstorming.
With this technique, you just pose a question and write down all the
answers that come to mind. You do not correct, edit, or contradict. You

just record everything that pops into your head in answer to the question you posed.

Although brainstorming can be done alone, many writers find it works best with small groups. In a group, something like a chain reaction occurs. When one person makes a comment, that comment sparks the thoughts of the other members. As an illustration, here is the brainstorming list produced in class when Joan Amato posed the question "What experiences can make people afraid of entering a hospital?"

1. They've read too much about the medical mistakes that can be made.
2. They've seen the film <u>Hospital</u>. That's enough to scare anybody forever.
3. They don't trust doctors.
4. They've been hospitalized previously and it arouses bad memories.
5. They've seen too many television programs where hospitals are where you die. If you have to go to the hospital for tests on television, you know your next step is the funeral parlor.
6. They hate the smell.
7. Everyone ignores you and treats you like an intruder.
8. The food is awful.
9. They can't stand being there; they are afraid of what's going to happen to them.
10. They can't afford it.
11. They fear catching the illnesses of other patients.
12. Hospitals make you think about death and dying. Who wants to think about that? It's morbid.
13. They take away your clothes and start sticking needles in you.
14. The surroundings are strange and unfamiliar.
15. They've had experiences where the doctor misdiagnosed an illness.

As you can see, brainstorming produced a number of potential answers to Joan's question. And that is precisely what makes this technique so useful: It provides a writer with an abundance of material. But, of course, not everything you write down during a brainstorming session will be useful. You have to examine the answers you have collected in light of your thesis statement and see what thoughts you might use and how you might use them. The following suggestions can help you make those decisions.

1. Don't immediately discard an answer that looks silly or pointless. On the surface, answer 6 ("They hate the smell") does not seem to be a useful answer. But if you explore it a bit, it becomes more valuable. Think for a moment about the smell in hospital halls. It smells like medicine, and medicine is associated with illness. If people are repelled by the smell in hospitals, in part they are repelled by the thought of the illnesses that can attack their body. The smell in hospitals is a reminder of the body's vulnerability to illness. Although it needs further development, this is a potentially fruitful answer to the question governing Joan's supporting paragraphs: "What are the experiences that create a fear of hospitals?"

2. Look for answers that are connected or related in some way. For example, answers 15, 1, and 3 show a relationship of cause and effect. Answer 3 claims that some people just do not trust doctors. Two causes for that effect are suggested by answer 1 ("They've read too much about the medical mistakes that can be made") and answer 15 ("They've had experiences where the doctor misdiagnosed an illness"). This is the kind of cluster of related ideas that you would want to indicate in the margins of your list. For what you have in those three answers are the bare bones of a supporting paragraph:

> Some people have lost faith in doctors.
>   They have been poorly diagnosed.
>   They have read about too many medical errors.

3. Next to each answer on your brainstorming list, try jotting down words, phrases, images, or sentences that you associate with them. What you want to do is find out what your answer means to *you*. Only then can you make it mean something for your reader.

4. Do not automatically eliminate an answer that fails to elicit any associations. The answer may be a good one, but you may not have enough information at your disposal to develop it. Take the time to look up your topic in the *Reader's Guide to Periodical Literature* (see Chapter 9, pages 280–281). Look for articles dealing with your thesis. Read them carefully. Then go back to your original answer. See whether you now have a richer response.

THE FIRST DRAFT

Even after Joan had analyzed the responses she produced through brainstorming, she still did not feel ready to write. Rather, she chose to discuss her thesis with several classmates to see what experiences they might provide. In addition, she went to the library and found an article called "Doctor Talk" (Diane Johnson, *The State of the Language* [Berkeley: U of Calif P, 1980] 396–398), which she felt supported her thesis. Having done all that, Joan finally felt ready to sit down and write her first rough draft.

Joan Amato

Hospitals are where we go to be cured of illness. They are the places that help and heal the sick. They should make us feel safe and secure. But that is not always their effect. There are people who, if told they need major surgery, will refuse it. For them the thought of being in the hospital is too terrifying. Then there are people who won't even visit a sick friend. When they walk through those doors, they panic. Initially at least, those reactions seem like a phobia, a fear without any real basis in experience. But fear of hospitals is not like fear of heights or fear of open spaces. It has a very real basis in experience.

When you walk into a hospital even as a visitor, the first thing you find out is that somebody else is the boss. There are places you can and cannot go, mostly cannot. You have to tell people who you are and why you are there. Everyone in uniform knows where they are going. Only the outsiders don't.

They take away your clothes and give you a ridiculous costume called a "Johnny Shirt." Most of the time you just sit and wait, wondering what's going to happen to you. No wonder hospitals seem a place of loss. What you lose is yourself! You can't call the doctor when you're ready. He calls you when he's ready. And then he talks to you in a language you can't possibly understand.

This is what the writer Diane Johnson calls "Doctor Talk." It's language that uses science to control and confuse. The only thing you know is that, with words that big, it's got to be serious. When my father was in the hospital. We used to wait for hours to see the doctor, and when we did we knew less than we did before. Not only did we not understand what he was talking about, but he made it clear we were wasting his valuable time. And it <u>was</u> valuable. We couldn't believe the bill when we got it.

But the people in the rooms are the most depressing. Seeing them, you realize you are human and very fragile. They have tubes in their noses and needles in their arms. If you feel good when you walk in, you feel sick when you walk out.

And hospitals make you think about death. A hundred years ago, people died at home with their families. But now they get carted off to hospitals to die, and we cannot help but associate the place with the image of death.

Reading this first rough draft as though it were a finished essay, you would find countless things to correct. The "voice" or "tone" Joan uses fluctuates (see Chapter 7). At the beginning she treats both her topic and her audience with a certain formality and seriousness. But by the end, she sounds as though she is having a casual conversation with a friend, and it is not always clear that she feels deeply about her topic. Sentences like "if you feel good when you walk in, you feel sick when you walk out" make it sound as though she is making fun of her topic.

In addition, the draft strays from her first tentative thesis. At times, Joan discusses the way hospital procedures can generate fear. But at other times, she describes situations that produce anger rather than anxiety.

Moreover, some sentences do not seem to follow logically from one another, nor do some paragraphs. There are grammatical errors and fragments.

Despite those problems, however, this is a successful first draft. It shows that Joan can explain her tentative thesis about the fear of hospitals. She does have some specific experiences in mind that can answer her readers' questions. But it also shows that, if she chooses, she can develop a different thesis altogether: "Hospital procedures seem designed to produce hostility in patients and visitors alike." To be successful, a first draft need only allay the fear that haunts every writer: "I just don't have anything to say." Judged on this basis, Joan's first draft was a success.

After having produced this first draft, Joan was ready to do nothing — that is, to take a complete break from her writing. Such pauses or breaks in the writing process are essential. In some mysterious way, they allow writers to separate themselves from their work. After a break, it becomes possible to view the paper as a reader might. Whenever you are drafting a paper, it is important that you allow the paper to rest between drafts. When you return to it, you will find it easier to read your draft as though someone else had written it. The ability to assume this stranger's perspective on your own writing is essential to communication.

EXERCISE 3

Read over the thesis paragraph you wrote for Exercise 2. Write down the question or questions you think your readers will raise. Make a list of many potential answers. Select three or four answers that you think you could develop in the supporting paragraphs of your essay.

Write a first draft of your essay.

ANALYZING THE FIRST DRAFT

To analyze a first draft effectively, you have to know what you are looking for. Although each individual draft raises its own specific set of questions, there are some general questions that can help you start the revision process.

1.   If the purpose of my essay is to make readers understand my thesis as clearly as I do, have I provided enough specific explanation to make that possible? Will my readers clearly understand how the particular details or illustrations I use explain what I say in the thesis paragraph? What more can I do to clarify my thesis statement?

2.   Does my draft tell me that my thesis is too general for the limitations of my paper? Am I discovering that I need ten pages rather than two in order to explain my thesis? How can I further restrict my thesis?

3.   Is there any point in the draft where I lose sight of the thesis altogether and start discussing an entirely different thought? Does this new idea seem to take over the paper? Should I think about developing a new thesis statement based on this idea?

4.   Are there places where I assume too much about my readers' previous knowledge of my ideas? Do I need to provide more specific details to make my general statements clearer to readers unfamiliar with what I say?

5.   Have I collected specific facts or figures without making sure that they add up to some kind of generalization?

6.   Are there any places where I simply pad my paper by making the same point twice with different words?

7.   Are there places where I force my readers to infer or guess connections that I should make explicit for them.

As a way of illustrating how you might use these questions, let us analyze Joan Amato's first draft paragraph by paragraph.

1   Hospitals are where we go to be cured of illness. They are
     the places that help and heal the sick. They should make us
     feel safe and secure. But that is not always their effect. There
     are people who, if told they need major surgery, will refuse it.
     For them the thought of being in the hospital is too
     terrifying. Then there are people who won't even visit a sick   *Is this a clear statement of
     friend. When they walk through those doors, they panic.   my thesis?*
     Initially at least, those reactions seem like a phobia, a fear   *Do I need to say anything
     without any real basis in experience. But fear of hospitals is   else to clarify message?*
     not like fear of heights or fear of open spaces. It has a real   *what questions would
     basis in experience.   readers raise?*

Paragraph 1 reveals that Joan is still refining her thesis statement for her
readers. In order to make it even clearer and avoid misinterpretation, she
has now made a definite distinction between the fear she describes and
phobias, fears that have no basis in actual experience.

2   When you walk into a hospital even as a visitor, the first
     thing you find out is that somebody else is the boss. There   *How does this support
     are places you can and cannot go, mostly cannot. You have to   thesis?*
     tell people who you are and why you are there. Everyone in
     uniform knows where they are going. Only the outsiders   *Is this the "basis in
     don't.   experience"?*

In paragraph 2 Joan tries to explain her thesis by defining, very specifically,
what happens when a person enters the hospital: "There are places you
can and cannot go, mostly cannot." But at this stage, it is not clear what
generalization Joan is trying to draw from this specific experience. Above
all, it is not clear how this paragraph answers that important question:
What causes fear of hospitals?

   Yet if you think about it for a moment, you will see that Joan is working
on an answer. However, she is working implicitly rather than explicitly.
She has not directly stated the conclusion she has in mind. She seems
to be relying on her readers to draw that conclusion for her. For the
most part, in academic writing, that is a mistake. To successfully relate
this section more directly to her thesis, Joan should state rather than
imply the generalization she has in mind.

   That means she has to work out what she wants to say, given the
details she has produced in the draft. In effect, she has to probe her
mind, clarify for herself what she wants to say, and then clarify it for
the reader. She has to ask herself why it would be frightening to be in

a situation where people tell you what to do. One answer might be that such situations make people feel unimportant and dependent. They do not feel able to assert their individual needs. If something goes wrong in that setting, they feel out of control and unable to correct the situation. Indirectly Joan is working on a supporting paragraph that makes the following point: In a hospital setting where patients and visitors have to abide by rules they don't always understand or approve of, it is easy to feel as though the world has gotten out of control — as though the individual is totally at the mercy of the institution. But if Joan is to communicate that to a reader, she has to work much more by explication (direct statement) and much less by implication or suggestion.

3   They take away your clothes and give you a ridiculous
     costume called a "Johnny shirt." Most of the time you just sit
     and wait, wondering what's going to happen to you. No
     wonder hospitals seem a place of loss. What you lose is
     yourself! You can't call the doctor when you're ready. He calls
     you when he's ready. And then he talks to you in a language
     you can't possibly understand.

what am I trying to say here?

How do you "lose your-self?"

am I getting away from the thesis?

what's the connection?

In the first half of paragraph 3, Joan does become more explicit about what she wants to tell her readers. Describing some specific hospital procedures, she explains how she thinks they affect the individual: "No wonder hospitals seem to be a place of loss. What you lose is your sense of yourself as a grown-up and competent individual who can change and control his surroundings."

But by the second half of that same paragraph, it is no longer quite so clear what Joan wants to say to her readers. Although she does describe a disheartening experience with a doctor, she does not explain the significance of that experience in terms of her thesis. At this point it is not clear how that experience fosters fear — anger, perhaps, but not fear. Actually, it is not until paragraph 4 that Joan really begins to make her point.

4   This is what the writer Diane Johnson calls "Doctor Talk."
     It's language that uses science to control and confuse. The
     only thing you know is that, with words that big, it's got to
     be serious. When my father was in the hospital. We used to
     wait for hours to see the doctor, and when we did we knew
     less than we did before. Not only did we not understand what
     he was talking about, but he made it clear we were wasting

his valuable time. And it <u>was</u> valuable. We couldn't believe the
bill when we got it.

How does this support thesis?

In paragraph 4, Joan makes her point much more explicitly: When patients
and their family are faced with scientific explanations they do not understand,
they believe the worst. Even the mildest ailment sounds like a serious
disease, and they grow frightened. But this section needs to be carefully
rethought and revised. Joan has to show how the experience she describes
creates a fear of hospitals. If she cannot make this connection, she has
to eliminate that experience from her paper — unless, of course, she
decides to make it the basis for an entirely new thesis: "The language
doctors use to talk to their patients confuses much more than it enlightens."

5   But the people in the rooms are the most depressing.
       Seeing them, you realize you are very human and very
       fragile. They have tubes in their noses and needles in their
       arms. If you feel good when you walk in, you feel sick when
       you walk out.

Keep

*Develop —
watch tone here.*

The relationship between the thesis paragraph and paragraph 5 is much
clearer. In this paragraph Joan says very explicitly why hospitals can be
frightening: "They make you realize how physically fragile you really
are." She has even presented some specific details to explain how that
realization takes place: When you enter a hospital, you see other human
beings whose bodies have been attacked by disease and are now invaded
by machines and needles.

6   And hospitals make you think about death. A hundred
       years ago, people died at home with their families. But now
       they get carted off to hospitals to die, and we cannot help but
       associate the place with the image of death.

Expand

Like paragraph 5, paragraph 6 shows a clear-cut relationship to the thesis
paragraph. It explains that people fear hospitals because they associate
them with death: "A hundred years ago, people died at home with their
families. But now they get carted off to hospitals to die, and we cannot
help but associate the place with the thought of death."

       This analysis of Joan's first draft illustrates some of the things a writer
should consider when examining a first draft. When inexperienced writers
analyze their first draft, they often have the wrong questions in mind.

They ask themselves where they have made grammatical errors and where they must turn fragments into complete sentences. But those questions are irrelevant at this point in the writing process. No matter how fragmentary and no matter how spotted with errors, a first draft can be counted a success if it gives you answers to the following questions:

1. Are you still committed to your first thesis? Or has your first draft made it clear that you really want to explore a very different controlling idea?

2. If you are still content with your tentative thesis, do you have the answers, no matter how roughly expressed, to questions your readers might raise about the thesis? What portions of your draft provide the most effective answers? What answers need to be sharpened, abbreviated, or eliminated altogether?

The answers to those questions should not just be recorded mentally. They should be noted on your paper as well. When you finish analyzing a draft, takes notes in the margin as Joan did on her first draft (pp. 59–61). Write down what you hope to change. Indicate what portions of your paper you hope to keep. Also indicate what portions you think you will eliminate. In general, have some record of what you thought about as you analyzed your first draft.

Once you have recorded potential revisions, the next step (once again) is to do nothing further for a few hours — if time permits, for a few days. During your break, do not try to think about your paper. Do something else while you let the unconscious part of your mind continue working.

Using the foregoing questions, analyze *your* draft, thinking about changes you would like to make. Note those changes on your paper.   EXERCISE   4

THE SECOND DRAFT

When you return to your paper after a break, you will be amazed at how much easier it is to see your work through the eyes of your readers. You will now be able to recognize many of those places where you treated your audience as though they were mind readers who could, with just a few faint clues, figure out what you intended to say.

After your break, however, you should not just sit down and start writing the second draft. Instead, read the first draft through again. Pay careful attention to the notes you made in the margins. Ask yourself whether you still agree with what you said in them. You may want to revise them, adding or eliminating points. Most important, jot down any ideas that occurred to you while you were away from your paper. Sometimes the spontaneous thoughts that come to you while you are away from your paper are the most interesting.

As Joan's second draft illustrates, a lot can happen during the time you are letting your paper rest.

Fear of Hospitals   Joan Amato

1   Hospitals are where people go to be cured of their illnesses.
Places of healing, they should make us feel safe and secure.
But for many of us, hospitals are places to be avoided. Told by
a doctor to enter a hospital for even minor surgery, many
people feel tremendous anxiety and foreboding. Despite
reassurances to the contrary, they are convinced they will die
if they have to be treated in a hospital. For some people, even
visiting a hospital is an anxiety-producing experience. When
they walk through hospital doors they grow panicky and
nervous. Although initially such fear of hospitals may seem
to be another odd and inexplicable phobia, like fear of great
heights or of open spaces, I think it is very different. There
are reasons why people panic at the thought of entering
those hospital doors.

In this draft Joan has changed her thesis paragraph to further define and specify her topic. She is talking about fear of hospitals as it is experienced by two different groups. She mentions people who are told to enter a hospital and do so, expecting the worst to happen. She also cites people who feel anxiety even when they are just visitors. She is *not* discussing people who are told to have major surgery to save their lives and won't go. To do so would be to undermine her thesis that fear of hospitals is not an irrational or unreasonable reaction.

2   The image of hospitals offered on television is one reason
why some people fear them. For years, television shows with
a hospital setting have been a part of daytime and nighttime
programming, and whether daytime or nighttime, whether
"General Hospital" or "St. Elsewhere," those television
programs suggest that hospitals are where you go if you

have a mysterious and incurable illness. They are not the
place where you have simple and relatively uninteresting
ailments like gall bladder problems or kidney stones. On
television, a person can enter a hospital with little more
than a swollen ankle. But by the time the program is over,
that same person usually has a life-threatening disease.

3   It is diseases like these, mysterious and terrible, that keep
viewers tuning in. But at the same time they create an image
of hospitals as the last resort of the incurably and terribly ill.
After a few hours of "Trapper John, M.D." or "St. Elsewhere,"
it's easy enough to assume that you can enter a hospital
relatively healthy but sooner or later the doctors will find
something terribly wrong.

These two paragraphs show that Joan has decided on an entirely new
answer to that central question: What are some of the experiences that
make people fear hospitals? Note, too, that she has eliminated altogether
her earlier discussion of hospital procedures and their effect on patients.
This was her response to comments that the essay seemed to go in two
directions, one part describing the fear people have about being in a
hospital and the other explaining patients' anger and frustration at hospital
procedures. In a longer paper, she might have been able to combine and
discuss the two. But within the limits of this assignment, it was not
possible to address both issues.

4   In some ways, the real, rather than the television
experience, is not much more reassuring. When you walk
through the doors of a hospital you can't help but recognize
how fragile the human body really is. Even if you are a
visitor rather than a patient, you can't avoid seeing people of
all ages moaning in pain. They lie in their beds with tubes in
their noses and plastic bags over their mouths, each one a
reminder of potential suffering and illness. Given the sight of
so much suffering and so much pain, it is easy enough to
think that some day it could be your turn. One day you could
be the patient rather than the visitor.

At this point Joan is refining an idea drawn from her original draft.
She is making more explicit connections between her ideas. In this revised
paragraph, she carefully explains why a person begins to feel more vulnerable
to illness after entering a hospital, even if such a visitor is perfectly healthy.

5   Even more terrifying, each patient is a reminder of death.
       Seeing people in pain, you can't help but wonder if they will
       ever get well. In our society, few people die at home anymore
       as they once did, surrounded by friends and family. Hospitals,
       not houses, have become the places that handle terminal or
       incurable illness. As you catch a glimpse of those people
       suffering or in pain, you can't help but wonder if they come
       to the hospital to die. Thinking about the death of strangers,
       you can't help but think about your own.

Here Joan continues to rework and enlarge the ideas derived from her
original draft as she explains why we associate hospitals with death. Note,
too, how she is trying to make her voice more consistent. The flippant
— almost humorous — tone of the first draft has disappeared.

Having finished her second draft, Joan was ready to analyze it. But
once again, this kind of analysis is most effective after a break or pause.

Read your first draft aloud. Read the notes in the margin. Jot down   EXERCISE 5
any additional ideas that came to mind while you were away from your
paper. Ask yourself, again, what your readers need to know in order to
understand your thesis. Then write your second draft.

ANALYZING THE SECOND DRAFT

By the time you begin analyzing your second draft, you are probably
hoping that the third draft will be your last. And that is certainly possible.
Joan's second draft, for example, resolved most of the problems her
instructor pointed out in the previous section. But there is no guarantee
that three drafts (or even five) is the magic number for completion. In
general, if you have worked out answers to the questions for revision
presented on page 58, you are ready to think about a final draft. But
those answers may emerge after four drafts rather than two. There is no
fixed rule about the drafting process.

However, even if your second draft has resolved the problems posed
by the first, do not just sit down and start writing. Above all, do not
assume you can just recopy your second draft, merely correcting your
punctuation and spelling. Instead read your second draft very carefully.
Try to separate yourself from your work as much as possible and approach
it as your readers might. Remember, they are intelligent but relatively
uninformed about your particular thesis. Nevertheless, by the time they
finish reading your essay, they should understand it as clearly as you do.

At the point when you think about writing your final draft, you need to do everything possible to encourage your readers' understanding. To this end, you should consider the following questions for final revision.

1. Have I given my readers the clearest possible introduction to my thesis?

This is the time to look carefully at your thesis paragraph. If your thesis statement is open to more than one interpretation, think about providing specific examples that would reduce the possibility of misinterpretation. If your thesis statement requires background information, you want to be sure your readers have it. If your thesis statement uses any terms you think might not be part of your readers' general knowledge, be sure to define them.

2. Do the ideas in my supporting paragraphs clearly explain my thesis?

To answer this question, make a skeleton outline of your paper. You can do this by writing out a short form of your thesis statement. Then go through your essay paragraph by paragraph and ask yourself what each paragraph contributes to the controlling idea. Indented under the thesis statement, write out your answers. As an illustration, here is Joan's outline:

Thesis: The fear of hospitals has a basis in our experience.
1. Television tells us over and over that hospitals are where they treat the mysteriously and incurably ill.
2. Hospitals tell us that we are vulnerable to illness.
3. They force us to face the reality of death.

Outlining in this way serves a useful function. It can tell you immediately where your paper might have lost *unity*. That is, it can reveal where you might have included ideas that are not relevant to the explanation of your thesis.

For example, if the outline for Joan's essay had contained the supporting sentence "Trauma centers in hospitals are essential for saving lives," she would have know immediately that she had to rework the paragraph or paragraphs containing this idea. The reason is simple: Initially, at least, it appears to have nothing to do with her thesis.

3. Have I used paragraphing as an effective guide to meaning?

When you indent for a new paragraph, your provide much more than just a pause or a break for your readers. You also prepare your readers for a change in your thinking. The indentation for a paragraph signals that you could be moving from a general explanation to a specific example, reversing your position altogether, or pointing out an important exception.

For your readers, paragraphing is a visual signal that guides their expectations. When you read Joan's final draft, notice the changes in paragraphing. For example, she has split her first thesis paragraph in two, and she now uses the first paragraph to provide some background about her topic.

4. Do I use a consistent voice throughout my paper?

Your writer's "voice" depends on two things: your relationship with your readers and your attitude toward your material. To a great extent both are limited by the academic environment. Very few instructors will encourage you to write for an audience of old friends. You will be expected to treat your readers as interested and intelligent acquaintances.

In addition, most of your instructors expect your attitude toward your material to be fairly serious. Although they might occasionally assign papers wherein you can be flippant and breezy about your thesis, those papers will be rare. It is not that your instructors do not have a sense of humor and do not want you to have one either. They simply know that most academic writing limits the range of voices a writer can adopt, and they are not going to encourage you to use a voice that would be fine for the editorial page of a newspaper but inappropriate for a college essay. (For further discussion of voice, see Chapter 7, "The Writer's Voice.")

From this point of view, notice the way Joan's voice has changed in the final draft of her essay. It no longer fluctuates between serious and flippant. Throughout the essay, Joan now speaks with a voice that emphasizes her respect for both audience and thesis.

5. Have I made the connections between sentences and paragraphs clear enough so that my readers have no difficulty following the trail of my thoughts?

In the process of reading your paper, your audience has to recreate the connections you had in mind when you followed one sentence with another and one paragraph with another. To help them do that, you have to give them sufficient guidance. (For more specific information on how to do this, see Chapter 6, "Writing a Coherent Essay.")

6. Have I used the final paragraph of my essay to give my readers a sense of completion or conclusion?

In the sample essay Joan used a restatement of her thesis, with some slight modification, to make her last paragraph into an effective conclusion. But you might want to consider some other possibilities:

a. Use the final paragraph or paragraphs to explain the significance of your thesis — in effect to tell your readers why they should pay attention to what you have said.

b. Use the final paragraph to offer a solution to the problem described in your paper.

c. Because you may very well not be able to solve the problem you describe, you can use the final paragraphs to stress the importance of solving the problem in the future. For example, you can predict what might happen if the problem is not solved.

d. In general, you should have little difficulty concluding your paper if you remember one basic rule of thumb: Do not end on an unfamiliar note that you haven't developed. Overall, an abrupt ending is better than a confusing one.

FINAL EDITING

When you can answer "yes" to all the foregoing questions, you are ready to think about final editing. The following questions suggest some general guidelines for the final editing process.

1. Are there any general words that should be exchanged for more specific ones?
2. Are there any cases where the choice of words is not suitable for a formal essay? Are there any words that are too informal and conversational for a written paper?
3. Are there any sentences that are ambiguous (could have more than one meaning)? Should they be rewritten for greater clarity?
4. Are all commas, colons, and semicolons used correctly?
5. Do all subjects and verbs agree?
6. Are there any problems with pronoun reference?
7. Are there any superfluous or excess words that you can eliminate?
8. Have you eliminated all sentence fragments?

All these questions are covered either in the sections on sentence combining or in "Pointers for Final Editing" at the end of this book (pp. 323–351). Refer to one or both if you feel unsure about any one of these eight guidelines for editing your final draft.

Here, fully revised and edited, is the third and final draft of Joan Amato's paper:

Fear of Hospitals   Joan Amato

Hospitals are where we go to be freed from the pain and
discomfort of illness. It would seem to follow, then, that hospitals
should make us feel safe and secure. But some people don't have
that "logical" reaction at all when they think of entering hospital
doors. Told by a doctor to enter a hospital for some minor surgery,
many people react with anxiety. They are convinced that the
doctor is not telling them the truth. They are convinced they are
going to die. For others even visiting a hospital is an anxiety-
producing experience, and they will do anything to avoid it.

Initially, such reactions might seem silly and unreasonable. But,
in fact, they are not. There are reasons why people feel dread,
anxiety, even panic at the thought of going to the hospital. Anxiety

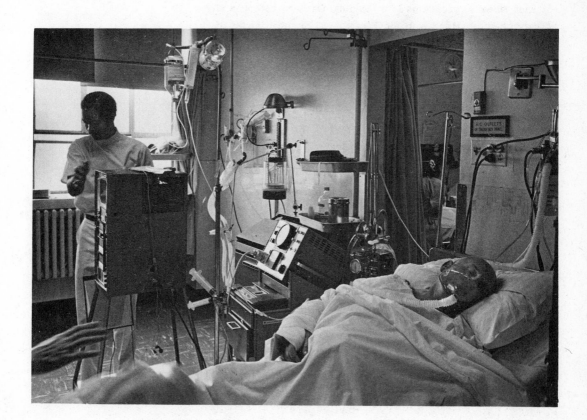

or panic about being in a hospital is not a phobia like fear of great
heights or fear of open spaces. On the contrary, the fear of
entering a hospital has a basis in our experience, both the real
and the televised.

The image of hospitals on television is certainly one reason why
many people feel enormous anxiety even if they are facing nothing
more serious than a gall bladder operation. For years, television
programs with a hospital setting have been very popular. But on
television, almost no one in a hospital ever has a minor or
insignificant illness. Even the patient who enters the hospital
relatively healthy does not stay that way. Sooner or later, someone
detects the first signs of incurable illness. The ratings demand it.
The television audience is not interested in programs about kidney
stones or hemorrhoids.

By emphasizing the mysterious and incurable diseases that
attract viewers, programs like "Medical Center," "Marcus Welby,"
"Trapper John, M.D.," and "St. Elsewhere" have consistently won
high ratings over the last decade. Yet that emphasis has helped
create the fear of hospitals I describe. After watching these
programs, you can easily imagine that no one enters a hospital as
a healthy human being and stays that way for very long. Sooner
or later, the dreadful illness hiding in that human body will be
diagnosed and the prognosis will be fatal.

The real experience of being in a hospital is not much more
reassuring. When you enter a hospital either as a patient or a
visitor, you are confronted with the body's weakness. As you walk
through hospital halls, it is impossible to avoid seeing people who
are seriously ill. They have tubes in their arms and plastic bags
over their faces. While some sleep quietly, others moan in pain.
After being faced with those images of human pain and suffering,
you have to recognize how vulnerable the human body really is to
the threat of illness.

But more frightening than anything else is the fact that death is
associated with hospitals. A century ago people died at home. But
in this country, that has changed. Nowadays the terminally ill go
to hospitals for their care and treatment. Consequently, when you
see someone lying in bed and moaning in pain, it is hard not to
wonder if that person came to the hospital to die.

Outside the walls of a hospital, death is remote and far away for
most of us. It is something that happens to other people. But

inside hospital walls, death is a very real presence. It can no
longer be avoided or ignored. In the face of that presence, it is no
wonder that some people feel anxiety — even panic — at the
thought of walking through the doors of a hospital. Places of
healing or not, hospitals still remind us of a reality that most of
us would like to forget.

Read over your second draft the first time with the questions for revision   EXERCISE 6
in mind. In the margins of your paper, make notes indicating potential
changes. Then write your third draft.

Put this draft away for a couple of hours or overnight. Then read over
your final draft and edit it for grammatical and stylistic errors. If you
have to make so many corrections that your paper starts to look messy,
type or write it over. The best ideas can be defeated or diminished by
sloppy presentation.

Given what you have learned and applied in this chapter, what specific   EXERCISE 7
pieces of advice about drafting and revising would you offer a class of
incoming freshmen? Give your advice in the form of a list or an essay,
whichever you prefer.

Write a paper in which you challenge a traditional or conventional point of view.

GETTING STARTED

With several of your classmates, read through the following list of topics and decide, as a group, what you think is the traditional or accepted opinion (or opinions) on each topic. Ask yourselves what point of view you have heard expressed over and over again. For example, given the topic "the army," one class's response was immediate: "Being in the army builds character."

- ☐ Life in the city
- ☐ Life in the country
- ☐ Anger
- ☐ The army
- ☐ Honesty
- ☐ Fat people
- ☐ Being alone
- ☐ Teen-age marriages
- ☐ Final exams
- ☐ Youth

GETTING ORGANIZED

Once you have a group consensus about the traditional or conventional perspective on these topics, pick one that particularly interests you and consider specific situations or contexts that might challenge or undermine that traditional perspective. For example, if you define *character* as a sense of personal independence and authority, you might write a paper questioning the army's ability to build that particular kind of character, and your essay would explain a thesis such as the following: "Army discipline forces men and women to renounce much of their personal independence and freedom."

Begin by thinking about the specific contexts or situations that could challenge the conventional perspective on your topic. Write a thesis statement that expresses your individual perspective. Then write a two-to-three-page essay clarifying that thesis for your readers.

Suggestions for
Your Writer's Notebook

SUGGESTION 1

Maxims can be defined as short statements that communicate a general truth about human behavior. Imagine that you had used one of the following maxims in talking to a friend. In response, that friend looked at you blankly, clearly without the vaguest idea of what you meant. What would you say to communicate what you had in mind?

1. "Most of our virtues are nothing but hidden vices." — La Rochefoucauld
2. "A true gentleman is one who is never unintentionally rude." — Oscar Wilde
3. "Truth is stranger than fiction." — Mark Twain
4. "The eagle never lost so much time as when he submitted to learn of the crow." — William Blake
5. "It is better to have pain than paralysis." — Florence Nightingale
6. "Generosity is the vanity of giving." — La Rochefoucauld

SUGGESTION 2

Try inventing some of your own maxims about life. I like this one from student Jeni Snyder: "The less bread you have the more baloney you get."

SUGGESTION 3

Select some famous person about whom you could write. Brainstorm your subject, jotting down every descriptive detail that comes to mind. Select those details that you consider most characteristic, and write a brief paragraph in which you describe your subject without naming her or him. Read your paragraph or paragraphs to the class. See whether they can tell who your subject is. To prolong the suspense a bit, you might want to put the most revealing characteristics last. Here are two examples:

Born in Georgia, he was a gentle man who swore to move mountains through peaceful means. "I have a dream," he shouted and his audience marched behind him, defying all obstacles. But the dream died in Memphis, with the explosion of an assassin's bullet.

Middle-aged but still strutting his stuff to the roar of teen-
age crowds. Ruby-red lips and shaggy brown hair, the man
can't get no satisfaction even though he's a millionaire.

SUGGESTION 4

When people talk at "cross purposes," they are generally using the
same words but giving the words different meanings. Sometimes their
problems can be solved by a better definition of terms. Read through the
following statements, decide which words or phrases could cause trouble
in a conversation, and see whether you can define them further to make
interpretation easier.

1. In America everyone is equal.
2. I love you.

3. I have tried to be a good friend to you.
4. The man is just horrible.
5. That's a happy marriage.
6. He's just wasted his life.

SUGGESTION 5

Given the writing you have done up to this point, how would you explain the following quotation?

> In all its phases, composing is conversation with yourself — or selves, since you are speaker, audience and critic all in one. (Ann E. Berthoff)

Combining Sentences

In Chapter 2 you combined separate sentences or independent clauses through the use of coordinate conjunctions such as *and, but, or, nor, for, so,* and *yet.* However, as you may know, you do not always need coordinate conjunctions to combine two separate sentences into one. You can also use a semicolon.

You can't really believe her; she never told the truth in her life.

Uniting separate sentences with a semicolon will not prove difficult for you if you keep one essential point in mind: When you use a semicolon to separate two clauses, both of those clauses should be capable of standing alone. That means you can use a semicolon like this: "She violently criticized his performance; among other things, she labeled it unoriginal, uninspired, and, most of all, unbearable." But you cannot use it like this: "She violently criticized his performance; calling it unspeakable." When you use a semicolon to combine clauses, each of those clauses must be able to function as a separate sentence.

You may find it easier to complete the following exercise in steps. **EXERCISE** Begin by combining everything that comes before the sentence introduced by the semicolon. Then combine everything necessary for the sentence that comes after the semicolon. Finally, combine both sentences.

Example:
1.   ∧ The prisoners had taken enough abuse
        This was *after ten years on Devil's Island.* [,]
   [;] They were determined to escape ∧ .
        They would do it *no matter what the cost.*
   Step 1: After ten years on Devil's Island, the prisoners had taken enough abuse.
   Step 2: They were determined to escape no matter what the cost.
   Step 3: After ten years on Devil's Island, the prisoners had taken enough abuse; they were determined to escape no matter what the cost.

Complete the following exercise.

1. ∧ She made her decision.
      She made it *during the discussion.* [,]
  [;] She would fire him ∧ .
      She would do it *on Friday.*

    _____

    _____

2. ∧ D. B. Cooper hijacked a plane ∧ .
      That was *ten years ago.* [,]
      He *stole a million dollars* [and]
  [;] He hasn't been heard from since.

    _____

    _____

3. Elvis Presley revolutionized ∧ music.
      This was *rock* music.
  [;] He combined the best of rock and roll ∧ .
      He combined it *with the best of rhythm and blues.*

    _____

    _____

4. Cults are dangerous.
  [;] They demand ∧ obedience ∧ .
      The obedience must be *complete.*
      The obedience is *from their followers.*

    _____

    _____

5. He had to admit the ∧ truth.
      The truth was *painful.*
  [;] He was a ∧ gambler.
      His gambling was *compulsive.*

    _____

    _____

6.   They found the ship ∧ .
         They found it *by chance.*
     [;] It was filled with ∧ treasures.
         The treasures were *priceless.*

     _____

     _____

7.   She had given up drinking ∧ .
         She had given up *smoking.* [and]
     [;] Her doctor had ordered it.

     _____

     _____

8.   ∧ His mind was made up.
         It was made up *from that point on.* [,]
     [;] He would defend his family ∧ ∧ .
         He would defend *his property.* [and]
         He would do it *against all intruders.*

     _____

     _____

9.   AIDS is a ∧ disease.
         It is a *devastating* disease.
     [;] It kills most of its victims.

     _____

     _____

10. The ∧ rain had begun to fall.
         The rain was *acid.*
     [;] The population had begun to fail.

     _____

     _____

Write five sentences imitating the sample sentence for pattern 3.   EXERCISE

1. _____

    _____

2. _____

_____

3. _____

_____

4. _____

_____

5. _____

_____

PATTERN 4

In pattern 3 you connected independent clauses with just a semicolon. However, you can also use the semicolon with words called *conjunctive adverbs*. (See list of common conjunctive adverbs on pages 82–83.) These are words that help define the relationship between the ideas contained in the sentences. In the following sentence, for example, the word *however* makes a connection between two clauses that might otherwise contradict one another.

The movie about nuclear warfare made him anxious and tense; however, he watched it.

You should be aware that conjunctive adverbs can appear between clauses:

The woman was bitten by a rabid dog; consequently, she had to have a series of painful injections.

Or they can appear somewhere near the beginning of the second clause:

Jim Morrison's rock and roll music is still very popular; Morrison, however, has been dead for almost twenty years.

EXERCISE

Depending on their position within a sentence, conjunctive adverbs require different punctuation marks. In the following exercises, the signals for the appropriate punctuation appear in brackets.

Examples:

1. The girl weighed only ninety pounds ∧ .
         She *still could not eat.* [and]
    [; consequently,]
    She sought treatment ∧ .
         The treatment was *for anorexia.*
    The girl weighed only ninety pounds and still could not eat; con-
    sequently, she sought treatment for anorexia.

2. The girl weighed only ninety pounds.
         She *still could not eat.* [and]
    [; , therefore,]
    She sought treatment ∧ .
         The treatment was *for anorexia.*
    The girl weighed only ninety pounds and still could not eat; she,
    therefore, sought treatment for anorexia.

Complete the following exercise.

1.   ∧ ∧ ∧ Musicians employ ∧ dissonance.
         There are *many* of them.
         They are *modern.*
         They play *jazz.*
         The dissonance is *tonal.*
    [; , therefore,]
    They attract an ∧ audience. [~~an~~]
         The audience is *only a small* one.

    _____

    _____

2. Communes were popular ∧ .
         That was *in the sixties.*
    [; however,]
    They are all but forgotten ∧ .
         That is *today.*

    _____

    _____

3. The movie ∧ aroused ∧ protest.
    The movie was *about nuclear warfare*.
    It aroused *a lot of* protest.
[; nevertheless,]
It was shown ∧ .
    It appeared *around the world*.

_____

_____

4. The troops ∧ were homesick.
    They were *in Lebanon*.
[; , nonetheless,]
They performed their duties ∧ .
    They did it *with determination*.

_____

_____

5. Jackie Onassis avoids ∧ reporters.
    She avoids *all* of them.
[; moreover,]
She refuses ∧ interviews.
    She refuses *all* of them.

_____

_____

6. Wayne Newton bought a ∧ hotel ∧ .
    The hotel is for a *resort*.
    The resort is *in the Poconos*.
[; furthermore,]
He is buying a casino ∧ .
    The casino is *in Atlantic City*.

_____

_____

7. He punished his son ∧ .
    It was *for the boy's misbehavior*.
[; afterward,]

He felt terrible ∧ .
    His feelings were *about what he had done.*

_____

_____

8. The house was falling apart.
    [; , moreover,]
    They had leveled the ∧ area.
        The area was *surrounding* it.

_____

_____

9. The patient wanted to give up ∧ ∧ .
        She wanted to *die.* [and]
        This was *after a long illness.* [,]
    [; however,]
    The doctors kept her alive ∧ .
        They did it *through artificial means.*

_____

_____

10. They fought ∧ .
        They did it *like cats and dogs.*
    [; still,]
    They stay married ∧ .
        They were married *for forty years.*

_____

_____

    Here is a list of words that are often used as conjunctive adverbs. Try using some of them in the next exercise.

TO SUGGEST THE ADDITION OF A RELATED IDEA:

furthermore	also
moreover	likewise
besides	similarly

To Suggest Emphasis or Repetition:

indeed   obviously

To Signal Modification or Reversal of Expectations:

nevertheless   conversely
nonetheless   still
however

To Signal Relationship in Time:

before   afterward
throughout   thereafter
now   meanwhile
earlier   finally
later

To Signal a Causal Relationship:

therefore   thereupon
consequently   accordingly

When combined, each pair of sentences should show the relationship   EXERCISE
indicated in the brackets.

Examples
1. Marilyn Monroe has been dead for more   [reversal]
       than twenty years.
    Her legend lives on.
    Marilyn Monroe has been dead for more than twenty years; none-
    theless, her legend lives on.
2. She is a tyrant to all her employees.   [causation]
    They despise her.
    She is a tyrant to all her employees; they, therefore, despise her.

Complete the following exercise.

1. Americans consume large   [reversal of expectation]
       quantities of junk food.
    They consider themselves a healthy people.

    _____

    _____

2. South Korean prize fighter Duk Koo Kim received   [causation]
       a wound to the head in the fourteenth round of a match.
    He died of brain injuries shortly after being carried out of the ring.

    _____

    _____

3. Scientists have taught several chimpanzees [reversal of expectation]
       to use sign language.
    They are being used in medical research that takes no account of
       their special abilities.

    _____

    _____

4. He is a man of unsavory character.   [emphasis]
    He is nothing but a crook

    _____

    _____

5. American jeans are popular in Europe.   [addition]
    McDonald's hamburgers, country–western music, and Coca Cola
    have also made their mark.

    _____

    _____

    Write five sentences imitating pattern 4.   EXERCISE

1. _____

    _____

2. _____

    _____

3. _____

   _____

4. _____

   _____

5. _____

   _____

CHAPTER 4

Five Useful Patterns
of Development

As you know from Chapter 3, supporting paragraphs anticipate and answer questions your readers might have about your thesis statement. However, different thesis statements provoke different kinds of questions. Depending on the thesis you are trying to develop, your supporting paragraphs can provide illustrations, describe effects, outline events, make comparisons, or define categories. There is no one single method or pattern of development that supporting paragraphs must assume in each and every essay.

To give you some idea of the options at your disposal, this chapter describes five methods of development that are frequently used by academic writers. Although these five methods can and often do overlap, this chapter introduces them individually to better explain and clarify their requirements.

Providing Illustrations

Imagine for a moment that, during a conversation with a friend, you claim that the people who write soap operas seem to be fascinated by the world of medicine. Imagine too that your friend responds with a puzzled "What do you mean?" You would probably respond by citing several specific examples of soap operas such as "General Hospital," "Guiding Light," and "Ryan's Hope" that have used hospitals and illness as a major source for their plots. Such a response is typical of the way people communicate ideas when they talk. Having made a general statement, they back it up with specific illustrations.

Exactly the same principle holds for writers. Having introduced their thesis, they frequently choose to develop it by providing specific illustrations. In Chapter 2, for example, Glenda Williams developed the following thesis statement: "Movies contribute a lot to the difficulties parents and teen-agers have communicating." Look now at the way in which she has developed that thesis statement through supporting paragraphs that offer specific illustrations of what she means.

Movie Parents   Glenda Williams

1   A good portion of the time my son seems to think that I am a fool, that all my years of living have taught me nothing worth knowing. He believes, I think, that anyone over thirty is bound to be dull, insensitive, and boring. I am not quite sure where this idea originated. <u>But I do know that the movies he most enjoys all serve to reinforce his negative opinion of adults and adulthood.</u>   *Thesis Statement*

2   I loved the movie <u>E.T.</u> as much as he did. It was the story of an adorable little being from outer space who happened to get stranded in a suburban home and almost died trying to get back to his own planet. It was so touching that I cried when the creature's heart almost broke because of homesickness.   *First Illustration*

3   <u>What I didn't find touching, however, was the portrayal of the adults in the film.</u> The mother was the most disorganized human being imaginable, and of course it was her children, not she, who cared for and shielded E.T. from harm. In fact, when she discovered his presence in her home, she immediately turned him over to the authorities for scientific research. And it was only when her son organized a band of his friends to rescue E.T. that the movie could have a happy ending. Left in the hands of the adults, E.T. would have been examined and probed until he died.   *Connection to Thesis Statement Explained*

4   <u>Christine</u>, the movie about a killer car, was another one of my son's favorites. I did not particularly want to see it, but my son raved about it so much that I thought I should. Naturally I hated it, partly because I just don't enjoy seeing people get run over, one after the other. <u>But what was more disturbing, once again, was the portrayal of the adults.</u> The hero's best friend and his girl friend, both teen-agers, were presented as sensitive and sensible human beings. But his parents, particularly his mother, were just awful.   *Second Illustration*

    Connection to Thesis Statement Explained

Throughout the film she pushes and nags him so much it is no
surprise that he finally blows up at her. As a matter of fact, you
want him to rebel. She is so impossible, you can't imagine him
tolerating her for one more minute. Watching the film, even I felt
that way. And the audience — most of them teen-agers — did too.
They all shouted and cheered when he screamed at her.

5   But the final insult was <u>Risky Business</u>. Here Joel, a senior in   *Third Illustration*
high school, falls into the hands of a dishonest and manipulative
but very sexy prostitute named Lana. Yet somehow the prostitute
never becomes the villain of the piece. On the contrary, the movie
ends with her cozily having dinner with the hero. Apparently the
two have become good friends. <u>If there are any villains to be found,</u>   *Connection to Thesis*
<u>it is, once again, the parents, who seem concerned with nothing</u>   *Statement Explained*
<u>except material things, with having the perfect home, the perfect</u>
<u>stereo, the perfect car.</u> With parents like these, it is no wonder the
hero gets into trouble: They haven't taught him anything except
how important it is to attend an Ivy League school, where you can
make the right connections.

6   When I see the movies my son loves, I feel as if I should give up   *Ending Restates Thesis*
trying to communicate with him. It is a losing battle. Every time
he enters a movie theater, he receives the same message: As a
teen-ager, he knows everything. As an adult, I know nothing. I
wonder if the people in Hollywood know what they are doing. Or,
more to the point, I wonder if they care.

Having claimed in her thesis statement that the movies her son sees
reinforce his negative attitude toward adults, the author of this essay uses
her supporting paragraphs to offer specific examples of what she means.
She offers the movies *E.T.*, *Christine*, and *Risky Business* as illustrations
of her claim. (You may remember that these were some of the examples
that emerged during her free writing.) She was able to use them, in an
expanded and more detailed form, in her supporting paragraphs.

Whenever you decide your readers need specific illustrations in order
to understand your thesis, consider the following guidelines for drafting
and revision.

1.   One isolated example rarely makes a general statement clear enough
for your readers. For this method of development to be effective, you
almost always need three or four specific illustrations.

2.   Develop each individual illustration as fully as you can. Imagine,
for example, that you wanted to illustrate the following thesis statement:

"Household pets can do more than provide companionship. They can also improve their owners' health." To effectively illustrate what you claim in that statement, you might want to develop a supporting paragraph around the following generalization: "Petting a dog can control high blood pressure." But you would not want just to introduce that general statement and leave it at that. Instead you would further develop it through more specific details, such as explaining how stroking the animal's fur soothes feelings of anxiety and stresss, a major cause of high blood pressure.

3.   Choose your examples carefully. Be sure they clearly exemplify your thesis. Above all, the relationship between the thesis and your supporting illustrations must be made clear to your readers. For example, in the model essay, Glenda did not simply cite the three movies and leave it at that. Instead she carefully explained how their plots helped reinforce her son's negative attitude toward adults. Remember: The relationship between your thesis and the illustrations you give might be clear to you, but that does not necessarily mean it is clear to your readers. It is up to you to explain the relationship between your thesis and the illustrations you provide in the supporting paragraphs.

The following exercise will give you some practice in using illustrations to explain your thesis.

From the following list, choose a tentative thesis you think you could effectively develop through illustration.

EXERCISE   1

1. Dogs are said to be man's best friend, but they are not always treated that way.
2. Cancer patients are often surprised and hurt by the way friends and family react to the disease.
3. Anyone interested in health and fitness has a number of magazines to choose from.
4. Babysitters should be prepared to face a variety of emergency situations.
5. For some people, taking a vacation is harder than going to work.
6. Sometimes it seems that parents and children speak totally different languages.
7. Students who return to school in middle age face some special problems.
8. Life on soap operas is anything but realistic.
9. At the present time, England dominates rock music.
10. For a young child, the simplest household object can become an instrument of death.

11. You can, of course, ignore all of these possibilities and discover your own thesis — one more suited to your tastes and interests.

After you have selected your tentative thesis, take at least fifteen or twenty minutes to brainstorm for examples. Remember to eliminate inappropriate examples only after you are through brainstorming. Then write a two-to-three-page essay using some of those illustrations to develop your thesis.

Tracing Chronological Order

At the root of that word *chronological* is the Greek word *chron* meaning "time." It follows, then, that papers using chronological order as a method of development focus on ordering events according to a particular sequence in time. In general, you should think about using this method whenever your thesis statement describes how something is done or created, happens, or develops. The following thesis statement, for example, suggests chronological order as a method of development: "With enough time and discipline, anyone can practice self-hypnosis." As you can see, that is precisely the form the supporting paragraphs take in the following model essay.

Self-Hypnosis   Emily Gage

1   Today everyone complains about the stress and strain of modern living. Yet those stresses and strains can be reduced — even eliminated — by anyone willing to practice self-hypnosis. <u>A simple method, self-hypnosis involves only fifteen minutes twice a day. To practice it, you need little more than time and discipline.</u>

Thesis Statement
Introduces Procedure
to be Explained
First Step

2   The first step is to find a quiet room where there is little noise or commotion from the outside. Then find an easy chair, where you can sit down comfortably without feeling cramped or confined. Feeling comfortable is extremely important.

3   When you sit down, make sure that both your feet are flat on the floor and that your legs are not crossed. When you have settled yourself in the most comfortable position, find a crack or a spot on the ceiling to focus on for a few minutes. As you focus on it, the spot will grow blurry and the noises from outside the room will subside.

Second Step

4   <u>At this point</u>, you can let your head drop to your chest. You can actually let it hang, as if you were a rag doll. This is the time to concentrate on your breathing, letting it become slower and slower. If your breathing does not slow down naturally, put your hands on your abdomen so that you can feel the movement of your breath as you inhale and exhale.

Underlined Phrases
Help Guide Readers
Through the Sequence
Third Step

5   <u>After your breathing has slowed its pace</u>, imagine any place where the predominant color is blue or green. Think about the ocean or the sky or about some trees or mountains. Concentrate on this image, blotting out everything else until you see it clearly, almost as if you were really there.

Fourth Step

6   <u>Once the image is clear</u>, try to lift first your arm, then your leg. When your arms and legs feel heavy — and they will feel heavy — tell yourself they are too heavy to move. This is the final stage of deep relaxation, and you should stay in it for ten to fifteen minutes, longer if you can. When you feel the time has passed, slowly open your eyes and look around you. <u>You will feel both rested and refreshed. Above all, you will feel more relaxed.</u>

Fifth Step

Ending Describes a
Result of Technique

In this essay, the thesis statement announces that self-hypnosis is possible for anyone who has the time and the discipline. Having introduced that thesis, the author anticipates the following question: "What exactly is this simple method that requires only a little time and discipline?" To answer that question, the supporting paragraphs outline and explain the individual steps in self-hypnosis.

Whenever you develop a thesis that suggests chronological order as the best method of development, you should consider the following points as you draft and revise your paper.

1.   Use your thesis statement to define clearly the overall direction of your paper: "Self-hypnosis is a simple method that anyone can practice." "Coal is formed when pressure is exerted on dead plant and animal material." Do not just plunge into the specific steps without telling your audience where you are going.

2.   With your essay in hand, your readers should be able to recreate physically the process you describe or to follow it mentally from beginning to end. Above all, they should understand how one step leads into another. That kind of clarity can be produced only by writers who thoroughly understand the process or procedure they describe.

To make sure the procedure or process you want to describe is clear in your own mind, consider outlining or diagramming the steps or stages involved in it before you even start drafting. Use lines, arrows, circles, or anything else you can think of to indicate relationships. Such diagrams are particularly useful when you are working out a complicated process like the development of coal:

STAGE ONE: Upper layer of matter gets heavy,
                          Exerts pressure on bottom layer,
                                  Causes temperature to increase.

STAGE TWO: Layer heats up ——→ hardens ——→ cools off,
                          Produces "peat" (a soft crumbly material)

STAGE THREE: Peat compressed ——→ heated ——→ hardens
                          Water forced out, leaving higher percentage of
                          carbon
                                  forms poor grade of coal called "ligite"

3.   Don't put all the steps into one long and confusing paragraph. Use paragraphing to indicate important divisions. Suppose, for example, your paper were organized to follow the making of an automobile on an assembly line. An ineffective paper would simply use one huge paragraph to describe that procedure. But a more effective one would put the three stages into three separate paragraphs: assembling the body shell, painting the body, and outfitting the body. Each paragraph would detail the specific steps involved in one of the individual stages.

4.   Sometimes the procedure or process you want to describe already has a clear sequence of steps. For example, if you describe how a car is put together on an assembly line, the order is there for you. You don't have to invent it. The process has already been divided into definite stages. But that is not always the case. The writer of the model essay, for example, had to provide much of the order, deciding where to combine several small steps into one. When you have to create your own order, you might want to play with several different alternatives before deciding on a sequence.

5.   Use "time words and phrases" to help your readers follow the sequence of steps you describe. Such words as *afterward*, *from then on*, and *next* can guide your reader from step to step without confusion. (For examples of "time words" used effectively, see the essay on chocolate at the end of this chapter.)

6.   If you decide to describe a process or procedure that might not be readily familiar to a general audience, think about what terms need

to be defined. For example, if you were describing how to take a good photograph, you might want to define terms such as *light meter* and *F-stop*. Remember, even if your instructor is an accomplished photographer, she will probably read your paper as though she were relatively unacquainted with the process you describe.

The following exercise will give you some practice in developing supporting paragraphs that exhibit chronological order.

The following thesis statements suggest chronological order as a method of development. Choose one that you think you could develop in a two-to-three-page essay.

EXERCISE 2

1. Planting a garden is a time-consuming process, but it is well worth the effort.
2. With a little instruction, anyone can learn how to tune up a car.
3. Washing a dog should be a simple procedure, but somehow it never is.
4. The first day of registration on college campuses is a nightmare for freshmen.
5. It is hard to believe, but under the right circumstances, a grain of sand can become an exquisite pearl.
6. The flow of blood through the body follows a definite path.
7. Anyone can give up smoking; you just have to follow a few simple steps.
8. When money is in short supply, it is a good idea to learn how to refinish old furniture and make it look like new.
9. Anyone who wants a loan, for whatever purpose, should be prepared for what seems like an endless chain of application forms.
10. Learning how to develop your own photographs takes time, but it can save you a lot of money.
11. If you think you can't develop any one of these thesis statements, feel free to create one that you can develop.

After you have selected or created a tentative thesis statement, try diagramming the procedure or process you intend to explain in your paper. This should help you decide whether you can, in fact, explain the process described in your thesis statement. Once you have a tentative thesis statement that you feel fairly sure you can explain, write a two-to-three-page paper that uses chronological order as a method of development.

Explaining Cause and Effect

The explanation of cause-and-effect relationships is an indispensable method of development for college writing. Throughout your college career, you will be expected to write essays that answer two kinds of questions: (1) Why did something happen? and (2) What is the result or consequence of its having occurred? These questions are implicit in such assignments as "Describe the effects of the Civil War on the Southern economy" or "Explain the economic factors that created the racial hostility in the early union movement."

Although you may not realize it, you are already familiar with this essential method for developing supporting paragraphs. In Chapter 3 Joan Amato used it to explain her thesis statement about fear of hospitals. Assuming that her readers would respond to that statement by asking what produced such a fear, Joan used her supporting paragraphs to describe some specific *causes*.

In the following paper, Marcy Federbusch explains a very different thesis, but she uses a similar method of development. And she concentrates more on effects than on causes. That difference was dictated by the requirements of her thesis statement: "In the pursuit of ratings, television news programs frequently slant — even distort — the news."

Slanting the News   Marcy Federbusch

1   In the pursuit of ratings, television news programs frequently slant — even distort — the news. Determined to win the biggest share of the audience, television broadcasting does not adequately or objectively report current events.

2   All three of the major networks rely on the findings of the A.C. Nielsen Company, an organization that tabulates the number of households viewing any particular broadcast and converts that number into a percentage of audience members reached. This percentage or "share" of the audience, then, determines the popularity of the show. The higher a show's audience "share," the more money advertisers will pay to present their products in a commercial aired during that show. Therefore, the networks make a profit that is directly proportional to the ratings. This means that every network is compelled to compete for bigger and better

Thesis Statement Defines Cause-and-Effect Relationship

More Specific Explanation of Cause

ratings, and this quest forces even news programs to search for stories that will excite though not necessarily inform.

3   In their endless search for interesting, exciting, or intriguing stories, broadcast journalists often resort to techniques that slant or distort the news they report. One such technique is called "staging." This occurs when an event is filmed not as it happened but as it was re-enacted. When news reporters arrive on the scene too late to film the actual occurrence, they may ask those involved to re-enact what happened before their arrival. Unfortunately, the television audience may view a "staged" event without ever knowing it has not seen the real thing.

First Specific Example of Effect Described in Thesis Statement

4   Yet another such technique is called "ambush interviewing." This is a technique that the news program "60 Minutes" has made famous. With this method of interviewing, a reporter unexpectedly approaches a subject and places a microphone in front of him, hoping he will be caught off guard and give a dramatic response, one that will stimulate viewer interest even if it is not directly related to the subject at hand.

Second Specific Example

5   "Tape doctoring" occurs in the editing room, where an interview can be spliced together to produce responses that are very different from those a subject may have intended. The point of this technique is to make the interview controversial — sometimes at the expense of accuracy.

Third Specific Example

6   A good part of the population likes to see the news rather than read about it. Given this fact, more attempts should be made to inform the television audience about the different techniques used to stimulate viewer interest. If members of the television audience knew about things like staging, ambush interviewing, and tape doctoring, they might prefer to have their news made less exciting but more accurate.

Ending Offers Possible Solution

The thesis statement in this example describes the relationship between a cause, "the pursuit of ratings," and its effect, "distortion of the news." But to make that statement clear for her readers, Marcy felt she had to answer two important questions: "Why are the ratings so important?" and "Just exactly how do television news programs distort the news?" In answer to these questions, her first supporting paragraph provided more specific information about the cause of news distortion (ratings are important to profits), while the remaining supporting paragraphs offered specific examples of the individual effects (staging, ambush interviewing, and tape doctoring).

Whenever you want to develop your thesis by explaining cause and effect, your chances of writing a successful paper will be improved if you consider the following guidelines as you draft and revise.

1.   Consider the possibility that your thesis statement describes not one cause-and-effect relationship but several chains of causes that also become effects. Take, for example, the thesis statement "In an attempt to avoid the chemical additives in meat, some people have turned to a vegetarian diet only to suffer from the symptoms of iron deficiency anemia." Diagrammed, it would look like this:

CAUSE	EFFECT	CAUSES	EFFECT
Additives in Meat	→ Vegetarianism	→	Anemia

What this diagram tells you is that the effect described in the sample statement, vegetarianism, is also a cause of something else, "anemia." With such a diagram, it is easier to decide which part of the chain you want to emphasize in your thesis statement and ultimately in your supporting paragraphs. You might choose to emphasize the cause-and-effect relationship between a meatless diet and anemia and simply summarize the cause-and-effect relationship between chemical additives in meat and the decision to become a vegetarian: "Eager to avoid chemical additives in meat, many people became vegetarians only to find themselves plagued by the symptoms of iron deficiency anemia.

Or you might choose a different emphasis: "Many people today have chosen to become vegetarians because they are afraid of the chemical additives in meat, additives that may cause serious illness." A good part of the time, diagramming will help you see and understand the chains of cause and effect underlying what appears to be the one simple cause-and-effect relationship expressed in your thesis statement. After diagramming your thesis statement, you will have a better idea of what you want to say in your supporting paragraphs.

2.   Do not assume that you have to cover every aspect of a cause-and-effect relationship. Instead, use your thesis statement to let your readers know that your supporting paragraphs will focus on one particular cause and effect even though you are aware of others: "Alcoholism is a complex disease produced by many factors. However, there is strong evidence that the child of an alcoholic may, in turn, develop a drinking

problem." With this statement the writer prepares his readers for supporting paragraphs that concentrate on one particular cause rather than several.

3. Do not assume that your readers will automatically understand your particular view of a cause-and-effect relationship. Be sure to give them sufficient explanation. Take, for example, the thesis statement "Because of the high incidence of rape, many feminists have begun to demand more restrictions on pornographic books and movies." That thesis statement implies a causal relationship: Reading or viewing pornographic material leads to the act of rape. Consequently, your supporting paragraphs would have to address the question readers might raise: *Is* there a connection between pornography and rape?

The following exercise will give you some practice in writing paragraphs that explain cause and effect.

Using the definition of a *problem* given in Chapter 2 (p. 26), write a tentative thesis statement about some issue that concerns or interests you, such as "Jogging is supposed to be good for you, but in my case it did more harm than anything else" or "Increasingly, funds for bilingual education are being cut, making it harder and harder for children who are not American-born to get a satisfactory education."

EXERCISE 3

Once you have a thesis statement defining a particular problem, write a two-to-three-page paper that explains the causes and effects involved in the problem you describe. To generate material for your supporting paragraphs, you can use discovery questions like the following:

What cause or causes can you find for this state of affairs? How did this situation come into being? When did it start? Why did it start?

What are the results or effects? Do these effects apply to everyone equally? What will happen in this situation over time?

Comparing and Contrasting

Consider for a moment this sample thesis statement: "Unlike the veterans of World War II, the veterans of Viet Nam received a cold, even hostile, welcome when they first returned home to America." With this as your thesis statement, you could certainly anticipate the following questions from your readers: "How did the reception that greeted the Viet Nam

veterans differ from the one accorded the veterans of World War II?"
"Was it really so different?" To answer those questions, your supporting
paragraphs would have to compare (discuss similarities between) and
contrast (discuss differences between) the two groups, and the result might
be an essay something like the one that follows.

Veterans of Two Wars   Joe Kelley

1   When the veterans of World War II came home from the
battlefields of Europe in 1945, America could not do enough for its
returning warriors. There were dancing in the streets, ticker-tape
parades, and a general atmosphere of joyous welcome. The
reception, however, was very different for the veterans who came
home from Viet Nam in 1975: On their return they were given a
cold, even hostile, welcome.

*Background Material
about Veterans of
World War II
Thesis Statement
Emphasizes Difference
Between Two Groups*

2   In 1945 everyone wanted to hear the war stories of the
returning veterans. No one had any questions about the justness of
America's entry into the war. Hitler and his allies were enemies
that had to be defeated no matter what the cost, and Americans
were proud of and grateful to the soldiers who had helped
accomplish that terrible and devastating task. With open arms,
they welcomed back those soldiers who had helped to win "The Big
One."

*Description of Welcome
Accorded Veterans
in 1945*

3   But in 1975, thirty years later, things were different. For over a
decade, Americans had been asking themselves what their country
was doing in Viet Nam. Unlike World War II, where the issues of
right and wrong were clear and sharp, the war in Viet Nam was
an ambiguous and confusing affair. There were those, in fact, who
firmly believed America should never have entered another
country's civil war. Given their political beliefs, those men and
women did not know how they should respond to the returning
soldiers. It was as though they wanted to forget the veterans of a
war they considered an embarassing and unjust mistake. Like the
previous generation of veterans, the Viet Nam vets had war stories
to tell, but few Americans wanted to listen. The veterans were
expected to return home, adjust to civilian life, and forget their
painful past.

*General Statement
of Difference*

*Specific Point
of Difference*

*Specific Points of
Similarity and
Difference*

4   To be sure, there were many people even at the war's end who
still supported the American presence in Viet Nam. But even they
were not always ready to open their arms wide to the returning

*Description of
Reception Given Viet
Nam Vets*

vets. <u>In 1975, the veteran in uniform was not the symbol of power and pride he had been three decades earlier.</u> On the contrary, he was a living reminder of the only war America had ever lost.

5   It has taken close to a decade for America to reconcile itself with its most recent veterans and to talk openly about the shabby treatment accorded them. Recently there have been articles in the newspaper and programs on television discussing the painful silence that greeted the returning Viet Nam vet. In a small way, Americans seem to be offering an apology. The question now is "Will the veterans of Viet Nam choose to accept it?"

Specific Points of Difference

Final Paragraph Comments on Possible Resolution

In this essay, the supporting paragraphs compare and contrast the receptions accorded two generations of veterans. However, you should be aware that the author does not always compare and contrast in exactly the same way.

Paragraph 1, for example, uses a point-by-point method of comparison. That means that, within the same paragraph, the author moves back and forth between the two subjects. Paragraphs 2 and 3, however, use a divided or block method of comparison. Paragraph 2 focuses solely on the veterans of World War II, whereas paragraph 3 focuses primarily on the veterans of Viet Nam.

Whichever method you choose for developing your thesis through comparison and contrast, you will be successful if you keep the following points in mind as you draft and revise.

1. The similarities and differences you describe must explain your thesis statement. Never let them become an end in themselves. For example, the essay on veterans did not spend a great deal of time describing similarities between the two groups, largely because the thesis statement required supporting paragraphs emphasizing difference rather than sameness.

2. Be sure that you are equally knowledgeable about the two people, ideas, or things you compare and contrast. Don't treat half of your topic with great specificity and then talk about the other half in the most general terms.

3. Look for similarities or differences that might not readily be apparent to the casual observer: "Traditionally spoken of in the same breath, Raymond Chandler and Ross McDonald actually wrote very different kinds of mystery stories" or "Although Richard Nixon and Jimmy Carter were political opposites, their biographies reveal very similar personality traits." It is this kind of originality that can stimulate your readers' interest.

The following exercise will give you practice in using your supporting paragraphs to compare and contrast two topics.

Make a list of paired people who are or were involved in very similar   **EXERCISE   4**
kinds of activities — for example,

☐ Jimmy Carter and Ronald Reagan
☐ Your mother and your father
☐ Muhammed Ali and Sugar Ray Leonard
☐ The Rolling Stones and Duran Duran

Using the following discovery questions, choose one pair of people and free write for at least twenty minutes.

1. What are the essential characteristics of each person?
2. What are the similarities or differences between the two?
3. What, in your opinion, is the most important point of similarity or difference?
4. What is the most obvious point of similarity or difference?
5. In what area are the two subjects most different or most similar?
6. Which member of the pair is better, more effective, or more successful?

Then use the material derived from your focused free writing to produce a thesis statement that makes one of the following claims:

1. Although the two people are normally considered very similar, the differences between them actually outweigh the similarities.
2. Although the two people are traditionally considered very different, the similarities between them actually override the differences.
3. Although the two are traditionally considered equal in their profession or activity, they are not. One is actually better than the other.

Write a two- to-three-page essay that explains your thesis statement by comparing and contrasting your two topics.

Using Classification

In the following model essay, the thesis statement claims that fictional detectives are not all alike even though they might appear so at first. "In fact, the heroes of mystery stories can be divided into two quite distinct categories." To develop that thesis statement for her readers, the author uses her supporting paragraphs to answer certain questions her readers might raise: How did you arrive at that number of categories? What are the characteristics of each category? Can you give specific examples of each category? In effect, what she has done in her supporting paragraphs is to explain her system of classification. She has shown her readers how to discover and identify the subgroups comprising a larger whole.

Amateurs and Professionals   Emily Gage

1   To the casual reader of mystery stories, the detective heroes who
solve the crimes may seem monotonously similar. In a way, that is
understandable because they all fulfill the same function: They
unravel the novel's mystery to discover the man or woman
responsible for the crime of murder. But to more devoted fans —
those likely to consume a mystery a night — there are definite
distinctions to be made. <u>If carefully examined, the heroes of</u>   *Thesis Statement*
<u>mystery stories actually fall into two quite distinct categories.</u>

2   On the one hand, there is the "<u>professional,</u>" for whom solving   *Paragraph Explains*
crimes is a business and a profession, a way of making money and   *Principle of Division*
earning a living. Opposed to the professional detective is the   *and Provides Labels*
"<u>amateur.</u>" This is the man or woman who solves crimes as a   *for Categories*
hobby. To the amateur, detection is a delightful pastime —
something to do for intellectual stimulation or pleasure, perhaps,
but never for money.

3   Led by heroes like Arthur Conan Doyle's <u>Sherlock Holmes</u> and   *Examples of "Amateur"*
G. K. Chesterton's <u>Father Brown</u>, it is the amateur detective who   *Detectives*
inhabits most of the early mystery stories written at the end of
the nineteenth century. <u>In such stories, the amateur typically uses</u>   *Characteristics of*
<u>intellect far more than muscle in order to solve the mystery</u>   *Amateurs*
<u>baffling everyone, including the always rather dimwitted police. He</u>
<u>alone sees the clues that the other, less clever characters have</u>
<u>managed to overlook.</u> It is only Holmes in <u>The Sign of the Four</u>
who notices that a normally ferocious watchdog did not bark when
the murderer entered. And he alone draws the correct conclusion:
The dog must have known the murderer. Similarly, only Father
Brown in "The Blue Cross" can unmask a murderer masquerading
as a priest. He is the only one able to detect the criminal's careless
observance of religious rite.

4   But the amateur was not just a creature of the late nineteenth   *Examples of More*
century. On the contrary, he remains alive and well in the   *Modern Amateurs*
twentieth. Among the most well known today is Dorothy Sayers'
Lord Peter Wimsey, the British lord who tracks down dangerous
criminals as easily as he discusses fine wine and exquisite
porcelain. Elegant and dashing, Lord Peter is the English cousin of
S. S. Van Dine's Philo Vance. And both men, although physically
strong, prefer to use their lightning intellect rather than their
fists. For them a crime is just one more delightful puzzle waiting
to be solved.

5   Most of the female detectives who exist belong to the amateur category, with Agatha Christie's elderly Miss Marple heading the list. Living in a quiet English village, Jane Marple spends most of her time knitting and tending flowers, but she always finds time to solve the murders she encounters on a very regular basis. With her blue eyes, pink cheeks, and fussy manner, Miss Marple is not so dashing as many of the male amateurs. But just like them, she arouses the admiration of everyone who knows her, particularly the police. And most of them, like Inspector Primer in the <u>The Sleeping Car Murder</u>, have to seek her out in order to find the solution to a baffling mystery.

Examples of Female Amateurs

6   Much younger than Miss Marple but just as clever, Amanda Cross's Kate Fansler teaches English literature. But she too cannot seem to avoid involvement in crime. At work or on vacation, she is always running across dead bodies that need to be explained. Astonishingly, in novels like <u>Death in a Tenured Position</u> and <u>The James Joyce Murder</u>, she manages to explain those bodies while still finding the time to attend a literary conference and proctor a final exam. The same can be said of Rebecca Schwartz, a feminist lawyer in San Francisco, who has a talent for tripping over bodies and solving crimes.

7   <u>For the professional detectives, however, there is little time for anything except crime. If murder is their business, it is hardly a lucrative one. Always in danger of having their phone disconnected or their lights turned off for lack of funds, the professionals have to solve crimes, not because they delight in puzzles, but because they need the money.</u>

Characteristics of the "Professional"

8   Probably the most famous members of this category are detectives like Raymond Chandler's Philip Marlowe, Dashiell Hammett's Sam Spade, and Mickey Spillane's Mike Hammer. Smart enough, these heroes still lack the flashy brilliance of the amateurs, and they triumph more through determination than genius. They lack all the privilege and prestige enjoyed by their amateur colleagues. On occasion, the police even suspect them of the very crimes they are trying to solve.

Examples of Professionals

9   Whereas the amateurs track down killers who are often as ingenious as themselves (men and women who use rare poison, tropical fish, or ancient dueling weapons to commit murder), the professionals seek far more ordinary criminals as they hunt the men and women who have neither the time nor the patience to commit elegant and exotic crimes. The murderers sought by the

Point of Contrast Between Two Groups

professionals use only the simplest and most common of weapons: guns, knives, and occasionally even their bare hands.

10   The amateurs live in a world where the police are dim but honest. But the same is not true of the professionals. In the fictional worlds created by Chandler, Hammett, and Spillane, the main difference between the criminals and the police is that the police wear badges. Corruption and violence are everywhere. No place is safe. To use Chandler's own words, the professional detective walks down "mean streets" (<u>Pearls Are a Nuisance</u>, 198).[1]

11   In contrast to the amateur detective who seldom has a serious involvement with members of the opposite sex, the professional frequently falls in love — particularly with dangerous women who would do him in if they could. But in the end, the professional detective always knows better than to give in to the charms of a female. In Hammett's most famous novel, <u>The Maltese Falcon</u>, Sam Spade sends the heroine off to jail for life, right after admitting that he loves her.

Taking Hammett one step further, Mickey Spillane in <u>I the Jury</u> makes Mike Hammer fall in love with a multiple murderess. But when Hammer discovers how dangerous his beloved really is, he has no difficulty disposing of her. He simply shoots her point blank in the stomach. Dying she asks him, "How could you?" His answer: "It was easy." (250)

Having announced in the thesis statement that the larger group "detectives" can actually be divided into two distinct subgroups, the author of the model essay uses the second paragraph to explain her principle of division. She tells her readers, that is, what criterion she has used to divide up the larger group: Although all the heroes of detective stories solve the crime in the end, they do not all do it for the same reason. Some detectives solve crimes for pleasure, whereas others do it to earn a living. In addition to announcing the principle of division, paragraph 2 provides specific labels for the two categories that emerge when that principle is applied — "amateur" and "professional."

The remaining supporting paragraphs explain the specific characteristics that identify the two different groups. After reading the model essay, it

---

[1]For more on the form of footnotes, see Chapter 9 (pp. 297–299).

is possible to list the specific attitudes and behaviors that characterize the two kinds of detectives.

AMATEUR	PROFESSIONAL
Solve crimes as a hobby	Solve crimes for money
Enjoy respect and prestige	Not respected
Police admire them	Police suspect them
Little romantic interest	Romantic interest
Criminals use exotic methods. Examples are Sherlock Holmes, Miss Marple, Father Brown, Lord Peter Wimsey	Criminals use ordinary methods. Examples are Mike Hammer, Philip Marlowe, Sam Spade

It is worth noting here that a different principle of division could have revealed different information about mystery stories. Let us say, for example, that the author had decided to use "nature of the crime" to develop her categories. Chances are she would have ended up with three categories rather than two: (1) stories dealing with crimes committed for love, (2) stories wherein the crime is committed for personal vengeance, and (3) stories in which the crime is committed for financial gain. Clearly, the characteristics defining those categories would have been quite different from the ones defining amateur and professional detectives.

The point, then, is this: If you have a choice about which principle of division to use, select one that reveals something significant about your subject. Your selection of an original and enlightening principle of division will go a long way to encourage your readers' interest.

Say, for example, that you were to write an essay about your classmates. Would you really be telling your readers anything of interest if you divided them according to height? But suppose you divided them according to the way they react to the instructor? Categories such as "hostile," "independent," and "passive" might yield some interesting information about the dynamics of the class.

Whenever you develop a thesis statement that seems to call for classification as a method of development, you would do well to consider the following guidelines as you draft and revise.

1.   Once you decide on a principle of division, make it clear to your readers. Let them know exactly what criterion you are using to divide the larger whole into smaller subgroups.

2.   Use one principle consistently. Do not begin by classifying teachers according to the homework assignments they give and then suddenly, without explanation, switch to classification on the basis of lecturing style.

3.   Your principle of division should account for all the members of the larger group. If it doesn't, find another principle of classification or reconsider your topic. Say you were writing an essay on "games" and had decided to classify them according to the style of the playing board. In time, you would probably want to change your principle of division so you could include games that don't use a board, like gin rummy and charades. Or you would consider further restricting your topic to "board games" rather than just "games."

4.   As much as possible, clearly identify the subgroups through specific labels, characteristics, and examples.

5.   Be sure to give each category the same degree of development.

6.   Whenever you can, compare and contrast the categories so that your reader has a clear understanding of the way they are similar or different. In the model essay, this is the purpose of such sentences as "The professionals have to solve crimes, not because they delight in puzzles, but because they need the money."

This last guideline leads directly to a point made on the first page of this chapter. The five methods introduced here can and usually do overlap. Sometimes you will combine chronological order with cause and effect or classification with comparison and contrast. I have introduced each method separately only to clarify what each requires to be an effective means of communication.

The following exercise will give you practice in using classification to develop your supporting paragraphs.

From the following list of topics, choose one you think you could write about.   EXERCISE   5

☐ Houses
☐ Sports
☐ Restaurants
☐ Movies

☐ Cooking methods

☐ Video games

☐ Dates

☐ Books

☐ Tests

☐ Friends

☐ Teachers

☐ Students

☐ If none of these topics interests you, feel free to select your own.

Now ask the following questions to explore your topic.

1. What principle of division or selection could be used to divide your topic into smaller categories?
2. Once you apply this principle of division, how many categories emerge?
3. Do these categories account for all members of the larger group?
4. What are some of the characteristics of these categories?
5. How different or how similar are the members of each group?

Write a tentative thesis statement that announces the specific number of subgroups or categories you have discovered. Then write a two-to-three-page paper that develops that statement by describing your system of classification.

Write an essay that traces the historical development of one of your favorite foods, such as pizza, chocolate, coffee, spaghetti, or tea.

GETTING STARTED

Begin by reading the model essay that appears on pages 109–111. Taken from the pages of *National Geographic*, this essay traces the discovery and development of chocolate and covers an enormous span of time — from 1502 to the present.

Once you have read the model essay, decide what food or drink you want to trace. Then, to find information about its development, look in the following reference works:

1. *American Heritage Cookbook and Illustrated History of American Eating and Drinking*
2. *Dictionary of Gastronomy* by Andre Simon and Robin Howe
3. *Encyclopedia of Food* by Artemas Ward
4. *The Wise Encyclopedia of Cookery*

Also check the indexes of encyclopedias such as the following. They may have information you can use.

1. *Encyclopedia Americana*
2. *Encyclopaedia Britannica*
3. *Collier's Encyclopedia*
4. *Compton's Pictured Encyclopedia and Fact Index*
5. *World Book Encyclopedia*

GETTING ORGANIZED

If you find information on your subject in the first book you open, do not stop there. Look at three or four different sources and see how each one describes the development of your particular food or drink. Compare sources, noting the dates and events emphasized in each one. Think about where they differ and where they are similar. In particular, be alert for those dates and events that appear in every account. Such repetition tells you that these are the crucial or most significant events. Those events cited in one account but not in any others are probably less important. Make three different lists of events, each one based on a different source.

Because the model essay covers centuries, the author obviously could not detail each and every event in the development of chocolate. Instead he selected what he considered the major or essential stages in the development of chocolate as a popular food.

To write your paper, you will also have to make some choices, emphasizing the most crucial or significant steps or stages over time. To get some sense of what they are, scan your lists for points emphasized in all the accounts you read. Then make a final list of what you think are the essential steps or advances in the development of your subject. Include all important dates. Using your final list, write the first draft of your paper.

SUGGESTIONS FOR REVISION
Reread your draft with the following questions in mind.

1.   Have you selected only the most significant events, when important advances or changes occurred? Have you avoided the tendency to include too many minor, insignificant dates and events?

2.   Have you made it as easy as possible for your reader to follow you over a large expanse of time? Have you provided enough chronological signposts, words such as *afterward, from then on,* and *thereafter?* Have you given dates whenever possible in order to guide your reader from stage to stage? (Note the words and phrases underlined in the model essay.

3.   Have you explained the individual stages clearly enough? Have you made it clear how one advance prepared the way for the next? Have you used paragraphing to help the reader grasp major shifts or advances in development?

Chocolate: Food of the Gods[1]
GORDON YOUNG

1   Cacao, as rich in history as in flavor, is said to have originated in the Amazon or Orinoco basin at least 4000 years ago. Christopher Columbus,

[1]From *National Geographic* (Nov. 1983): 666–669. Used with permission.

in 1502 was the first European to run across the beans, on his fourth voyage to the New World, but he virtually ignored them.

2   Two decades later Hernan Cortés found Moctezuma, the Aztec emperor, drinking cup after cup of *xocoatl* — a liquid so prestigious that it was served in golden goblets that were thrown away after use. Cortés sipped the bitter, spicy beverage, and when he returned to Spain in 1528, he took some of the wondrous beans back to his king, Charles V.

3   He was a man with his eye on a golden doubloon, this Cortés, much impressed by the fact that the cacao beans were used as Aztec currency (about a hundred beans would buy a slave). So when the Spaniards left the Aztec Empire, they took cacao beans with them, seeding "money plantations" on Trinidad, Haiti, and the West African island of Fernando Po, now Bioko. Later one pod was brought from that island to the mainland; from it grew the huge cacao trade now dominated by four West African nations.

4   The Spanish then added water and cane sugar (another New World import) and heated the brew. Soon chocolate was a favored drink of Spain's nobility. Meanwhile British and Dutch sea raiders were dumping "worthless" bags of cacao beans off captured Spanish ships.

5   The money plantations of Cortés gave imperial Spain a virtual monopoly of the cacao bean market for almost a century. Still, the sweet reputation of the drink began to drift throughout Europe.

6   Dr. Stephani Blancardi of Amsterdam declared about 1705 that tasty chocolate "is also a veritable balm of the mouth, for the maintaining of all glands and humors in a good state of health. Thus it is that all who do drink it possess a sweet breath."

7   One of his countrymen backed that claim with the report of a man who had died at the age of 100: "He subsisted for 30 years on nothing other than chocolate and some biscuits. Occasionally, he would take a little soup to eat. Yet he was so fit that, at the age of 85 years, he could still mount his horse without stirrups."

8   With chocolate generating such excitement, other European nations established their own cacao plantations. The English in the West Indies called theirs "cocoa walks" and soon were satisfying well-to-do countrymen with a blander chocolate drink mixed with milk. "To a coffee house to drink jocolate," Samuel Pepys's diary chronicled in 1664. "Very good."

9   It was not yet the drink of the European masses. Charles Dickens's Tale of Two Cities dwells on one nobleman's conspicuous consumption: "It took four men, all four ablaze with gorgeous decoration . . . to conduct the happy chocolate to Monseigneur's lips. . . . Deep would have been

the blot upon his escutcheon if his chocolate had been ignobly waited on by only three men; he must have died of two."

10   In the early 1700s chocolate houses sprang up in London to compete with coffeehouses. English Quakers sang the praises of the drink as a healthful substitute for gin. And then increased production and the industrial revolution, which mechanized chocolate making, brought the price within the public's reach. Though it was often thickened with alien substances (such as brick dust), its popularity soared.

11   Theobroma* came full circle back to the New World in 1765 when a chocolate factory was established in the Massachusetts Bay Colony. Thomas Jefferson expressed the hope that "the superiority of chocolate, both for health and nourishment, will soon give it the same preference over tea and coffee in America which it has in Spain."

12   In 1828 Conrad van Houten, a Dutch chemist, learned to press out some of chocolate's fat — a pale substance called cocoa butter — and make cocoa powder. Two decades later, when cocoa butter and sugar were added to a paste of ground beans, "eating chocolate" came on the scene. In 1875 the Swiss developed a way to make solid milk chocolate. New machines were developed to stir, or conche, the liquid chocolate in the process, vastly improving its smoothness.

13   Today chocolate lovers range from the affluent seekers of the good life to the kid at the candy counter. The food that chocoholics crave ranges from extravagantly lush (and extravagantly priced) assortments down to simple "chocolate bars" — which may contain no chocolate at all.

*Theobroma: literally "food of the gods," the name given chocolate in the nineteenth century.

Suggestions for
Your Writer's Notebook

SUGGESTION 1

Which of the papers you had to write for this chapter do you consider the most successful? Try to explain its success.

SUGGESTION 2

Think about what it would mean to write a fairy tale or a nursery rhyme for an audience of adults. The resulting stories or narratives would be very different, because you could assume an entirely different kind of knowledge and experience on the part of your audience. Look, for example, at this student's version of "Old Mother Hubbard."

Megan Donnelly

```
Old Mother Hubbard went to the cupboard
to give her poor dog a bone.
But when she got there, the cupboard was bare
And so the poor dog had none.
                              --Mother Goose
```

```
    The truth of the matter is that times were tough for Old
Mother Hubbard and me. Poor old mother had been on
welfare ever since they fired her from the candy department
at Sears, and it hit her hard. The loss of the job led her to
drinking vodka and whiskey, all day and all night. At first it
wasn't too noticeable, but then she started mixing my Gravy
Train with alcohol instead of water. One day she yelled at me
"Rover, I've no money left to feed you. I only have what's left
in the cupboard for you." And then she belched, a loud belch
that stunk like whiskey, right in my face. After she passed
out on her bed, I jumped upon the counter to check out the
cupboard: I had enough bones to last me for a month —
that's it. As the days wore on, things got worse and worse.
The drunker grandma got, the more she kicked me around,
and I resented it. She stopped petting me, bathing me, and
walking me. She even left me outside for an entire week. I
```

really began to hate her. Then one day she threw away my
favorite toy, my squeaky ball, and it was then that I lost all
love and affection for that wretched woman. So the next day,
Mother Hubbard, drunk as ever, went to the cupboard to get
me a bone. (This is where Mother Goose got her story,
although she never knew grandma was wasted.) And as the
story goes the cupboard was bare. Grandma just laughed.
Mother Goose's account says that "the poor dog had none,"
but Mother Goose got her story mixed up because I sure did
get some bones — Granny's bones.

SUGGESTION 3

According to Bruno Bettelheim, a well-known psychologist, fairy tales
are extremely important to a child's emotional life. In Bettelheim's analysis,
fairy tales have both "overt" and "covert" meanings. On the overt level,
they tell stories about princes disguised as frogs, animals who can speak,
and witches who can fly.

But on the covert level, they allow children to work through their
deepest anxieties about death, loss, and change. Viewed from this perspective,
"The Three Little Pigs" teaches a child that one with wit and intelligence
can overcome even the largest and strongest opponent and that being
small does not necessarily mean being helpless. Obviously you don't have
to be a psychologist to figure out why a child would be interested in that
theme.

Think of two or three of your favorite fairy tales. What were the ones
you liked to hear over and over again when you were a child? Write
them down. Just tell what happened when.

Then see whether you can interpret the story on the covert level as
well. If your favorite tale was "Snow White and the Seven Dwarfs," for
example, try to explain what the cruel stepmother might have meant to
you as a child or why it was important that Snow White died and came
back to life.

SUGGESTION 4

When Jakob and Wilhelm Grimm, the brothers who collected *Grimm's
Fairy Tales*, decided to gather together the stories of their childhood,
they traveled throughout the countryside talking to elderly men and women
who seemed to know endless numbers of fairy tales. The brothers wrote

them down as they heard them, trying to edit as little as possible. The results became perhaps the most famous fairy tale collection of all time.

On a less grand scale, see what fairy tales your own friends and relatives remember from their childhood. If possible, talk to people born in other countries. See what stories they have to tell. Compare and contrast their stories with those told by Americans who were born here.

SUGGESTION 5

Because she retold the story of Mother Hubbard from the dog's point of view, Megan Donnelly was able to give that tale an entirely new twist. Similarly, in a wonderful novel called *Grendel*, the author John Gardner retold the story of Beowulf, an Old English hero, from the point of view of the monster that Beowulf slays. The shift in point of view made the whole story change. Viewed from the monster's perspective, Beowulf and his men were no longer heroic. They became a bunch of mean-spirited drunkards concerned only with their own glory.

Try rewriting one of the following incidents from the animal's point of view.

1. You are walking your dog down the street and the dog is pulling so hard that it is not clear who is leading whom.
2. You are standing in front of a cage containing a panther that paces back and forth endlessly, seemingly unable to rest.
3. You are waiting for a chicken to hatch an egg so that you can collect the egg and make your breakfast.
4. You are sitting in the living room with your friend, who owns a doberman pincher. Your friend says the dog is harmless, but he keeps snarling at you. And you jump every time he makes a move.
5. You and your friend are standing in front of a cage of monkeys, laughing at their antics.

SUGGESTION 6

At some time in your life, there was undoubtedly someone whom you admired and imitated, someone whose presence, in fact, shaped your own personality. Write a description of that person. Try to give it enough vivid, specific details so that your reader can grasp how and why this person affected you so deeply.

SUGGESTION 7

Metaphors are figures of speech that compare two seemingly unlike things: "Love is a battlefield." "This house is a prison." "The man is a robot." But those comparisons have a purpose. As writer Howard Moss explains, "The power of metaphor is not merely descriptive but psychological; the link between two things we were not aware of is revealed to us."

Metaphors, then, are not just a means of decoration. They are a means of explanation. For example, the statement "The manager is a robot" compares the manager to some mechanical being in order to tell you that he is a rigid person without much spontaneity or life. In the same fashion, the simile "He was crazy as two waltzing mice" tells you, not that a person has ears and a tail, but that his actions are as strange as the appearance of two mice dancing a waltz.

Make up a metaphor or simile (similes use *like* or *as*) that you think could illustrate or bring out some aspect of each item appearing on the following list. (In some cases, if you choose to develop a simile, you may want to change the *a* or *an* to *the*.)

The first three have been completed by a student, Laura Kruper.

1. A black dog sleeping in the sun, *a shaggy black rug spread out to dry.*
2. The river winding through the mountains was *like a silver blue ribbon that went on forever*
3. The old white house with broken windows and a missing door, *a pale face with the eyes and the mouth open in pain.*
4. A racoon standing upright in surprise
5. A group of nuns all in black
6. A teacher leading a line of children across the street
7. An airplane flying very low and seeming to head for the roof of a house
8. Children playing in the snow
9. A huge red sun on the horizon
10. A perfect full moon

11. A meeting of businessmen all dressed in gray, three-piece suits

12. A cat's eyes wide open in the darkness

SUGGESTION 8

Think about the question "Who Am I?" For most of us the answer changes with the circumstances. We feel different, that is, in public than in private, or we appear to be one person on the outside but feel like an altogether different person on the inside. Try to write two paragraphs describing the contradictory aspects of your personality. Here is a sample, written by a student, to get you started.

Melissa Muñoz

One side of me is quiet and reserved. She is innocent, never daring to get in trouble. Her idea of a good time is going to a movie with one of her friends. She is always trying to please others; she pleases her parents by doing well in school. She pleases her boss at the snack bar in the hospital by always keeping busy, making sure she doesn't talk too much or waste time. She is very honest, never lying to her parents or teachers. If someone is unkind to her, she ignores it and tries to say something nice.

But there's another side of me that's anything but quiet and reserved. Only her closest friends see this side of her. She is noisy whenever and wherever she is supposed to be quiet. Even during class, she will talk constantly to her friends. She likes to loaf a lot, to watch T.V. and just veg out. She even likes to make fun of people, to do exactly what they don't expect and won't like. She just gets tired of being so good all the time, and she wants to know what it's like to be bad for a change. Luckily for all concerned, she doesn't appear very often.

SUGGESTION 9

How do you interpret or explain this quote from writer and critic Richard Lanham (*Revising Prose* [New York: Charles Scribner's Sons, 1979] 106)?

"Writing should enhance and expand the self; allow it to try out new possibilities."

Combining Sentences

Like pattern 1, this pattern concentrates on increasing the modification within a single sentence. Only this time you will modify not through single words or phrases but through whole clauses beginning with relative pronouns like *who, which, whom,* and *that.* Using relative clauses, you can create sentences like the following:

> Corporate executives who have driven
> themselves too hard frequently arrive at the top
> with a sense of failure rather than success.

Written as two separate sentences, the sample sentence would have looked something like this:

1. Corporate executives frequently arrive at the top with a sense of failure rather than success.
2. These corporate executives have driven themselves too hard.

Instead of writing those two separate sentences, it is possible to eliminate the repeated element in sentence 2 (*corporate executives*) and insert the second sentence as a relative clause beginning with *who.*

However, *who* is not the only relative pronoun you can use for this pattern. You can also use *that:*

1. The book ∧ has been banned from public schools.
   > *I chose* the book. [that]

   The book that I chose has been banned from public schools.

Or you might want to use *which:*

2. He has chosen a difficult path ∧ .
   > The path *will cause him much pain.* [, which]

   He has chosen a difficult path, which will cause him much pain.

You can also use *whose:*

3. The scientist has designed an army of robots ∧ .
   > The robots' *capabilities are hard to believe.* [, whose]

117

The scientist has designed an army of robots, whose capabilities are hard to believe.

And you can use *whom:*

4.   The artist ∧ was very pretentious.

> *I met* the artist *at your party.* [whom]

The artist whom I met at your party was very pretentious.

In the following exercise, you will add commas according to the signals given — a comma before the pronoun [, which] means that a comma should precede the dependent clause; a comma before and after the pronoun [, which,] means that the entire clause should be enclosed in commas. For an explanation of why commas are or are not used with relative clauses, you should review the rules appearing in the "Pointers for Final Editing" (pp. 323–351).

EXERCISE

1.   The murderer spotted the woman ∧ .

> The woman *was to be his next victim.* [who]

_____

_____

2.   The President addressed the union ∧ .

> The union *had supported him from the beginning.* [that]

_____

_____

3.   Alzheimer's disease ∧ has become a growing concern.

> Alzheimer's disease *plagues millions of Americans.* [, which,]

_____

_____

4.   Sally Rand was a burlesque queen ∧ .

> The burlesque queen *used fans in her act.* [who]

_____

_____

5.   In a fury, the gunman shot the sheriff ∧ .

> The sheriff *had arrested his brother.* [who]

_____

_____

6. After the accident, the ambulance attendants carefully picked up
   the victim ∧ .
   The victim's *neck was broken.* [, whose]

   _____

   _____

7. The chimps use a sign language ∧ .
   The sign language *has over a thousand words.* [that]

   _____

   _____

8. Unfortunately, the dog ∧ had to be destroyed.
   The dog *had bitten the child.* [that]

   _____

   _____

9. The candidate ∧ was incompetent.
   I picked the candidate. [whom]

   _____

   _____

10. After the hearing, the pilot ∧ cursed the committee.
    The pilot's *license was revoked.* [, whose,]

    _____

    _____

   Write five sentences using a relative clause. Try to use a different   EXERCISE
relative pronoun in each sentence.

1. _____

   _____

2. _____

   _____

3. _____

   _____

4. _____

_____

5. _____

_____

PATTERN 6

The sentence pattern featured in this section reintroduces the word *that*, previously used in relative clauses functioning as adjectives: "These are the articles *that I intend to publish*." This time, however, the word *that* appears in clauses functioning as nouns rather than adjectives. For example, the blank in the sentence "I know _____" could be filled with a noun such as "the truth," and the sentence would read "I know the truth." That blank could also be filled with a noun clause, "I know *that this is the truth*." Likewise, the blank in this sentence, "_____ guaranteed him a medal," could be filled with a noun ("*His injury* guaranteed him a medal") or a noun clause ("*The fact that he was injured* guaranteed him a medal").

The following exercise will give you practice working with noun clauses linked by the word *that* or by the phrase *the fact that*. However, you should realize that the use of these links is frequently optional.   **EXERCISE**

Example:
The manager thinks _____.
    He is the most important person on earth. [that]

Here we can combine the sentences with or without the word *that*.

1. The manager thinks that he is the most important person on earth.
2. The manager thinks he is the most important person on earth.

Finish the following exercise.

1. He told himself _____ ∧ .
    He was a lover. [that]
    He was not a fighter. [and]

_____

_____

2. _____ has not made her happy ∧ .

    She is rich. [The fact that]

    It has not made her *healthy.* [or]

_____

_____

3. It is not hard to predict _____ ∧ .

    He will fail. [that]

    He runs again. [if]

_____

_____

4. ∧ I tell myself _____.

    I do it *every day.*

    I won't eat at night. [that]

[, but]

I do it anyway.

_____

_____

5. _____ should not be taken into account.

    She lost her job. [The fact that]

[, but]

Everyone knows _____.

    It will be. [that]

_____

_____

6. ∧ He told me anyway.

    I tried to ignore _____. [although,]

    He was angry. [the fact that]

_____

_____

7. _____ is not necessarily a sign _____.
        Something pleases you. [The fact that]
        It is good. [that]

        _____

        _____

8. Everyone knew _____.
        The play was a flop. [that]
    [, but]
    She refused to give up ∧ .
        The engagement was over. [until]

        _____

        _____

9. I suppose _____.
        He will have to come. [that]
    [; , however]
    I must say _____.
        I don't want him to stay. [that]

        _____

        _____

10. The audience thought _____.
        The play was too long. [that]
    [, and]
    The reviewers thought _____.
        It was too short. [that]

        _____

        _____

    Write five sentences using a noun clause.   EXERCISE

1. _____

    _____

2. _____

    _____

3. _____

_____

4. _____

_____

5. _____

_____

CHAPTER 5

Paragraphing and the Paragraph

In the early drafts of your essay, you do not need to concentrate too much on the individual paragraphs. When you first begin writing, your primary concern is to discover what you want to say about the specific topic you have chosen.

But once you can answer that important question *"What* can I say about this topic?" another one arises: *"How* can I communicate that message so that my readers understand it too?" When this question becomes the focus of your drafting, it is time to start thinking more about paragraphing and the paragraph. The closer you come to a finished paper, the more you have to consider the form and content of individual paragraphs. Chapter 5 offers several suggestions that can guide and focus your thinking as you analyze and revise the paragraphs of your essay.

The Importance of Paragraphing

When you indent for a new paragraph, you provide more than just a pause or a break for your readers. You also tell them to be prepared for some kind of shift or change in the development of your thesis statement. You might, for example, be introducing a new answer to the question or questions raised by your thesis statement. Or you might be modifying what you have already said by citing a specific illustration or exception.

Through paragraphing, you give your readers the visual signals that will help them follow you as you develop your thesis statement. In short, you make it easier for them to grasp the message of your paper.

Therefore, when you revise, it is important that you think about the ways in which paragraphing can clarify the message you want to communicate. For an illustration of the contribution that paragraphing can make, read the following excerpts. The first one does not fully utilize the power of paragraphing; the second one does.

Sleeplessness   Joe Kelley

1   Every night millions of Americans go to bed only to toss and turn for hours, unable to sleep. Suffering from insomnia, they reach for sleeping pills or tranquilizers. But unfortunately, over time, both will disturb the body's natural rhythms and aggravate an insomniac's problem. <u>In the long run, it would be better if people suffering from chronic sleeplessness avoided pills altogether and concentrated instead on improving their sleep habits.</u>

Thesis Statement Raises the Question "What Are the Sleep Habits That Could be Improved?"

2   <u>Simply by paying careful attention to their nighttime eating habits, insomniacs can do a lot to ensure themselves a good night's sleep.</u> Foods high in carbohydrates, for example, stimulate the production of serotonin, the chemical naturally produced by the body prior to sleep. Anyone who wants to sleep well should consider, then, a snack high in carbohydrates like crackers, toast, or bagels. <u>What they should not consider are foods high in protein,</u> for proteins have the opposite effect on the body's chemistry. They interfere with the body's production of serotonin and work to postpone the onset of sleep. This means that a midnight snack consisting of a hamburger or a pizza can lead to hours of tossing and turning. But a better diet is not the only way to fight insomnia. There are other habits insomniacs can develop in pursuit of a good night's sleep. <u>They can also learn the importance of a fixed schedule for</u> both waking and sleeping. This means going to bed at approximately the same time every night and getting up just about the same time every morning. Adjusted to that particular rhythm of sleeping and waking, the body will automatically prepare for sleep at the accustomed hour. <u>Following such a schedule is particularly important on weekends, when the rigors of rising for work or school no longer apply.</u> Unfortunately,

Answer 1

Modifies First Answer

Answer 2

Modifies Answer 2

many people use the weekend to stay out and sleep late, a practice
that can upset the body's sleep schedule and encourage the return
of insomnia. Tempting as it is to throw caution to the winds on
weekends, anyone suffering from insomnia should think twice
before tampering with a fixed schedule for sleeping and waking.

In this example, the writer has not effectively utilized paragraphing to
introduce and highlight the material in the supporting paragraphs. Because
he has provided only one indentation, it appears as though he has given
only a single answer to the question raised by his thesis: "What sleep
habits need to be changed in order to cure insomnia?" But in fact he
has provided two: (1) Insomniacs should change their dietary habits, and
(2) They should develop a fixed schedule for sleeping and waking.

Unfortunately, he has not used paragraphing to highlight those answers
for his readers, and the result is a somewhat confusing answer to that
key question. Although it is easy enough to identify the first answer
introduced, it is not clear how the explanation of fixed scheduling is
related to dietary habits. Thus the one paragraph that exists does not seem
to have a single focal point or direction. It does not develop any one
controlling idea. But, like essays, paragraphs must develop one controlling
idea. When they do not, they can create confusion.

With this passage, you are left to sort out the author's answers to the
question raised by the thesis statement. Very little guidance has been
provided.

Although it is certainly possible for readers to do this much sifting and
sorting, they should not have to. It is the writer's responsibility to guide
them by means of careful paragraphing. As the following revision illustrates,
careful paragraphing can clarify the message of your paper.

Sleeplessness   Joe Kelley

1   Every night millions of Americans go to bed only to toss and
turn for hours, unable to sleep. Suffering from insomnia, they   *Thesis Statement Raises*
reach for sleeping pills or tranquilizers. But unfortunately, over   *the Question "What*
time, both will disturb the body's natural rhythms and aggravate   *Are The Sleep Habits*
an insomniac's problem. In the long run, it would be better if   *That Could be*
people suffering from chronic sleeplessness avoided pills altogether   *Improved?"*
and concentrated instead on improving their sleep habits.

2   Simply by paying careful attention to their nighttime eating   *Answer 1*
habits, insomniacs can do a lot to ensure themselves a good

night's sleep. Foods high in carbohydrates, for example, stimulate the production of serotonin, the chemical naturally produced by the body prior to sleep. Anyone who wants to sleep well should consider, then, a snack high in carbohydrates like crackers, toast, or bagels.

3   What they should not consider are foods high in protein. For proteins have the opposite effect on the body's chemistry. They interfere with the body's production of serotonin and work to postpone the onset of sleep. This means that a midnight snack consisting of a hamburger or a pizza can lead to hours of tossing and turning.   *Modifies Answer 1*

4   But a better diet is not the only way to fight insomnia. There are other habits insomniacs can develop in their pursuit of a good night's sleep. They can also learn the importance of a fixed schedule for both waking and sleeping. This means going to bed at approximately the same time every night and getting up at just about the same time every morning. Adjusted to that particular rhythm of sleeping and waking, the body will automatically prepare for sleep at the accustomed hour.   *Answer 2*

5   Following such a schedule is particularly important on weekends, when the rigors of rising for work or school no longer apply. Unfortunately, many people use the weekend to stay out late and sleep even later, a practice that can upset the body's sleep schedule and encourage the return of insomnia. Tempting as it is to throw caution to the winds on weekends, anyone plagued by insomnia should think twice before tampering with a fixed schedule for sleeping and waking.   *Modifies Answer 2*

   This is the same essay. But here the author has made more effective use of paragraphing. After reading the thesis statement, you no longer have to sort through a tangle of sentences that do not signal where the explanation of one idea ends and that of another begins. In this revised example, paragraphing has been used to introduce and highlight shifts in the writer's train of thought.

   As you revise, you should always consider the way which paragraphing can ease your reader's task. That means you should consider the following guidelines:

   1. If your thesis paragraph becomes overburdened with background information for your thesis, divide that paragraph into two. Use the opening paragraph to give the background and the second paragraph to

introduce the thesis statement. This was what Joan Amato did in the sample essay on fear of hospitals.

2. Always indent when you introduce an idea that has not been previously developed in the essay.

3. Each paragraph should develop only one controlling idea. A paragraph that develops more than one idea loses unity and can confuse your readers. It becomes hard for them to figure out the relationship between the sentences in your paragraph and the controlling idea it explains. (For more on paragraph unity, see the final section of this chapter.) Each time you introduce a new idea that further develops your thesis statement, indent for a new paragraph. If you cram all of your ideas into one long paragraph, they are sure to lose their effectiveness.

4. Paragraphs that develop one controlling idea but provide too much information about that idea can also be confusing. When a supporting paragraph starts to grow beyond five or six sentences in length, consider whether that one paragraph should be divided into two: a major and a minor paragraph. That way you can use the major supporting paragraph to introduce the controlling idea and the minor supporting paragraph to modify it. By using a major and a minor paragraph to develop one conrolling idea, you can offer your readers maximum development with minimum confusion.

5. Although short paragraphs of two or three sentences can be used effectively for emphasis, do not rely on them too heavily. Most of the time, two or three sentences are simply not enough to answer fully the questions your readers might raise.

The following exercises will give you some practice in thinking about the importance of paragraphing.

Read through the following passage and decide where you think there should be an indentation for a paragraph. Explain your reason for each indentation you suggest.   EXERCISE 1

Can Stress Be Good for You?
Susan Seliger

According to the latest research, the ability to control stress is within each person's power. It is the perception of and attitude about both self and environment that most influence whether a person will be hurt by stress. What researchers are finding is that bad stress is triggered not by the pressures of decision-making but rather by the feeling that one's decisions are useless, that life is overwhelming and beyond personal control. Those people making the decisions, the high-powered, high-pressure executives that many have believed are most vulnerable, turn out, therefore, not to be. And it is not that they are genetically more fit to cope that accounts for their rise to the top. It is their attitude. Yet, the notion that they are at risk has been perpetuated by those selling stress services to employers who are all too willing to spend money for stress counseling for their top people. Unfortunately, it's the underlings these managers supervise who are at far greater risk, people the employers pay little attention to. "An executive who makes a lot of decisions is better off than his secretary," says Dr. Kenneth Greenspan, director of the Center for Stress Related Disorders, at Columbia–Presbyterian Medical Center. "Secretaries — along with assembly-line workers — are at a great deal of risk from stress because all their decisions are predetermined: when they start work, when they stop, what they do. They fear that they can be easily replaced; they see themselves as victims. And that produces bad stress."

Now compare your system of paragraphing with the author's, which follows.

Can Stress Be Good for You?
Susan Seliger

1   According to the latest research, the ability to control stress is within each person's power. It is the perception of and attitude about both self and environment that most influence whether a person will be hurt by stress. What researchers are finding is that bad stress is triggered not by the pressures of decision-making but rather by the feeling that one's decisions are useless, that life is overwhelming and beyond personal control.

2   Those people making the decisions, the high-powered, high-pressure executives that many have believed are most vulnerable, turn out, therefore, not to be. And it is not that they are genetically more fit to cope that accounts for their rise to the top. It is their attitude. Yet, the notion that they are at risk has been perpetuated by those selling stress services to employers who are all too willing to spend money for stress counseling for their top people. Unfortunately, it's the underlings these managers supervise who are at far greater risk, people the employers pay little attention to.

3   "An executive who makes a lot of decisions is better off than his secretary," says Dr. Kenneth Greenspan, director of the Center for Stress Related Disorders, at Columbia–Presbyterian Medical Center. "Secretaries — along with assembly-line workers — are at a great deal of risk from stress because all their decisions are predetermined: when they start work, when they stop, what they do. They fear that they can be easily replaced: they see themselves as victims. And that produces bad stress."

Start paying attention to the individual methods of paragraphing that different authors use. Some authors like to use a very short paragraph periodically for strong emphasis. Others tend to rely on paragraphs of a consistent length. Still others alternate long paragraphs with short ones. Try to figure out for yourself what methods of paragraphing you consider the most effective. Which ones, that is, do you find easiest to read and understand?

EXERCISE 2

Read through two or three of your previous essays. Pay particular attention to your paragraphing. Do you have one set pattern? Do you rely primarily on long or short paragraphs? At every indentation for a paragraph, ask yourself why you chose to create a paragraph in that particular place. Were you trying to highlight a specific exception to the general rule you had already introduced? Were you introducing a new idea? Were you reversing what you had already said in the previous paragraph? If you can not think of a reason for your paragraph, consider other places in your paper where indenting for a paragraph would have been a more effective signal.

EXERCISE 3

The Topic Sentence

When you write your first draft, you begin by asking yourself what questions your readers might raise about your thesis statement. By generating answers to those imagined or anticipated questions, you also generate the controlling ideas of your supporting paragraphs. You define for yourself what ideas you must introduce and explain in the supporting paragraphs if your readers are to understand your thesis statement.

In the first stages of drafting, your main concern is to flesh out the controlling ideas of your supporting paragraphs. Through drafting, you want to discover whether you can provide the specific details that will make the controlling ideas of your individual paragraphs answer the questions your readers might raise. Once you feel confident that you can develop the controlling ideas of your supporting paragraphs, you should also consider the function of the topic sentence.

THE FUNCTION OF THE TOPIC SENTENCE

The topic sentence is to the paragraph what the thesis statement is to the essay. It announces the controlling idea to your readers. Though not all paragraphs present their controlling ideas in topic sentences, a good many would be improved if they did. They simply would be clearer and more direct if they contained one sentence that was more general than the rest and summed up the controlling idea of the entire paragraph.

Accordingly, when you are revising your essay and beginning to think about creating your final draft, check to see which paragraphs would benefit from the addition of a topic sentence. That means you should ask yourself a series of questions:

☐ Does this paragraph clearly express one controlling idea?

☐ Is that idea stated in a topic sentence or implied by the supporting sentences in the paragraph?

☐ If it is implied, would the addition of a topic sentence make it easier for my readers to grasp the message of the paragraph?

Consider the following paragraph:

> At the age of seventy Meyer Lansky, a key figure in the criminal underworld for many years, wanted to retire to Israel. But Israel would not claim him despite his Jewish heritage. After several legal battles, he was finally expelled. Lansky then offered a million dollars to any country that would give him a home. Argentina, Brazil, Paraguay, Bolivia, Peru, and Panama all refused. As a result he was forced to return to the United States and face charges of tax evasion. Eventually cleared of those charges, Lansky retired, aging and angry, to Miami Beach.

Every sentence in this paragraph records a precise event of action. On the level of individual supporting sentences, there is little chance for confusion or misinterpretation on the reader's part. But when we take the paragraph as a whole, it is not immediately clear what the writer wants to say about Lansky and his unsuccessful attempts to find a homeland.

Was the paragraph written to create sympathy for Lansky or to condemn him? In short, what is the point of this paragraph? That question no longer arises when that same paragraph is rewritten with a topic sentence:

> *When no country of his choice would accept him because of his criminal past, Meyer Lansky, a key figure in the underworld for over fifty years, finally suffered the consequences of his crimes.* At the age of seventy, Lansky wanted to retire to Israel. But Israel would not claim him despite his Jewish heritage. After several legal battles, he was finally expelled. Lansky then offered a million dollars to any country that would give him a home. Argentina, Brazil, Paraguay, Bolivia, Peru, and Panama all refused. As a result, he was forced to return to the United States and face charges of tax evasion. Eventually cleared of those charges, Lansky retired, aging and angry, to Miami Beach.

Topic Sentence

In this revised version of the sample paragraph, the first sentence is a topic sentence. More general than the remaining supporting sentences, it sums up the controlling idea of the entire paragraph: After many years, Lansky finally discovered that crime had its consequences. The remaining, more specific sentences further develop and explain the idea contained in that sentence. Given this revision, a reader no longer has to guess what the writer had in mind. The point of the paragraph is clearly stated in the topic sentence.

THE PLACEMENT OF THE TOPIC SENTENCE

If you do decide that a paragraph needs a topic sentence, you should also think about *where* it would be most effective. Do not assume you have to make the first sentence the topic sentence. This is a very effective position for the topic sentence, but it is not the only one. You have other alternatives at your disposal.

One alternative is to use the *last* sentence rather than the first. This alternative is particularly useful for thesis paragraphs where the topic sentence of the paragraph is also the thesis statement for the entire essay. This placement is useful because it allows you to prepare your readers with the background they need in order to fully grasp the message of your essay. The following paragraph is a good example.

> In the twenties, there was Jack Dempsey, famous in fight circles as the "Manasas Mauler." Dempsey, in turn, was followed by

fighters like Joe Louis, celebrated as the "Brown Bomber" and Jake La Motta, notorious as the "Bronx Bull." Today, the names are, if anything, even more colorful: There is "Marvelous Marvin," "Boom Boom Mancini" and Hector "Macho" Camacho. *Sooner or later, if a fighter is any good, he gets a nickname; for a fighter, it is equivalent to being knighted.*

Yet another alternative is to use the first sentence of a paragraph as the introductory sentence that presents background about the topic. The *second* sentence then introduces the controlling idea by modifying or reversing what was said in the first.

For most of his life, automotive executive John De Lorean was the proverbial golden boy; he was the man who had everything — all the wealth, power and success any man could desire. *Yet it took less than twenty-four hours for De Lorean to fall from the heights of success to the depths of humiliation.* Arrested by the Federal Bureau of Investigation in October of 1983, De Lorean was arraigned on charges of conspiracy to possess narcotics with the intent to distribute them. As if stunned by the whole affair, De Lorean appeared before the judge like a man in a dream. Normally talkative and witty, he stared blankly ahead never saying a word. Rumpled and unshaven, he was the exact opposite of his normally neat and well-groomed self.

Here the first sentence introduces the topic of the paragraph, "John De Lorean." It also provides some background — his career had been a phenomenally successful one. It is the second sentence, however, that actually presents the controlling idea: In a short time, De Lorean lost almost everything.

Introducing the topic sentence in this way has certain benefits. First, writers in all different areas or disciplines make use of this statement–counterstatement method of organization. That means your readers will be familiar with this pattern and will use their expectations to guide their understanding. Hence it is easier for you to communicate your ideas quickly and easily. Second, this method makes your writing more convincing because it is one way to acknowledge an opposing point of view at the outset. In effect, it tells the reader that you have taken contradictory information into account and are still sure of your own ideas.

Still another alternative is to begin the paragraph with a *question* that arouses the reader's interest. Following that question comes the answer, and the answer is the controlling idea of the paragraph. Here is one student's example.

Renée Mariano

Why do people dream? <u>They dream for many reasons, not the least of which is to escape the normal limitations of reality.</u> If during the day we are confined by a job and a life we find intolerable, it is not unusual to dream of flying through the skies, unfettered and uninhibited by anything or anyone. It is not unusual for a person who is shy and withdrawn in the waking world to dream at night of walking naked through a crowded room, delighted by the shock and outrage provoked.

Here it is the question that introduces the topic. But it is the answer that presents the controlling idea: There are many reasons why we need to dream, but escaping reality is one of the most important.

As pointed out above, this method arouses reader interest. But it serves another purpose as well: It increases your chances of being understood correctly. When they encounter such a question, your readers know automatically that the answer will be the controlling idea of your paragraph. Thus, again, your organization allows you to make use of your readers' expectations.

Another common alternative method is to use *the first and the last* sentences of the paragraph. Say, you have a paragraph that already states the controlling idea in the very first sentence. You may still find it useful to repeat that controlling idea in the final sentence. This method is ideal for material you think is complicated or may be difficult for your audience to understand. Through restatement you try to double their chances of comprehending. This is precisely what the author of the following paragraph has done.

It is comforting to believe that foreign policy is based purely on rational decision making, but research suggests that is not necessarily true. Two political scientists, Ole R. Hosti of Duke University and Alexander George of Stanford, have analyzed various examples of such decision making in foreign policy and have found that rationality governs the more trivial decisions. When the problem is of a more serious and consequential nature, there is a marked increase in irrational rather than rational thinking.

Unfortunately, even with the high ranks of foreign policy decision makers, rationality is rarely the reality.[1]

In this example the first sentence introduces the controlling idea: Even at the highest levels of foreign policy, decisions are not always guided by reason. In turn, the supporting sentences explain how the author arrived at that conclusion and restate the controlling idea: Even in the high ranks of foreign policy, decision making can be an irrational process.

When you revise, check to see whether any of your paragraphs would benefit from the addition of a topic sentence. If you decide that some would be improved by the addition of a topic sentence, consider what would be the most effective place for it. The following exercise will give you some practice.

Give two different essays to two different classmates and ask them to analyze every paragraph in those essays. That means they should write the controlling idea of each paragraph in the margin. If they identify any paragraphs in which, from their point of view, the controlling idea is not clear, it is your job to dispel their confusion by revising to include a topic sentence.

EXERCISE   4

The Importance of Supporting Sentences

Revising your paragraphs to include topic sentences can help ensure communication between you and your readers. However, a topic sentence cannot do all the work of a paragraph. Even if you revise a paragraph to include a topic sentence, you still have to pay attention to the supporting sentences you have used to develop and explain it. To be effective, they should provide the specific illustration and explanation that can prevent misinterpretation or confusion on your readers' part. Ultimately you have to treat your supporting paragraphs in the same way you treated your thesis paragraph. You have to ask yourself what questions your readers might raise about the controlling idea of each supporting paragraph. By answering those anticipated questions, you can fill out or develop your

[1]Adapted from Morton Hunt, *The Universe Within* (New York: Touchstone Books, 1982) 129.

supporting paragraphs with the necessary specificity. The following paragraph will serve as an illustration.

> [1]The blues, it is sometimes thought, speak only of the pangs of love. [2]Thousands of poems do indeed exist dealing with every aspect of love betrayed and frustrated, but the themes evoked by the blues cover a much wider range. [3]The singer can bemoan with equal readiness catastrophes to crops and damage wrought by flood and tornado, the ravages of sickness, the harmfulness of drink, cruel deeds of the police, and hardships brought on by economic crisis. [4]Ever since blacks started their mass migrations from the rural South to the cities in the North, they have often entrusted to the blues their expression of longing for the regions they have left, or the recurrent desire to abandon the heartless city and let the train bear them off to sunnier skies.*

In this paragraph, the author introduces the controlling idea in the second sentence: The range of the blues is much wider than most people normally assume. Having said that, the author can expect a question from her readers: Just how wide is the range of the blues? To answer that question, the author uses supporting sentences 3 and 4 to illustrate the variety of blues themes. In effect, she uses the supporting sentences to specify and particularize the phrase "wide range." Because she cannot be sure that her readers' idea of a "a wide range" is the same as hers, she offers them specific examples of the meaning she intends.

In the following paragraph, the author does not make adequate use of his supporting sentences. For the most part, they are on the same level of generality as the topic sentence. They do not provide the kind of specific details necessary to communicate the controlling idea with clarity.

> [1]Quite apart from the question of drugs — which don't always work — it is all too possible to demonstrate that many psychiatrists have very little understanding of what they are doing. [2]Allegedly experts on the psyche, they have little real knowledge of how the human mind functions. [3]When it comes to distinguishing the sane from the insane, psychiatrists are as much in the dark as any other human being. [4]They cannot really divine or explain the workings of any other mind except their own.

---

*Jean Wagner, *Black Poets of the United States: From Paul Lawrence Dunbar to Langston Hughes* (Urbana: U of Illinois P, 1973) 34.

In this paragraph, the first sentence is the topic sentence introducing the controlling idea: It is easy to demonstrate that psychiatrists do not really know what they are doing. But except for sentence 3, which defines the area of expected competence, the author does not attempt to answer the questions raised by the topic sentence, questions such as "What precisely should psychiatrists be able to do that they do not do?" "How can this be demonstrated?" In this paragraph, the supporting sentences do little more than repeat the controlling idea, only in different words. That means the paragraph needs to be revised. Compare now the following paragraph, where the supporting sentences do what they are supposed to do — clarify and explain the controlling idea through specific detail.

[1]Quite apart from the question of drugs — which don't always work either — it is all too possible to demonstrate that many psychiatrists have very little understanding of what they are doing. [2]In 1972, Professor David Rosenhan of Stanford University decided to try an experiment. [3]He and a number of other accomplices entered twelve public and private psychiatric hospitals in California, Oregon, Pennsylvania, New York, and Delaware. [4]In each case, the experimenters complained of hearing voices, but they acted normally in every other way. [5]As soon as they were admitted to the hospitals, they told the doctors that the voices had stopped. [6]They behaved normally and said they wanted to leave the hospitals. [7]In many cases, other inmates somehow realized that the experimenters were imposters but the doctors did not. [8]Every one of the researchers had difficulty in getting out of the hospital. [9]The average hospitalization was nineteen days, although one experimenter was held for fifty-two days. [10]All but one of them, when finally discharged, were diagnosed as having schizophrenia in remission. [11](The other was said to be manic-depressive also in remission.) [12]'We now know,' Rosenhan concluded 'that we cannot distinguish insanity from sanity.' [13]Perhaps not. [14]But if the mental patients themselves could make that distinction by detecting the impostors, then who is 'we'?*

Here, the author makes good use of his supporting sentences. Having introduced his controlling idea in a topic sentence, he uses his supporting sentences to illustrate, very specifically, what he means when he claims that psychiatrists have little understanding of what they are doing.

*Otto Friedrich, *Going Crazy* (New York: Avon Books, 1977) 26.

In revising your paper, it is important that you think about the supporting sentences in your paragraphs. They should provide enough specific illustration and explanation so that your readers fully understand each and every idea you present in support of your thesis.

Select one of your previous papers and read through the supporting paragraphs very carefully. Look for those paragraphs where you could develop the controlling idea in more specific detail. Revise them.   EXERCISE 5

The Unity of Paragraphs

Chapter 4 talked about the way a paragraph outline can help you check the unity of your entire essay. However, individual paragraphs should be unified as well. In short, be sure that every sentence within each individual paragraph furthers the development of one controlling idea. Eliminate or rewrite any supporting sentence that does not perform its function. (The one exception here is transitional sentences appearing at the end of paragraphs — more about them in the next chapter.)

Like supporting paragraphs in an essay, supporting sentences in a paragraph fall into two groups:

1. Major supporting sentences directly develop the controlling idea; they provide details, examples, or reasons that further explain it.
2. Minor supporting sentences develop the major ones. They provide additional information about a thought introduced in a previous sentence.

It is often on the level of *minor* supporting sentences that paragraphs go astray. Take the following paragraph:

   [1]From the very beginning, 3-D movies have concentrated on plots with more action than ideas. [2]Made in 1952, the very first 3-D movie to be successful was called *Bwana Devil*; it specialized in lions that jumped into the audience's lap. [3]*Bwana Devil* was followed by a succession of equally mindless horror films like *The Creature from the Black Lagoon, The Maze, House of Wax*, and *It Came from Outer Space*. [4]All of these films cost a great deal of money but only *The Creature from the Black Lagoon* and *House of Wax* made a profit. [5]Even simpler in plot than the

horror movies made in 3-D were the slightly pornographic films like *The Playgirls* and *The Bellboy,* or the even more mindless *The Stewardesses.*

In this example, the first sentence is the topic sentence of the entire paragraph. More general than the remaining sentences in the paragraph, it announces the controlling idea: 3-D movies have concentrated more on action than thought. Sentence 2 then offers a specific example of how mindless the first 3-D movie was. Sentence 3 continues developing the controlling idea through more specific examples of mindless 3-D movies. Sentence 4, however, moves away from the controlling idea expressed in the topic sentence and challenges the unity of the paragraph. Although sentence 4 is a minor supporting sentence that provides more information about sentence 3, it does not further develop the idea expressed in the topic sentence: From the very beginning, 3-D movies have concentrated more on action than ideas. Irrelevant or unrelated to the controlling idea, sentence 4 would have to be eliminated.

The unity of sentences is even more crucial in paragraphs without a topic sentence. When such a paragraph does not consistently focus on one main idea, it can leave your readers wondering exactly what it was you intended to say. Compare the following two paragraphs.

> [1]It is not unusual for top corporate executives, suffering from an exhausted physical and emotional state commonly known as "burnout," to abandon their careers after years of hard work and struggle. [2]They simply give up and drop out, unable to stand the pressure. [3]Nurses have been known to do the same thing. [4]Following years of rigorous training, they abandon their chosen profession, dissatisfied and unhappy with their careers. [5]In recent years perhaps the most attention has been paid to teachers, who have begun, in increasing numbers, to exhibit the depression and anxiety associated with burnout.

Here every sentence in the paragraph contributes to one controlling idea: Burnout affects a wide variety of people in many different professions. But look what happens to that paragraph when the sentences are not unified around one main idea:

> [1]It is not unusual for top corporate executives, suffering from an exhausted physical and emotional state known as "burnout," to abandon their careers after years of struggle. [2]They simply give up and drop out, unable to stand the pressure. [3]Nurses have been known to do the same thing. [4]Following years of rigorous training, they abandon their chosen profession, too tired to continue. [5]For it seems that the frustration and pressure of nursing can make even the most dedicated and idealistic dissatisfied and miserable. [6]As if that weren't enough, there is always the problem of prestige: Doctors are admired and rewarded for their work while nurses are not. [7]But in recent years, perhaps the most attention has been paid to teachers, who have begun, in increasing numbers, to exhibit the depression and anxiety associated with burnout.

With the addition of sentences 5 and 6, this paragraph has begun to go in two directions. On the one hand, it seems devoted to describing the way burnout affects different groups. But it also seems to concentrate on the particular plight of nurses. This paragraph needs to be revised to express only one controlling idea. The sentences focusing more on the problem of nurses can be eliminated or rewritten, or they can take their place in a minor supporting paragraph that probes the details of burnout within specific professions.

Exactly how you handle irrelevant material is up to you. The crucial thing is to make every sentence work to support *one* central or controlling idea. If each and every sentence does not in some way contribute to the purpose of the paragraph, your writing loses unity. You should always revise with this idea in mind.

The following exercises will give you some practice in thinking about the unity of paragraphs.

The following paragraphs may contain an irrelevant sentence. Read the paragraphs over to discover that one sentence.

EXERCISE 6

Example:

¹Female alcoholics have more difficulty than males do seeking and getting the appropriate medical treatment, largely because society still penalizes them more than their male counterparts. ²Uncomfortable in general with the subject of alcoholism, most people are even less comfortable confronting the fact that fifty percent of America's alcoholics are women. ³While a man stumbling out of a room, barely able to stand up, is considered an unpleasant sight, a woman who does the same thing is considered disgusting. ⁴Still, alcoholism in women has begun to increase. ⁵Just as important as these differing social perceptions is the simple fact that female alcoholics have different needs than male alcoholics do. ⁶Many women, for example, will not undergo treatment unless they can find a facility that also provides child care, and, in general, few facilities offer any such service.

IRRELEVANT SENTENCE ___4___

Finish the remaining paragraphs in the same fashion.

1   ¹Today electroshock therapy is not the same terrifying, even dangerous, procedure it once was. ²When electroshock therapy, also known as ECT, was introduced in the early forties, the

patient had to be strapped down so that the ensuing convulsions would not produce serious, even fatal, bone fractures. [3]Terrified by the procedure, many patients had to be literally dragged into the therapy room. [4]In the famous movie *The Snake Pit*, the heroine, played by Olivia DeHavilland, received several shock treatments that were supposed to bring back her memory. [5]Today, however, doctors control injuries through the use of muscle relaxants. [6]In addition, because patients receive a mild anesthetic before the treatment takes place, they are no longer terror-stricken at the thought of electric shock therapy, and the procedure can even be handled on an out-patient basis, with patients calmly checking in for treatment.

IRRELEVANT SENTENCE _____

2   [1]Scientists are beginning to believe that animals, from insects to mammals, have greater mental capacities than anyone has previously realized. [2]To prove that animals do in fact think, they cite as examples reptiles that carefully camouflage themselves when approaching their prey. [3]In fact, these animals make conscious attempts to assume a disguise. [4]In a similar vein, scientists also point to the example of the heron, who uses one of its own feathers to lure unwary fish into its waiting mouth. [5]Initially it seemed that, in the animal kingdom, it was only the tool-using chimps who revealed such complicated thinking abilities, but increasingly chimps are being joined by a whole range of animals previously considered far less intelligent.

IRRELEVANT SENTENCE _____

3   [1]To many people the name of Chuck Norris is not even vaguely familiar, but to admirers of karate films, Chuck Norris is the master, the American successor of Chinese martial arts champion Bruce Lee. [2]When Lee died in 1973, Chinese and American promoters tried to find someone to replace him, but no one seemed able to take Lee's place — no one, that is, until Chuck Norris played a black-belt trucker in a 1977 movie called *Breaker, Breaker*. [3]Norris went into films when the late Steve McQueen encouraged him to take a chance. [4]But it was not until 1979, when Norris starred in a film called *Good Guys Wear Black*, that his place as Lee's successor was firmly established. [5]When

that film made millions in profits, producers stopped looking for
another Bruce Lee and instead began talking about some day
discovering another Chuck Norris.

IRRELEVANT SENTENCE _____

4   [1]Anxious over an upcoming test, I camp out in the kitchen,
calming my anxiety with steady doses of chocolate cookies and
milk. [2]Nervous about an interview, I start eating in the morning
and finish up just before I go to bed at night. [3]I don't even have
to like what I'm eating. [4]Sometimes I do, sometimes I don't.
[5]What I eat really doesn't matter. [6]What's important is that I
continue munching and chewing, almost without stopping, every
hour on the hour. [7]For me, eating is related to nerves far more
than to nutrition.

IRRELEVANT SENTENCE _____

Take one of the essays you wrote for the previous chapter and analyze   EXERCISE 7
every single paragraph. Begin by writing down the controlling idea of
each paragraph. Then go through each paragraph sentence by sentence
and ask yourself how every sentence contributes to the controlling idea.
If you discover a sentence that is not related to the controlling idea, make
the appropriate revisions.

Writing   The Summary
Assignment

Write a one-paragraph summary of the article "Challenging Darwin," which begins on page 147.

GETTING STARTED

When you write a summary of an article, your goal is not to rewrite it. Instead, you want to reduce it to about one-quarter of its original length. To accomplish that objective, you need to take the following steps:

1. Read the article at least twice.
2. If you are working with your own text or a xerographic copy, underline or take notes in the margin. Circle any key terms, names, or numbers you think are especially important. Pay particular attention to any phrases or sentences that the author has highlighted via quotation marks, italics, or boldface type.
3. After the second reading, make a paragraph outline of the entire article. Begin your outline by writing down the thesis statement of the entire article. Indented and below this thesis statement, write a topic sentence for each paragraph.
4. Underneath each topic sentence, jot down any specific details or examples you think were essential to explaining that sentence.

GETTING ORGANIZED

Make the thesis statement of the article the topic sentence of your one-paragraph summary. Using your outline to guide you, decide which controlling ideas from the individual paragraphs are essential to explaining that topic sentence. Use those ideas to develop the supporting sentences of your paragraph.

REVISING

Once you have a rough draft of your summary, go back and reread the article. Check to see whether you have left out any words, dates, or terms that are essential to the development of the thesis statement.

Before beginning your own summary, read the model article, outline, and summary provided on the following pages.

Mummy Autopsies

Lygeri Koromvokis

1   Long before the ancient Egyptians were embalming their dead, South American Indians were making mummies, the all-natural way: They were wrapping the bodies in reeds and leaves or cotton and "sun-baking" them dry in shallow desert graves. Today, these dehydrated preserved corpses have become fertile ground for research into the history of human disease. In the past decade, more than 2500 mummies, some as much as 5000 years old, have been excavated from desert coastal valleys in Peru and Chile.

2   In a study funded by the National Geographic Society, a team of medical detectives has x-rayed, dissected, and rehydrated each mummy in a search for clues to how these people lived and died. According to Dr. Marvin J. Allison, professor of clinical pathology at the Medical College of Virginia, "People died from the same causes 5000 years ago as they do today."

3   The findings indicate that health in rural parts of western South America has improved little over the past five millenia. In some ways, it seems even to have deteriorated. Unchanged are adult height and life span, both of which are nutrition-related factors. And respiratory disease — tuberculosis, for instance — still ranks as the major cause of death in Latin America. Infant mortality and child illness, however, appear to have been lower 5000 years ago than they are today, according to Allison, and there were fewer diseases caused by viruses. Toothaches were also less common, because hunting and gathering provided a diet high in protein instead of the carbohydrate-rich foods that came with agriculture.

4   In documenting how little the causes of death have changed, the study also refuted some long-held myths. It had been thought for example, that the Europeans introduced tuberculosis to the Western Hemisphere. But Allison has discovered well-preserved tuberculosis bacilli in people who died centuries before Columbus set foot on the New World. Similarly, many anthropologists believed that South American natives, until they mated with European settlers, had only type-O blood. But after examining tissue samples from the mummies, Allison has found that many Indians had A- and B-type-blood. Allison believes that the primitive health conditions that exist in this part of the world are due to the unavailability or unpopularity of modern medicine. However, his studies have demonstrated the success of primitive skull surgery, practiced by the Indians, apparently without benefit of either anesthetics or antiseptics.

Outline

Thesis Statement: In South America, mummies have become
important for research into human disease

1. People today die from the same causes as they did 5000
   years ago.
   a. Expert Marvin J. Allison cited.
   b. X-rayed, dissected, rehydrated 2500 mummies.
2. Research on mummies shows that health in rural parts of
   South America may have deteriorated rather than improved
   a. Height and life span about the same.
   b. Tuberculosis still major cause of death.
   c. Infant mortality and childhood illness may have been lower.
   d. Toothaches less common.
3. Study of mummies refuted long-standing myths.
   a. Europeans did not introduce tuberculosis
   b. Many Indians had type-A-type-B blood even before arrival of
      Europeans.
4. Studies demonstrate success of primitive skull surgery.
   a. No anesthetics
   b. Scraped away pieces of the skull
   c. Patients recovered with little incidence of infection.

Summary

   Research on mummies more than 5000 years old indicates that
time has not improved the health standards of people living in
rural parts of South America. According to medical expert Dr.
Marvin J. Allison, time has not necessarily improved the health of
people living in these areas. Adult height and life span remain
unchanged, and respiratory diseases like tuberculosis still rank as
a major cause of death. Surprisingly, the incidence of infant
mortality and childhood illness appears to have been lower 5000
years ago. Research on the mummies has also revealed that
primitive skull surgery practiced without anesthetics was
apparently successful. Patients recovered with relatively little
incidence of infection.

   Write a one-paragraph summary of the following article.

Challenging Darwin

Dina Ingber

1   Charles Darwin is under scientific siege. His basic evolutionary premise — that all life forms evolved from one common ancestor — is not in dispute. The debate rages over how.

2   One conflict concerns the Darwinian concept called "gradualism": minute genetic changes occur from one generation to the next, accumulating over the course of billions of years, until eventually a totally new life form develops. If this were true, the fossil record should show evidence of every level of development. But it doesn't.

3   Niles Eldredge of the Museum of Natural History in New York and Stephen Jay Gould of Harvard have proposed an alternative theory: "punctuated equilibria." Change, they say, comes not in steps but in leaps.

4   "Our theory is based on the observation that new species seem to appear suddenly and then to hang on for five to ten billion years without change," explains Eldredge. "So it is reasonable to assume that changes take place over a few thousand years — in a spurt — not over billions of years."

5   Other scientists challenge Darwin's belief that change came about randomly; they claim, as Jean Baptiste de Lamarck first did in 1809, that the environment induces changes that are passed on to the next generation. According to Darwin, for example, a single animal born by chance with longer legs is able to run faster, and because this trait increases the chance of survival, the animal and its long-legged offspring live on; other shorter-legged members of the species die off. Lamarck's view was that, forced to run fast to escape enemies, animals stretch their legs, and this acquired trait is passed on to the next generation.

6   Preliminary experiments of Drs. Edward J. Steele and Reginald M. Gorczynski at the Ontario Cancer Insitute lend support to Lamarck. They showed that mice given an artificial immunity to disease produced pups with the same immunities. Similarly, Dr. Neil J. Skolnick, of the Albert Einstein College of Medicine, showed that rats with artifically induced susceptibility to disease passed it on.

7   Darwin said only those genetic changes that improve fitness to survive are retained. But, according to David Raup, of Chicago's Field Museum of Natural History, even genetic changes that do not improve survival prospects are sometimes retained merely by chance. This would account for the existence of various animal characteristics — such as certain body proteins and possibly even the direction in which a snail's shell spirals — that seem to have no survival value.

Suggestions for Your Writer's Notebook

SUGGESTION 1

One way to develop an eye for vivid and expressive details is to cultivate the habit of making lists. Just pick a place or an object, observe it for a while, and then list everything you see, smell, or hear, recording even the most insignificant detail.

SUGGESTION 2

The great nineteenth-century scientist George Buffon believed that thought began with observation, and he counseled his followers to "gather facts in order to have ideas." Use one of your lists to put Buffon's advice into practice. Read it through several times. Then try to discover some conclusion or inference that you can draw from the specific details you have observed and recorded. Here are one student's list and a first draft and final version of her paragraph.

My Husband's Desk   Glenda Williams

A desk calendar with SEPTEMBER in capital letters
A box of multicolored paper clips
Books, all sizes and shapes, everywhere
Papers, scraps, pads, pieces, crumpled pages on the floor
A coffee cup with day-old coffee in it on top of the Webster's
Two jars of rubber cement with lids half off and cement
dripping down the sides
Two old post cards from the Grand Canyon
Pens, pencils, crayons, magic markers
Drawers half open with papers sticking out
Staples
Elastic bands
A box of index cards, alphabetically ordered

Draft 1

A quick glimpse of my husband's desk reveals a man not interested in tidiness. In the middle of the desk is a coffee cup, half-filled with day-old coffee. The cup is surrounded by numerous odds and ends. There are two jars of rubber cement, flanking each side of the coffee cup. The jars are half opened, and there is cement dripping down the sides. Luckily the cement has fallen only on the desk calendar, which bears the word SEPTEMBER. Books are everywhere, as are writing instruments; there are pens, pencils, magic markers, and crayons lying all over the desk. Paper is almost as plentiful.

Revised Version

A quick glimpse of my husband's desk suggests a man not impressed by the virtue of tidiness. In the middle of the desk, perched on top of Webster's dictionary sits a coffee cup, half-filled with day-old coffee. Next to the coffee are pens and pencils of all kinds, ball points, fountain pens, magic markers, colored pencils, even a few crayons. Paper is almost as plentiful. There are scraps of it, pages of it, whole piles of it. A few pieces have fallen on the floor, while some, the crumpled pages, have clearly been thrown there. Peeking out from beneath the papers are books of every color, size, and shape. Somehow, out of all of this mess, my husband produces scientific reports that are masterpieces of clarity and organization, but you could never tell that from his desk!

SUGGESTION 3

Making lists can help you explore yourself as well as the world around you. Lists like the following can do more than develop your ability to see and record details. They can also help you discover who you are and what you think.

Unimportant but Irritating Things

1. Meetings that last more than an hour.
2. People who shake my hand hard enough to hurt.
3. Anyone who tells a joke and gives me a sharp poke in the ribs to make me laugh.
4. People who call me Liz rather than Elizabeth.
5. People who talk in the movies.
6. Black dog hair all over my white clothes.

SUGGESTION 4

Start analyzing and collecting verbs that express a metaphorical relationship. Take, for example, the following sentence: "The dog *exploded* with pleasure when his master appeared." In this example, the verb used compares the dog's pleasure to an explosion, and that comparison vividly communicates the dog's excitement and happiness much more effectively than the verb in the sentence "The dog showed its pleasure when its master appeared."

Compare as well the following sentences:

1. Her rigid upbringing *had affected* her already timid spirit.
2. Her rigid upbringing *had imprisoned* her already timid spirit.
3. Unexpectedly, the teacher *caught* the students whispering.
4. Unexpectedly, the teacher *swooped down upon* the whispering students.

As you read, collect examples of verbs that rely on an implied comparison between two things, actions, or events. When you write, consider where you might use verbs that draw their power from an implied comparison.

SUGGESTION 5

Collect sentences that you like and imitate their form. Here are two examples from two students.

Megan Donnelly

"But most of all this little man, barely a hundred pounds and sadly unfitted for outdoor life, mastered the forest, noting all things that occurred therein." (James A. Michener, Chesapeake)

But most impressive the fat midget, hardly three and one half feet tall and physically inadequate for major league soccer, mastered the sport, remembering all intricate strategies of the game.

Joe Kelley

"She heard of Weinstein's death, his suicide by drowning, from the English department secretary, a handsome white-haired woman who kept a transistor radio on her desk." (Joyce Carol Oates, "In the Region of Ice")

He got the news of Alice's accident, her wreck by drunk driving, from the kindergarten teacher's student aide, a preppy blonde girl who always wore a peace button on her shirt.

Combining Sentences

In pattern 5 you worked on combining sentences through the use of relative pronouns like *who, which,* and *whom.* Pattern 7, however, introduces another set of connectives or linking words. These words are called *subordinate conjunctions,* and they connect or link clauses that function like adverbs to express the following set of relationships:

1. *Cause and Effect:* because, inasmuch as, since, once, not that
2. *Opposition and Contrast:* although, though, no matter how, whereas, even though
3. *Specific Condition:* if, unless, as soon as, when, whenever, provided that, with the provision that, in case of
4. *Manner:* as though, as if, like, as
5. *Time:* when, whenever, till, until, while, in the meantime, before
6. *Place:* where, wherever

Here are some examples of subordinate clauses that express particular relationships. The following subordinate clause shows one cause of an action:

> *Because animals used in Hollywood films have repeatedly met with unnecessary accidents and harm,* many people have begun to demand more stringent regulations for the use of animals on the film.

This subordinate clause shows under what conditions an act will take place:

> *If they will give up their guns,* the police will cease firing.

This subordinate clause tells when something happens:

> *Every time the production of a new Broadway musical begins,* thousands of young dancers dream about becoming the star.

This subordinate clause indicates place:

> *Wherever his master goes*, that faithful dog is sure to follow.

One important thing to look for when you are revising your papers is a pair of separate sentences that could actually be combined into one sentence containing a subordinate clause. Look carefully, for example, at the following:

1. Karen Silkwood was on her way to meet a reporter for *The New York Times* the night she died. Many people assume the young woman was murdered.
2. Because Karen Silkwood was on her way to meet a reporter for *The New York Times* the night she died, many people assume the young woman was murdered.

In the second example, the first sentence has been turned into a subordinate clause that modifies the second, giving one reason why some people claim Karen Silkwood was murdered. In this example, subordination expresses more clearly the relationship between the two sentences and the ideas they contain.

The following exercises will give you some practice in patterns of subordination.   **EXERCISE**

1. He went away ∧ .
       She married somebody else ∧ . [because]
       That somebody else *was more reliable* ∧ . [who]
       He *didn't go away for long periods of time*. [and who]

    _____

    _____

2. ∧ He tried to collect the debris.
       The storm was over. [when,]
    [, but]
    The task was too much for him.

_____

_____

3.   ∧ She passed the test ∧ .
        It looked difficult. [although,]
        She did it *with flying colors.*

_____

_____

4.   ∧ They gave her husband up for dead.
        He had been missing in action for so many years. [because]

_____

_____

5.   ∧ You will follow my orders ∧ .
        You live in my house. [while]
     [, and]
     You will respect my rules.

_____

_____

6.   ∧ He never praised me ∧.
        I worked for him. [as long as]
     [, but]
     I liked him anyway.

_____

_____

7.   ∧ He started to have ∧ ∧ hallucinations.
        He had been snorting cocaine. [because]
        The hallucinations were *bizarre.*
        The hallucinations were *frightening.* [and]

_____

_____

8.   Aspirins ∧ may reduce heart attacks.
        They are taken regularly. [, if,]

_____

_____

9. The plane crashed ∧ .
     The landing gear failed. [because]

_____

_____

10. The judge will give him a ∧ sentence ∧ .
     The sentence will be *brief.*
     He pleads guilty. [on the condition that]

_____

_____

Write five sentences using subordinate conjunctions to introduce a   **EXERCISE**
dependent clause. Use a different conjunction in every sentence.

1. _____

   _____

2. _____

   _____

3. _____

   _____

4. _____

   _____

5. _____

   _____

PATTERN 8

Pattern 8 introduces the appositive. *Appositives* are single words or phrases that modify or identify nouns. For example:

> At the age of seventy Meyer Lansky, *a key figure in the criminal underworld for many years,* retired to Israel.

In this sentence, the italicized phrase is an appositive, that is, it re-names and re-defines the subject, Meyer Lansky.

Appositives function much like relative clauses; they contain ideas that could be expressed in a simple sentence. Compare these two sentences:

1. Alexis Colby of *Dynasty* takes orders from no one. She is a woman of means.
2. Alexis Colby of *Dynasty*, *a woman of means*, takes orders from no one.

The following exercise will give you practice working with appositives.   EXERCISE
Once again directions for punctuation appear in brackets. Pay careful attention to those following the appositive. Appositives may or may not be enclosed in commas. For example the following appositive requires commas:

1.   Peter Arnot ∧ spoke to an ∧ audience
        He was *the translator of Antigone.* [, ,]
        The audience was *enthusiastic.*
     Peter Arnot, the translator of *Antigone*, spoke to an enthusiastic audience.

However, this example does not:

2.   The play ∧ was ∧ well-attended.
        It was Sophocles' *Antigone.*
        It was *remarkably* so.

     The play *Antigone* was remarkably well attended.

For an explanation of when to use commas with an appositive, see "Pointers for Final Editing" (pp. 323–351).

Complete the remaining exercise:

1.   ∧ The building ∧ was slated for destruction.
        It was *because of urban renewal.* [,]
        It was *an old vaudeville theater.* [, ,]

[, but]

The townspeople protested.

[, and]

The city relented.

_____

_____

2. He is a ∧ speaker ∧ ∧ .

     He is very *eloquent*. [an]

     He is *a man inspired by a mission*. [,]

     The speaker *will make his party a winner*. [, who]

_____

_____

3. Boy George ∧ dresses in ∧ clothing.

     Boy George is *the lead singer of Culture Club*. [, ,]

     The clothing is a *woman's*.

[; nevertheless,]

The group is enormously popular.

_____

_____

4. ∧ ∧ My date ∧ arrived ∧ .

     She arrived *promptly*.

     She arrived *at eight o'clock*. [,]

     She was *a tall woman with glasses*. [, ,]

     She arrived *at my home*.

_____

_____

5. Karen Carpenter ∧ died ∧ ∧ .

     She was *a talented singer and musician*. [, ,]

     She died *at the age of thirty-two*.

     This was *after a long struggle with anorexia nervosa*. [,]

_____

_____

6. ∧ The play ∧ was revived.
        This was *after more than twenty years.* [,]
        The play was *Death of a Salesman.*
[, and]
Dustin Hoffman played the lead.

_____

_____

7. The dog ∧ became his best friend ∧ .
        The dog was *a mangy old hound.* [, ,]
        The dog *followed him everywhere.* [and]

_____

_____

8. _____ annoyed everyone.
        The speaker ∧ *arrived late.* [the fact that]
        The speaker was *a British lord.* [, ,]
[, and]
The audience grumbled ∧ .
        This was *throughout the lecture.*

_____

_____

9. The detective ∧ grew sick ∧ .
        He was *a veteran of twenty-years on the force.* [, ,]
        This was *at the sight of the* ∧ *body.*
        The body was *mutilated.*

_____

_____

10. The short story ∧ was written by William Faulkner.
        The short story was *"Barn Burning."*
[, but]
It was ∧ attributed to Robert Penn Warren.
        This was done *incorrectly.*

_____

_____

Write five sentences using an appositive.   EXERCISE

1. _____

   _____

2. _____

   _____

3. _____

   _____

4. _____

   _____

5. _____

   _____

CHAPTER 6

Writing a Coherent Essay

As a writer, your ability to communicate a message to your readers depends on your willingness to act as their intellectual guide. This means it is your responsibility to provide the cues or signals that will guide them along the path of your thoughts.

On the basis of the signals you provide, your readers must constantly connect what they *have* read with what they *are* reading. At all times they should be able to see the relationship between the given and the new, the familiar and the unfamiliar, the first sentence and the last. An essay that allows them to make such connections quickly and easily is said to be coherent, and that is high praise indeed.

But praiseworthy or not, a coherent essay is not unattainable for a student writer. On the contrary, there are a number of very specific things you can do to increase the coherence of your writing. Although the following chapter does not explore every method for creating coherence, it introduces four of the most essential: (1) repetition and reference, (2) limitation of the number of inferences your readers must draw, (3) transitional markers and sentences, and (4) parallelism.

Using Repetition and Reference

WITHIN PARAGRAPHS

Your writing will become more coherent almost immediately if you consider a general principle of learning: It is easier to understand and remember unfamiliar information when it can be linked to the familiar. Therefore, when you revise your paper, you should do everything possible to show your readers how each new sentence is connected to prior sentences. You want to make it easy for them to see the relationship between the unfamiliar and the familiar, the given and the new.

One way to do this is to create sentences that *force* your readers to remember previous ideas at the same time that they process new ones. You can create such sentences by consciously building chains of repetition and reference. That is, you can repeat and refer to key terms all the way through your writing. Look, for example, at the following paragraph. Here the author repeats or refers to the key term *initiation* in order to make the controlling idea echo throughout the paragraph. That verbal echo helps the reader process the new information in each succeeding sentence.

> [1]The end of childhood is marked in many of the world's societies by some kind of initiation rite. [2]Initiation ceremonies sometimes involve circumcision and the revelation of hitherto secret knowledge: almost always they entail a change in diet and the relaxation of previous taboos — as, for example, the drinking of coffee and wine at dinner by older children in modern societies. [3]Among the southern Bantu, initiation ceremonies take place when a sufficient number of boys have reached the appropriate age or when the chief's own son has done so. [4]The male child is now separated both symbolically and in fact from the mother's household. [5]Initiation makes him aware of a network of obligations that bind him to other huts and to other families; he learns to measure prestige by the ability to offer hospitality and by the company in which he eats.[1]

The first sentence in this paragraph introduces the controlling idea: Many societies mark the end of childhood with some kind of initiation rite or ceremony. Note too that the first sentence ends with the phrase *initiation rite* and that the second sentence immediately repeats the word *initiation*. Although you can overdo it, this is one very nice way of using repetition to link your ideas: You can repeat in the opening of your new sentence some form of the word or phrase that ended the previous sentence. Such explicit repetition of a word that is central to the controlling idea

[1]Peter Farb and George Armelagos, *Consuming Passions* (New York: Washington Square P, 1980) 98.

keeps that controlling idea in your readers' minds as they process new information. Employed in this way, repetition makes it easier for your readers to follow the progress of your thoughts.

Be aware, too, that *where* you repeat words or phrases central to the controlling idea is important. In the foregoing paragraph, the word *initiation* is explicitly repeated three different times in the subject position (sentences 2, 3, and 5). When you use repetition to make an idea echo throughout your paragraph, be sure that some of that repetition appears in the subject position.

On a more implicit level, the pronoun *they* in the second sentence serves the same function as repetition. By referring to the phrase *initiation ceremonies*, it keeps the controlling idea firmly anchored in the reader's mind. Like careful repetition, careful reference can be a very effective way of helping the reader weave new information into old.

Furthermore, the authors do not use repetition and reference only in the opening sentences of the paragraph. On the contrary, this paragraph reveals a carefully constructed chain of repetition and reference designed to guide readers from the first sentence to the last. Sentence 3, for example, begins with an unfamiliar topic, "the southern Bantu." But, to help their readers see the relationship between this new material and what has already been said, the writers explicitly repeat the key word *initiation*. This repetition helps a reader anticipate the appropriate connection: The southern Bantu will supply a specific illustration of the controlling idea.

Sentence 4, in turn, is linked to sentence 3 by its reference to the words *boys* and *son* via the phrase *the male child*. That phrase acts as a verbal substitute for or equivalent to those previous words. It signals that the authors are still pursuing the same subject, the initiation rite of Bantu boys. In sentence 5, the authors return to explicit repetition of the key word *initiation*. That repetition makes it easier for readers to link the information conveyed in the final sentence with what appeared in the opening one.

BETWEEN PARAGRAPHS

Such a carefully constructed chain of repetition and reference can be useful not only within paragraphs but also between them. In the following excerpt, the author uses both to help his readers move quickly and smoothly from paragraph to paragraph as he explains how human expectations can shape experience.

From Taking Charge of Your Health

NORMAN COUSINS

1   Robust expectations are important. The human body has a tendency to move along the path of the mind's expectations. I learned recently of a study made of about one hundred patients awaiting similar surgery. The patients were divided into two groups. One group dreaded the surgery, regarded it as mutilation, and tried to do everything possible to avoid going into the operating room. Members of the second group viewed surgery as an opportunity to liberate their bodies from a dangerous intruder. Careful observation of all patients following surgery revealed that those who had high expectations had a much more rapid recovery than those who feared the worst.

Paragraph 1 introduces the idea that expectations can shape or control experience, and it provides two significant examples. Paragraph 2 (below) pursues that idea but introduces a new element — subconscious rather than conscious expectations. Note how carefully the author uses both repetition and reference to help the reader make the appropriate connections.

2   *An even more dramatic example of the way even subconscious expectations can be translated into reality occurred not long ago in a Louisiana hospital.* There was a sudden outcropping of deaths from heart stoppage during anesthesia. An investigation was ordered. The heart arrests were tracked down to two anesthesiologists who would inform patients of the risks of anesthesia just before the patients were wheeled into the operating room. Even though the patients were not conscious during the surgery, their subconscious labored under the burden of the information they had just received. In defense of the anesthesiologists it should be said that they were required to inform the patients of their risk. The problem, however, was in the timing and manner of their communication.

The opening sentence of this paragraph introduces a new topic, subconscious expectations. But at the same time it carefully repeats the controlling idea: "Expectations can shape reality." In addition, that opening sentence refers to the previous paragraph through the phrase *An even more dramatic example.* That phrase not only explicitly introduces the new illustrations that are "more dramatic" but also implicitly refers to the less dramatic examples cited in the previous paragraph. In this way, that phrase helps the reader make the appropriate connection between the given and the new.

3   *The approach of the other anesthesiologists at the hospital was totally different.* They didn't wait until just before the patients had to go into surgery. They made a point of discussing the procedure well before the critical hour; they explained that the law required them to inform the patients of the worst that could happen but that adverse results were extremely rare. Then they would dwell on the good results that were expected of the surgery. The two anesthesiologists involved in the tragic deaths had usually followed this procedure but had become very busy and found it necessary to rush through the requirements in a few instances. It goes without saying that, on completion of the investigation into the tragic deaths, corrective procedures were instituted and the hospital's excellent record was restored.

In this paragraph the opening sentence explicitly tells the reader to expect something "different." But note how that word *different* forces you to think about what went before, to question how the new approach differs from the old. The phrase *the approach of the other anesthesiologists* does the same thing. You cannot think about the approach of the other anesthesiologists without thinking about the approach already discussed. The explicit repetition of the key word *anesthesiologist* is important here too. Replace it with the word *doctors,* and you will find it takes longer to make the appropriate connections between paragraphs 2 and 3.

The author's decision to choose words that create a web of repetition and reference is one good reason why the foregoing essay is so coherent. As you read it, you are never lost. You can always, quickly and easily, connect what has already been said with what you are reading.

If you revise with the following suggestions in mind, you can create the same kind of coherence in your own writing.

1. Use repetition and reference to create verbal echoes of your thesis statement. You want your readers to know, throughout your paper, how the supporting paragraphs are related to your original thesis.

2. By the same token, use repetition and reference between sentences so

that your readers can always weave unfamiliar information into the familiar.

3. *Where* you use repetition and reference is important. The openings of both sentences and paragraphs are powerful places. Use them to build a careful chain of repetition and reference that will guide your reader through your paper.

4. Careful word choice can forge the chain of references you need for effective coherence. Using synonyms and pronouns is one obvious way to create a chain of references. But there are more subtle ways as well. You can also use words that are closely associated with the key terms you want to refer to. Consider an example: "The party had come to a disastrous end. Colored hats, streamers, and noisemakers were scattered all over. Amid them all sat the hostess, crying her eyes out." Here the first sentence announces that the party had ended in failure. In the second sentence, the words *colored hats*, *streamers* and *noisemakers* all function to suggest the word *party*. It doesn't need to be explitly stated. And using the word *scattered* in this context keeps the idea of disaster in the reader's mind.

The following exercises are designed to help you think about and use repetition and reference to create coherent pieces of writing.

Collect three or four paragraphs that you think are particularly clear **EXERCISE 1** and coherent. Identify those places where the author used some form of repetition and reference to create coherence. An example follows.

A growing number of social scientists and mental health professionals are now studying contemporary American loneliness. Some say that we are more lonely than in the past. Others argue that we just think we are. More persuasive is the evidence that the physical and emotional consequences of loneliness pose greater dangers than anyone thought. Dr. Stephen E. Goldston, director of the Office of Prevention at the National Institute of Mental Health in Washington, an organization not known for its interest in subjects of merely philosophical value, believes that "persistent and severe" loneliness can lead to alcoholism, drug abuse and suicide. Recently his office convened a conference to raise the question of whether such loneliness can be prevented or cured.[2]

[2]Louise Berkinow, "Alone: Yearning for Compassion in America," *New York Times Magazine* (15 Aug. 1982): 25.

Imagine that you had produced the following very rough draft of a
paper. You want now to rewrite it for greater coherence. Produce a draft
that may not be a finished product but that is definitely more coherent.
Although you may make any other changes you want, be sure to use
some kinds of repetition and reference.

EXERCISE   2

1   Observe people making sandwiches for any length of time and
one thing becomes quite clear: Not everyone prepares a sandwich
in the same way. There are at least three distinct groups, each one
with its own set of methods and attitudes.

2   Messiness is an outstanding characteristic. They just want to eat
it as soon as possible. Speed is essential; appearance is irrelevant.
Mayonnaise and mustard go on any which way. They may be
smeared inside or outside the sandwich. Slices of luncheon meat
are piled on top of one another, with the corners left protruding
outside the bread. Pickles and tomatoes are slapped on top of
one another, with no attention paid to symmetrical form. The
sandwich resembles the leaning tower of Pisa, ready to topple at
any moment.

3   There is the meticulous sandwich maker. The sandwich is a work
of art. He gathers together all of his materials, bread, meat, spread,
and various garnishes. He carefully spreads mayonnaise or
mustard on each slice of bread and arranges the layers of
luncheon meat so that they lie neatly on top of one another. In
the same way, pickles and tomatoes must be placed symmetrically
in each corner. The final product has all the unity and design of a
carefully constructed brick wall.

4   In the third group neither taste nor appearance is important.
Nutrition counts, and every attempt must be made to make the
sandwich have the appropriate balance of carbohydrates, proteins,
vitamins, and minerals. Luncheon meats are poison. Only
ingredients like fresh tofu, alfalfa sprouts, and sesame seed paste
are acceptable. Sandwiches prepared by members of this group
frequently look and taste disgusting. But they are nutritionally
sound. That's all that counts.

Limiting Inferences

WITHIN PARAGRAPHS

No writer ever provides every last bit of information the reader needs to make the appropriate connections between sentences and paragraphs. At some point she always expects her readers to make *inferences*. She expects them, that is, to read between the lines, to use what is explicitly said in order to understand what is implicitly suggested but not directly stated. Take, for example, the following:

> He had been late for work four days out of five. When he came
> to work on Friday, he received notice that he had been fired.
> His employer had finally lost patience with him.

In this example the author clearly expects her readers to make the appropriate inference: The man was fired because he was consistently late. Here the writer assumes that her readers have enough knowledge about the world of work to know that employers consider repeated lateness grounds for dismissal. That writer's assumption does not seem unreasonable. But compare the following:

> For some people, working at a computer becomes like an addiction.
> It is something they want to do twenty-four hours a day. In some
> cases, the purchase of a computer has been the first step toward
> a divorce.

In this example the author assumes that his readers can, with very little assistance from him, construct the following chain of inferences:

1. Some married couples purchase computers.
2. After that purchase, one member starts working on the computer and becomes addicted to doing so.
3. This creates friction in the marriage, with one member becoming increasingly unhappy.
4. The addiction to the computer is so strong that nothing can be done about it.
5. In despair, the unhappy spouse files for divorce.

What this chain of inferences suggests is that the author is making too
many demands on his readers. He is forcing them to supply information
he should have supplied himself.

To a degree, your readers will be willing to supply information not
explicitly offered in your paper. But if they need to create a long chain
of inferences to understand the relationship between your sentences, you
are asking too much of them. Instead you should provide more information
and reduce the number of inferences your readers have to make. Here,
for example, is a revised version of the previous paragraph.

> For some people, working at a computer becomes an addiction,
> something they want to do twenty-four hours a day. Citing this
> phenomenon, marriage counselors have begun to use the term
> *computer widow* to refer to the woebegone spouses of those men
> and women who neglect their marriage because they cannot tear
> themselves away from the computer screen. In some cases the
> addiction can actually destroy the marriage, and the only solution
> is a divorce that leaves the addicted spouse free to spend most
> of his or her waking hours at the computer.

Here the number of inferences the reader must draw has been significantly
reduced, and the result is a far more coherent piece of prose.

PLACING INFORMATION PROPERLY

However, just adding information to reduce the number of inferences
your readers have to make is not enough. *Where* you place that information
is also important. Usually your readers need it at the beginning of sentences,
not at the end. If they have to wait until the end, chances are they will
put down your paper in annoyance. Certainly, being faced with too many
paragraphs like the following could produce that result. In this example,
the author has not always provided enough information, and when he
does, it is in the wrong place.

> [1]Sometime around the end of March, most people begin to
> dream of enjoying the summer sun. [2]They see themselves sporting
> a pot belly or flabby thighs, those unwanted souvenirs of holiday
> overindulgence. [3]Enrolling in exercise classes, they stretch and
> strain, all for the sake of whittling those thighs and flattening
> those bellies. [4]No amount of exertion seems too much to ask.

In this example, sentence 1 explains that March brings with it pleasant dreams of summer. After that sentence, the second sentence comes as a shock because it discusses not pleasant dreams but unpleasant ones. Puzzle over the two sentences for a bit and you can infer the appropriate connections: (1) If you have pleasant dreams of summer, you imagine yourself on a beach or a tennis court. (2) You see yourself in shorts or a bathing suit. (3) Imagining yourself in a swimsuit, you realize you have gained too much weight during the winter. This is another example of sentences that overburden the reader.

Unfortunately, sentence 3 does not make the reader's task much easier. Nothing more is said about dreams. Suddenly there is a new subject, exercise classes where people stretch and strain without complaining. When the writer finally reveals the connection between dreams of summer and exercise — people want to whittle away those unsightly bulges in order to look good — it is too late. The reader has either inferred the appropriate connection or given up in annoyance. By the final sentence, "No amount of exertion is too much to ask," it is easy enough to forget what the first sentence in the paragraph had to do with the last.

With two essential changes, this paragraph can become much more coherent. (1) Additional information should be provided so that the reader is not forced to construct a long chain of inferences. (2) Information already in the paragraph should be placed at the beginning of a sentence rather than the end. Look at the difference these revisions make.

> [1]Sometime around the end of March, most people begin to dream of enjoying the summer sun. [2]With anticipation, they imagine themselves on the beach or the tennis court. [3]Unfortunately they also imagine themselves in shorts or bathing suits that reveal their pot bellies and flabby thighs, souvenirs of holiday overindulgence. [4]Inspired by the desire to whittle those thighs and flatten those bellies, both men and women enroll in exercise classes, where they willingly stretch and strain, pant and perspire without complaint. [5]Because they are determined to be lean by summer, no amount of exertion seems too much to ask.

Here again, the first sentence announces that March brings with it pleasant dreams of summer. But note the change in sentence 2. It now supplies a specific summer dream. Sentence 3, in turn, explains how pleasant dreams of being on a tennis court or a beach lead to more unpleasant ones about flabby bodies. In the previous paragraph the reader had to infer the appropriate connections. But in this paragraph the writer makes the connections clear and explicit.

Sentence 4 contains much the same information as sentence 3 in the previous paragraph, but that information is in a different place. Now the reader learns at the beginning of the sentence, rather than at the end, how dreams of summer lead to strenuous exercise classes. In much the same way, the opening of sentence 5 explicitly links dreams of summer and the willingness to work hard in exercise classes.

BETWEEN PARAGRAPHS

In the following paragraphs, the author does not rely on repetition and reference alone to bind his paragraphs together. He also provides enough information so that his readers are never left to develop long chains of inferences by themselves.

The Tire Trap
STEPHEN S. HALL

1   Unfortunately for Americans, mosquitoes do not take tires for granted. They take them for homes. Scientists would be hard pressed to design a better breeding chamber for mosquitoes — and disease.

This paragraph introduces the thesis of the entire essay: Acting as breeding grounds for mosquitoes, old tires foster disease. Now observe how the next paragraph echoes the controlling idea of that thesis statement and introduces new information about a specific breed of mosquito.

2   *The larvae of* Aedes triseriatus, *the mosquito that infects young children with La Crosse encephalitis virus, thrive in old tires.* The tires retain water nicely and fill up with a kind of nutrient-rich debris that larvae voraciously devour. By some estimates, the mosquitoes that hatch in tires are larger, live longer, and emerge as much as four weeks earlier than adults that hatch in tree holes. Some 4,867 larvae — and 12 separate isolates — were harvested from a single tire found outside Chardon, Ohio, near Cleveland.

Having described, in general terms, the danger of mosquitoes breeding in tires, the author uses the first sentence of the second paragraph to tell his readers how to connect the second paragraph with the third. The third paragraph will illustrate the danger described in the second.

3   *The danger of such situations is borne out by fieldwork by the Vector-Borne Disease Unit of Ohio's department of health; in Ohio, there have been 558 cases of La Crosse encephalitis — and five fatalities — since 1963.* Follow-up studies on 69 diagnosed cases in 1981–82 showed that tires were present in 72.5 percent of the cases and were considered the "predominant source" of A. *triseriatus* 54 percent of the time.

A less conscientious writer could have have begun the previous paragraph with only the second half of the first sentence, "In Ohio, there have been 558 cases of La Crosse encephalitis — and five fatalities — since 1963." He could have assumed that his readers would infer the appropriate connection: This is a specific example of the dangers just described. But he chose not to do that. Instead he chose to make his readers' task easier and defined for them the relationship between the two paragraphs. "The danger of such situations is borne out by fieldwork by the Vector-Borne Disease Unit of Ohio's department of health."

4   *Statistics linking old tires to cases of encephalitis are confirmed by haunting personal anecdotes.* A 1983 case in Perry County, Ohio, for example, occurred at the rural home of a man who was in the business of recyling tires. Public health investigators found hundreds of tires and large numbers of A. *triseriatus* mosquitoes at the site. The victim: the man's two-year-old daughter. A puzzling 1977 case in a suburb of Milwaukee, well outside the endemic area, made sense when it was found that a neighbor of the victim had previously lived in a rural area north of La Crosse — and had hauled old tires along to Milwaukee when he relocated.

The author *could* have begun the fourth paragraph simply by describing the 1983 case. The reader could have inferred the appropriate connection: This paragraph offers more specific and more personal examples of the statistics discussed in the previous paragraph. But this author is extremely careful and conscientious. He won't take the chance of losing or confusing his reader. Thus his opening sentence refers to the "statistics" of the previous paragraph and tells the reader to expect some "personal anecdotes" hidden behind the numbers.

Deciding when you have to provide additional information and reduce the number of inferences your readers must make is often complicated. But you are more likely to make the right decision if you remember that no two minds work exactly alike. Even if your readers have the same knowledge at their disposal, they may well combine it in different ways.

Remember too that your instructor, in assuming the role of academic reader, will not be so cooperative a reader as you might expect. To test your ability to write coherently, she will frequently read your paper as though she were relatively uninformed about your particular thesis. As you grow more specialized in a subject and more experienced as a writer, your instructor may encourage you to write as one expert to another. But at first she may well do just the opposite. Playing the role of someone unfamiliar with your thesis, she will expect you to make it familiar by providing the appropriate information.

The following exercise will give you some practice in thinking about when and where you need to provide more information for your readers.

Select at random two or three paragraphs from essays that you have written. Number every sentence in each paragraph, and then identify the inferences you expect your readers to draw in order to understand how one sentence connects with another.

EXERCISE 3

What you want to discover with this exercise is whether you are consistently expecting your reader to draw the inferences that will connect your sentences. If you are, you should consider revising to add the appropriate information and reduce the number of inferences your readers have to make. Here is an illustration:

> [1]On the movie screen, robots may be a match for human beings. [2]However, they are actually very specialized and very stupid. [3]Robots like R2D2 do not exist. [4]Robots are just being designed to find their way around randomly placed objects, and even that simple capability is still very much a thing of the future. [5]Robots may be cute, even cuddly, in the movies. [6]However, they are anything but social beings. [7]They have been known to forget their own strength and hurl both people and objects across the room.

Readers must make at least six inferences in order to connect these sentences properly.

☐ 1 to 2: The writer is no longer talking about the world of movies but about reality.

☐ 2 to 3: The writer is talking about a particular movie, *Star Wars*.

☐ 3 to 4: Now the writer is talking about real robots.

☐ 4 to 5: Here the writer provides the information to make the connection, but it comes too late in the sentence.

☐ 5 to 6: Here the reader has to infer that the writer is again talking about real robots.

☐ 6 to 7: Here again, the reader has to infer that the author is continuing a discussion of real (not movie) robots.

In this case, the additional information highlighted below could reduce the number of inferences the reader has to draw and make the resulting paragraph far more coherent.

REVISED VERSION
[1]On the movie screen, robots may be a match for human beings, *but in reality,* they are very specialized and very stupid. [2]*At present,* robots like R2D2 *in the movie "Star Wars"* simply do not exist. [3]*In real life,* robots are just being designed to find their way around randomly placed objects, and even that simple capability is still very much a thing of the future. [4]*Although in the movies* robots may be cute and even cuddly, they are anything but that in reality. [5]*On the contrary,* robots have been known to forget their own strength and hurl both people and objects across the room.

Transitional Markers and Transitional Sentences

WITHIN PARAGRAPHS

Transitional markers are words and phrases like *furthermore, moreover, however,* and *for example.* (A more comprehensive list appears on pages 177–179.) Placed at the opening of sentences, they signal relationships and tell your readers what they can expect from the sentence to come. As an illustration of what transitional markers can do for your writing, read and compare the following passages.

[1]My boss had a stormy marriage. [2]He and his wife quarreled up until the day she died.

Given those two sentences, you have certain expectations about what could follow. They lead you to expect more negative information about that apparently unhappy marriage. But look now at the way the passage actually continues.

[1]My boss had a stormy marriage. [2]He and his wife quarreled up until the day she died. [3]They loved one another very dearly. [4]After her death, he was devastated and died shortly thereafter. [5]In my opinion, the man died of a broken heart. [6]That sounds romantic, but it's probably accurate.

Given the ideas presented in sentences 1 and 2, sentence 3 comes as a shock. It seems flatly to contradict what came before. More to the point, when presented in this way, the idea in sentence 3 seems to destroy the coherence of the passage. But it does not have to. The addition of a transitional marker could help make the passage more coherent.

[1]My boss had a very stormy marriage. [2]He and his wife quarreled up until the day she died. [3]*Nevertheless*, they loved one another dearly. [4]After her death, he was devastated and died shortly thereafter. [5]In my opinion, he died of a broken heart. [6]That sounds romantic, but it's probably accurate.

The addition of the transitional marker *nevertheless* makes a big difference. Placed at the beginning of sentence 3, it serves to reconcile the apparent contradiction between the ideas of sentences 2 and 3. It signals that the reader should expect the opposite of what has just been said and should understand that such oppositions can coexist. Transitional markers such as *nevertheless, however, furthermore,* and *moreover* are useful devices for guiding and controlling your readers' expectations.

However, as useful as transitional markers are for making what you write more coherent, like any other device, they have their limitations. Compare the following paragraphs. The first one is overburdened with transitional markers. The second one is not.

1   An organization called MADD, Mothers Against Drunk Driving, has decided to take firm action against those who drink and drive. *For example*, the organization has started a letter-writing campaign publicizing the need to increase the penalties for drunk driving. *Consequently*, a number of states have instituted stiffer penalties that include both heavier fines and longer jail sentences.

Moreover, MADD has also begun to demand that the media increase coverage of serious auto accidents involving drunk drivers. *In summary*, MADD is an organization determined to make a difference.

2   An organization called MADD, Mothers Against Drunk Driving, has decided to take firm action against those who drink and drive. An important part of that action is a letter-writing campaign publicizing the need to increase the penalties for drunk driving. *Consequently*, a number of states have instituted stiffer penalties that include heavier fines and longer jail sentences. MADD has *also* begun to demand increased media coverage of serious auto accidents involving drunk drivers. Dedicated to the goal of their organization, to wipe out drunk driving, the members of MADD are determined to make a difference.

Whereas the first paragraph relies too heavily on transitional markers, the second does not, and the result is coherent without being tedious.

Functioning in much the same way as transitional markers, transitional sentences are another useful device for improving the coherence of your writing. They too can signal relationships and guide your readers' expectations.

In the following paragraph the author wants to introduce the idea that an American writer has been underestimated. But as the paragraph stands now, it moves too abruptly from the negative view to the positive one. It does not really take into account the expectations aroused by the opening sentence.

[1]In general, the majority of critics view Mary Wilkins Freeman as a writer of very limited talents. [2]From their perspective, Freeman's short stories, written in the late nineteenth century, reveal little more than a gift for detailed and accurate description. [3]Freeman did a great deal more than describe landscape and transcribe dialect. [4]Her stories show that, in addition to having a gift for description, she was an astute psychologist. [5]In her best work, she brilliantly explored the effects of repressed rebellion, showing how fully she understood that emotions long denied can have dangerous consequences. [6]Failing to find an acceptable outlet, they invariably find some more unacceptable and more dangerous form of expression.

In this paragraph the first two sentences develop the idea that Mary Wilkins Freeman was a writer of limited talents. Reading them, you expect to hear more about the traditional viewpoint. But the author does not want to fulfill those expectations; he wants to re-evaluate Freeman's work. To do that without destroying the coherence of his writing, he needs to prepare the reader more carefully. One way to do that is to add a transitional sentence.

[1]In general, the majority of critics view Mary Wilkins Freeman as a writer of very limited talents. [2]From their perspective, Freeman's short stories, written in the late nineteenth century, reveal little more than a gift for detailed and accurate description. [3]*Yet common as such critical evaluations might be, they do not do their subject justice.* [4]Freeman did a great deal more than describe landscape and transcribe dialect. [5]Her stories show that, in addition to having gift for description, she was an astute psychologist. [6]In her best work, she brilliantly explored the effects of repressed rebellion, showing how fully she understood that emotions long denied can have dangerous consequences. [7]Failing to find an acceptable outlet, they invariably find some more unacceptable and more dangerous form of expression.

Transitional Sentence

In this revised example, the transitional sentence creates an effective bridge between the opening sentences and the remainder of the paragraph. The result is a more coherent paragraph.

BETWEEN PARAGRAPHS

Transitional sentences and transitional markers are not limited to use within paragraphs. They can create equally effective bridges between paragraphs.

1   Mystery surrounds the early life of the black poet Countee Cullen, and there are a number of conflicting stories about his past. By one account, he was born in Baltimore and named Countee Leroy Porter. Because his father died shortly after the boy's birth, he was raised by an ailing mother, who had great difficulty supporting herself and her son. To avoid raising her son in poverty, she decided to give him up for adoption.

2   *In direct contrast,* Cullen's widow claimed that the poet was

born in Louisville, Kentucky, and was adopted while he was still a baby by the Reverend Frederick Asbury Cullen, who gave the poet his last name. According to this account, Cullen was not raised in affluence. But he also wasn't raised in poverty, and the circumstances of his childhood were far from bleak. *Still, even this is not the final version.*

3   There has *also* been speculation that the poet was actually the illegitimate son of the Reverend Cullen and was adopted by him, although the adoption was never legalized. This account places Cullen's childhood in Harlem, and it fits more closely with the poet's own account of his life. Although Cullen said little about his past, he always claimed that the Cullens were his real parents, and he denied the existance of a previous mother and father.

Here the opening paragraph offers the first account of Cullen's life, and the second paragraph introduces another version. To move the reader smoothly from one account to the other, the writer opens the second paragraph with a transitional marker, *in direct contrast*. But the second paragraph also contains a transitional sentence: "Still, even this is not the final version." Given this sentence, the reader is prepared for yet another conflicting account of the poet's life.

Transitional markers and transitional sentences are not the only ways to create coherence, but they can be extremely effective if used with care. The following exercises will give you some practice.

Read through the paragraphs on pages 179 and 180 in order to determine where transitional markers or sentences could help guide your readers' expectations. Then revise each paragraph to add them. Here, for your reference, is a list of commonly used transitional markers.

EXERCISE 4

TO SIGNAL THE ADDITION OF RELATED IDEAS, EXAMPLES, AND REASONS

furthermore	moreover	in a similar
again	in addition	manner (or
further	similarly	fashion)
first	also	in the same
second	likewise	vein
too	for example	by the same
for instance	finally	token

| add to this | as an illustration | thus it follows along the same lines |

To Signal Special Emphasis or Repetition

| indeed | in fact | in other words |
| obviously | that is | above all |

To Signal Reversal or Modification

nevertheless	all the same	at the same time
but	still	on the other hand
however	conversely	despite that fact
yet	to be sure	notwithstand- ing
for all that	nonetheless	
on the contrary		

To Signal Relationships or Order in Time

afterwards	finally	earlier
then	before	thereafter
later, later on	soon	simulta- neously
when	while	at present, currently
meanwhile	at that point	recently
first	second	
	next	

To Signal Conclusions, Results, or Summaries

finally	therefore	consequently,
as a result	thus	as a conse- quence
on the whole	to conclude	in summary
accordingly	thereupon	to sum up
		in the end

Note: Context changes the function of a transitional marker. In different settings, the same word plays different roles. Take, for example, the word *finally*, which appears in two columns, the one for conclusions and the one for time.

Example:

Historically, human beings have treated animals as creatures without the capacity for thought. Scientists have recently begun to show that animals, from insects to mammals, have the capacity for conscious reasoning. They have discovered that reptiles, after seeing their prey, carefully camouflage themselves in preparation for attack. The heron will pluck one of its own feathers and use it to lure unwary fish into its waiting mouth.

Revised Version:

Historically, human beings have treated animals as creatures with no capacity for reason or thought. However, recently scientists have begun to show that animals, from insects to mammals, have the capacity for conscious reasoning. They have discovered, for example, that reptiles, after seeing their prey, carefully camouflage themselves in preparation for attack. Along the same lines, a heron will pluck one of its own feathers and use it to lure unwary fish into its waiting mouth.

1. Uncomfortable in general with the subject of alcoholism, most people are even less comfortable confronting the fact that fifty percent of America's alcoholics are women. They simply refuse to admit the problem exists. The number of female alcoholics is increasing. Ignoring the problem has not made it go away.

2. There was a time when home video games could not compete with those in the amusement arcades. The home video games are easily a match for those found in the arcades. Intelevision and Odyssey have added voice modules to their home games so that private homes, like the arcades, can ring with machine-produced noise. Graphics for home games have been enormously improved and compare favorably with those designed for arcade use.

3. During the brief time he lived, the young Canadian athlete Terry Fox proved to the world that he was an extraordinary human being. In

1979 doctors told the boy he had to have his leg amputated because of cancer. Following the operation, Terry decided to run a 3000-mile marathon throughout Canada. He wanted to use the run as a way to raise money for cancer research, with donations being made according to each mile he completed. Against all odds and all expectations, Terry ran for miles. He had to give up. His body could no longer match his spirit. He had fulfilled his goal: He had raised thousands of dollars for cancer research.

4.   When David Bowie first became a musical presence in the 1960s, he presented himself as a flashy London dandy. By the seventies, his stage persona had changed, and he was the bisexual Ziggy Stardust. With his red hair, heavily painted face and outrageous costumes, Bowie definitely stood out in a crowd. By the end of that decade, yet another David Bowie emerged. This man was a flamboyantly but still tastefully dressed aristocrat. In his 1983 concert tour, he appeared on stage looking like a businessman or a college professor.

The Principle of Parallel Form

In the simplest terms, the principle of parallel form is as follows: Whenever possible, make elements that are equal in function equal in form.

He searched everywhere: *under the rugs*, *behind the pictures*, and *in the closets*.

The italicized phrases all perform the same function in this sentence. They are adverbs defining place. Because they all perform the same function, they also assume the same parallel form; they all appear as prepositional phrases.

The use of parallel form is not limited to the single sentence. You can also use parallel form to signal the relationship between major and minor supporting sentences in a paragraph.

[1]Contrary to long-standing traditions affirming infant ignorance, researchers continue to discover that babies know much more than we think they do. [2]They know, for example, how to imitate their elders, how to reproduce on their miniature faces the expressions of the adults who surround them. [3]They know, too, how

to distinguish the simple from the complex. [4]Studies of their eye movements, for example, reveal that they pay more attention to objects showing variety in line, color, and form. [5]With more uniform objects, they quickly become bored. [6]Babies also know how to express their affection, how to show their caretakers that they appreciate kindness. [7]When pleased with their care, babies will wave their hands, make sucking sounds, and gurgle.

Sentence 1 introduces the controlling idea of the paragraph: Babies are not ignorant; they know much more than we think they do. That topic sentence commits the writer to telling the reader what babies *do* know, and sentence 2 promptly gives the first illustration of infant knowledge. Sentence 3 gives the second. But in addition to noting the parallel content of these sentences, you should also note that they are quite similar in form. For the reader, such similarity in form is a signal. It announces that the two sentences contain different but equally important illustrations of infant understanding. They are both major supporting sentences.

Sentence 4, however, does not continue the same grammatical form. In this case, the absence of parallel form is also a signal. It tells the reader that the author is not introducing a new illustration but is modifying the previous one. Sentence 4, then, is a minor supporting sentence.

With sentence 6 the writer returns to parallel form, and that return signals a new illustration in another major supporting sentence. Sentence 7, by dropping the parallel form, tells the reader to expect some modification of the previous sentence.

When you employ parallel form in your writing, you are helping your readers sort out the information provided in your paragraph. More specifically, you are telling them when to expect a major supporting sentence and when to expect a minor one.

As you might have guessed, the use of parallel form within an essay does much the same thing. It tells a reader when to expect a major supporting paragraph and when to expect a minor one. The following essay provides an illustration.

Video Games: A Threat to Teen-agers?   Renée Mariano

1   On February eighth, the village of Bradley, Illinois, barred children under the age of sixteen from playing video games in local amusement arcades. On the very same day, the city of

Marlborough, Massachusetts, prohibited youths under eighteen
from using the arcades at night and during school hours. These
are just two examples of the many cities across the country that
have had to take legal action against the teen-age mania for video
games. For many parents and administrators, video games are a
threat to teen-agers' emotional and intellectual growth.

Thesis statement

2   Critics of the games argue that they encourage the waste of both
time and money. They maintain that, instead of doing homework or
playing sports, teen-age addicts concentrate on improving their
scores in Pac Man or Donkey Kong. While disposing of their time,
the games also dispose of their money — in great quantities. At a
quarter a game, a really addicted teen-ager can spend five or ten
dollars in a long afternoon, and most teen-agers simply don't have
that kind of money.

*Major Supporting
Paragraph*

3   Unfortunately, many students get it by sacrificing money their parents give them for lunches and books. For them, the games have become more important than such inessentials as food and textbooks. Obviously, parents who have found out about this exchange have been less than delighted.

Minor Supporting Paragraph

4   Critics also argue that the games encourage a casual attitude toward violence and aggression. In most cases the goal of video games is to destroy your opponent through the use of weaponry, and teen-agers spend hours shooting down that last battleship or space invader. In the minds of some, this is a dangerous way to spend the afternoon, for it encourages the idea that violence and destruction are fun and without real consequence.

Major Supporting Paragraph

5   Like television, then, video games may encourage our society's tendency to take violence lightly, to see it as a source of amusement rather than horror. Of course, all of this remains to be proved. But there is a chilling question to consider: What does happen to the mind of a teen-ager who spends every afternoon in the video arcade and every evening in front of the tube?

Major Supporting Paragraph

The foregoing essay consists of five paragraphs. Paragraph 1 introduces the thesis statement: "For many parents and administrators, video games are a threat to teen-agers' emotional and intellectual growth." To develop that thesis statement, paragraph 2, a major supporting paragraph, offers the first example of the threat it describes, and paragraph 3 further modifies that example.

Paragraph 4, also a major supporting paragraph, introduces another specific illustration of the dangers video games can pose for teen-agers. As you can see, paragraphs 2 and 4 open in much the same way. Here the author is using parallel form to signal that both paragraphs function in the same way: They introduce new illustrations of the thesis statement. Paragraph 5, however, because it does not introduce a third equally important illustration, does not maintain the parallel form established by paragraphs 2 and 4.

Used carefully, parallel form can be an effective device for guiding your reader within paragraphs or between them. The following exercise will give you some practice in employing parallel form.

In this exercise, concentrate on giving ideas of equal importance similar form. All the information you need to complete the paragraphs is provided

EXERCISE   4

below the lines you are to write on. You just have to give that information the appropriate parallel form.

Example:

   Research in learning suggests that, in the long run, getting good grades depends more on effective study skills than on a high I.Q. Whereas students with good grades prepare for exams way in advance, reviewing their notes periodically, students with poor grades wait until the last minute and then cram. Unfortunately, cramming does not produce the desired results. While students with high grades usually organize their time, planning when and where they will complete their assignments, students with low grades ignore schedules altogether and hope they will find the time for their work. Unfortunately, that time never seems to present itself and the work doesn't get done. **Whereas students with high grades ask questions in a lecture, trying to clarify points they don't understand, students with low grades frequently allow their attention to drift. When the lecture is over, they don't remember a word.**

Additional Information:

   Students with high grades ask questions in lectures. They try to clarify points they don't understand. Students with low grades frequently allow their attention to drift. When the lecture is over, they don't remember a word.

   1.   For some people being alone is a death sentence. If they are alone for more than an hour, they feel nervous and uneasy. They are anxious but they don't know why. Anxiety just seems to be in the air they breath. If they are alone for over twenty-four hours, they grow desperate. Companionship must be found at any cost, and even a bore is better than no one. _____

_____

_____

_____

_____

_____

Additional Information:
People who spend a week alone start feeling that the walls are closing in. They start to have panic attacks, during which they can neither think nor concentrate.

2.   Although Americans envy Europe's intellectual attainments, they are usually uncomfortable thinking of themselves as intellectuals. Instead, Americans prefer to see themselves as practical inheritors of a pioneer spirit that carved civilization out of a land where no book could be found. They like to think of themselves as a people of emotion, full of more feeling than logic, guided more by enthusiasm than reflection. _____

_____

_____

_____

Additional Information:
Americans are more comfortable seeing themselves as a nation of doers rather than thinkers. They are a people concerned more with practice than theory.

3.   The nineteenth century was the era of spiritualism, of ghost stories, table rapping, and spirit mediums. Stunned by the scientific discoveries that challenged the role of God in the life of man, many people turned to the spirits for answers. There was the celebrated Mrs. Guppy who could, through gentle communication with the spirits, make the dead reappear before the living. There were the sensational Fox sisters, two young teen-age girls who traveled throughout Europe and America interpreting messages from the dead. Then, _____

_____

_____

_____

Additional Information:
Even in the early twentieth century, it was claimed that clever Hans, a horse from Germany, solved mathematical problems by tapping his foreleg.

4.   The world of Adolf Hitler has disappeared. But unfortunately, many of the basic attitudes and prejudices that were part of his world view still exist. Despite the tragedy of World War II, you can still hear men and women who talk about the superiority of one race, one sex, or

one religion over another. You can still hear the complaints of those who refuse to be contaminated by the presence of those who are inferior — not fit, in fact, to be alive. And most frightening of all, _____

_____

_____

_____

Additional Information:
Even today, there are still those who would honor the name of Adolf Hitler. They wear the uniforms and the insignia of the Nazi party.

A synthesis is an essay that combines the views of different authors on the same topic. Beginning on page 194, there are three articles on the use of computers. You are to write a synthesis of those three articles.

GETTING STARTED

Using the steps introduced at the end of Chapter 5, write a summary of each article. After you have finished your summaries, consider how the three articles are related to one another. The following questions can help you discover a relationship.

1. Does one article make a point that the other contradicts or denies?
2. Does each article illustrate a different aspect of the same thought?
3. Do the articles illustrate different steps in the same process?
4. Does one article describe a general cause, while the others emphasize specific effects?
5. Does one article explain an idea on a general and impersonal level, while the others offer personal anecdotes about the same subject?

GETTING ORGANIZED

Once you have decided how to unite or connect the three separate articles, write a thesis statement that expresses that connection. Your thesis statement should resemble these examples:

> Though all three authors agree that the educational system must be improved, they have very different plans for improvement.

> Each author describes the horror of the concentration camp, but only one does so from a personal point of view.

> All three authors express their contempt for pornographic material, but they do so for different reasons.

Once you have your thesis statement, use your individual summaries as the basis of your supporting paragraphs. But remember that those summaries now have a purpose beyond themselves. They should explain your thesis statement. That means you can probably condense your summaries further, eliminating any material that is not related to the thesis statement. You should also revise each of the original summaries so that it states the author's name and the title.

It also means that you must tell your readers how each article is related to the controlling idea of the whole paper. This explanation should come in the opening sentence or sentences of your supporting paragraphs. Here is where you tell your readers how this particular article affirms or denies what was said in the other articles. For an example, see the underlined sentences in the model synthesis, which starts on page 192.

REVISING

When you revise your synthesis, you need to concentrate on communicating explicit connections that you have found between separate pieces of writing. But you also have to concentrate on unifying what may be the different styles of the separate articles. Although the different articles may have very different voices (for more on the writer's voice, see Chapter 7), your synthesis should adopt one consistent tone toward the audience and the material.

The following articles and model synthesis can help you get started.

Can Psychologists Tip the Scales of Justice?

JAMES L. GOBERT

1   In the third week of a controversial murder trial, the defense calls to the stand an expert medical witness for a lengthy, highly technical examination. The prosecutor counters with a searching cross-examination. Defense counsel objects to his adversary's line of questioning, tempers flare and the judge chastises both attorneys for their outbursts. While the jury rivets its attention on the lawyers, they in turn speculate about the jurors. Are they offended by the bickering? Have they lost or gained sympathy for the defendant? The answers to these questions cannot be obtained directly, for lawyers are expressly forbidden to contact jurors.

2   But one of the attorneys has a better insight into what the jurors are thinking. Unknown to the judge, jury or opposing counsel, she has placed in the courtroom a "shadow jury," made up of persons whose demographic,

economic and personality profiles approximate those of the real jurors. Each evening she meets this shadow jury, ascertains its reactions to the day's developments and plots the next day's strategy.

3   Shadow juries are a recent development in an emerging trend: use by lawyers of behavioral scientists and behavioral-science theory to improve their chances in a trial. From a psychological perspective, these developments constitute a breakthrough in the application of theory to practice. From a legal perspective, they may threaten one of our most precious institutions, trial by jury.

4   The involvement of psychologists and other behavioral scientists usually begins at the jury selection stage, when a trial is often won or lost. Attorneys are well aware that a jury with strong psychological predispositions toward one side may be far more important than the weight of the evidence in deciding a case and strive to select those whose predispositions favor their clients. The trick is to discover these persons without letting the opposite lawyer realize it, for overtly biased jurors will be excused from serving.

5   At the outset of a trial, the attorneys or the judge questions prospective jurors to discover prejudices that would prevent them from fairly deciding the case, a process known as *voir dire*. Jurors who are clearly biased can be challenged for cause and removed from the panel. In addition, each attorney has a limited number of peremptory challenges to eliminate jurors without having to prove partiality.

6   In questioning jurors and making peremptory challenges, lawyers have traditionally relied on their experience and intuition to empanel a jury that is unbiased or, better yet, biased toward their client. Clarence Darrow, for example, reputedly advised defense attorneys against selecting Germans because "they are bullheaded;" Swedes because "they are stubborn;" Presbyterians because "they know right from wrong but seldom find anything right;" and Lutherans, prohibitionists and the wealthy because they are prone to convict. Conversely, Darrow favored Irishmen and Jews, because "they are easiest to move to emotional sympathy;" old men, because "they are generally more charitable and kindly disposed than young men;" and persons who laugh, because they hate to find anyone guilty.

7   In the past decade, lawyers have increasingly turned to psychologists and other behavioral scientists to help them with jury selection and trial strategy. Psychologists can teach lawyers how to spot persons with authoritarian personalities or low esteem, and tell them how such individuals will likely react to different kinds of evidence and presentations. Psychologists

can also explain how different personalities interact in groups. The latter information is particularly critical since a jury verdict is ultimately a group decision-making process.

8   More specifically, psychologists can conduct demographic and attitude surveys of people in the various areas and neighborhoods from which the jury is to be empaneled. Based on their findings, they can tell the lawyers what characteristics (such as age, sex, occupation, education and recreational preferences) are typical of people whose attitudes are the most likely to favor the client's case.

9   In addition to providing general information, psychologists can, as the lawyers or judge conduct *voir dire*, scrutinize the reactions of jurors for behavioral clues to their feelings toward the attorney and the attorney's client. A juror's verbal response may not be nearly as revealing as the fact that his hands are clenched, that his legs are crossed or that he seems unwilling to look the lawyer in the eye. Armed with these insights, lawyers can shape *voir dire* more effectively and use peremptory challenges more accurately.

10   Once a trial starts, psychologists can help lawyers assess the jury's reaction to various lines of questioning, arguments and overall trial strategy. They can create a shadow jury to work as a sounding board. Tactics the shadow jury views unfavorably will likely be looked upon with equal skepticism by the real jury. New lines of argument can be tried out on the shadow jurors for their reaction, much as a Broadway-bound show polishes its production out of town before braving the audiences of Manhattan.

Exhibit A: Language
Our Trials Are a Labyrinth of Words:
How You Talk Is Often More Important
Than What You Say
LORI B. ANDREWS

1   More than two centuries ago, Jonathan Swift satirized lawyers, describing them as "a society of men among us, bred up from their youth in the art of proving by words multipled for that purpose that white is black and black is white."

2   Perhaps today's lawyer does not deserve so scathing a criticism, but at its heart is one undeniable fact: Far from being a straightforward fact-finding mission, a trial is a labyrinth of language, with the words of the

judge, lawyers and witnesses creating numerous obstacles that prevent juries from making accurate decisions.

3   Since at least 1975, social scientists have fervently studied our trials, approaching the courtroom interchanges with the careful scholarship previously saved for studies of rare languages in distant lands. They have found the psychology of language in the courtroom to be more intricate and influential than they had ever imagined.

4   During a trial, the judge, attorneys, plaintiffs, defendants and witnesses may all be using different styles of speech, each with its own psychological force. Some of the effects of the language used are intentional, while others are inadvertent.

5   The judge refers to himself in the third person in order to underscore his authority. He turns himself from mere human to neutral decision-maker by using phrases like "approach the bench" instead of "Come up here and talk to me."

6   The language used by attorneys is also chosen for its influence. In rape cases, prosecutors may refer to the incident in language that accentuates force and aggression, while defense attorneys may use terms suggesting romance to subtly convey the victim's consent to and responsibility for the alleged rape.

7   A lawyer's linguistic style can mean the difference between winning and losing a case. One study of 38 criminal cases found that the prosecutors who won cases made significantly different use of language than those who lost them. Winning prosecutors asked more questions referring to the witness, spoke longer and made more assertive statements than did losing prosecutors.

Eyewitnesses: Essential but Unreliable
Their Evidence Is Often Vital and Sometimes Unique,
but It Can Also Be Misleading and Dangerous
ELIZABETH F. LOFTUS

1   The ladies and gentlemen of William Bernard Jackson's jury decided that he was guilty of rape. They made a serious mistake, and before it was discovered, Jackson had spent five years in prison. There he suffered numerous indignities and occasional attacks, until the police discovered that another man, who looked very much like Jackson, had committed the rapes.

2   If you had been on the jury, you would probably have voted for

conviction too. Two women had positively identified Jackson as the man who had raped them in September and October of 1977. The October victim was asked on the witness stand, "Is there any doubt in your mind as to whether this man you have identified here is the man who had the sexual activity with you on October 3, 1977?" She answered "No doubt." "Could you be mistaken?" the prosecutor asked. "No, I am not mistaken," the victim stated confidently. Jackson and other defense witnesses testified that he was home when the rapes occurred. But the jury didn't believe him or them.

3   This is just one of the many documented cases of mistaken eyewitness testimony that have had tragic consequences. In 1981, Steve Titus of Seattle was convicted of raping a 17-year-old woman on a secluded road; the following year he was proven to be innocent. Titus was luckier than Jackson; he never went to prison. However, Aaron Lee Owens of Oakland, California, was not as fortunate. He spent nine years in prison for a double murder that he didn't commit. In these cases, and many others, eyewitnesses testified against the defendants, and jurors believed them.

4   One reason most of us, as jurors, place so much faith in eyewitness testimony is that we are unaware of how many factors influence its accuracy. To name just a few: what questions witnesses are asked by police and how the questions are phrased; the difficulty people have in distinguishing among people of other races; whether witnesses have seen photos of suspects before viewing the lineup from which they pick out the person they say committed the crime; the size, composition and type (live or photo) of the lineup itself.

Synthesis   Gene Coleman

On television, at least, justice is done when the defendant goes to court for a trial by a jury of her peers. But in reality, the decision about guilt or innocence is not that easy to make. <u>In different ways, the following sources all suggest one very important and very disturbing theme: Trial by jury is an accepted and cherished</u>   *Thesis Statement*
<u>part of our legal system, yet in many ways a jury is continuously open to manipulation and influence that can seriously hinder its ability to make a just decision.</u>

   <u>James J. Gobert, in an article titled "Can Psychologists Tip the</u>   *Topic Sentence*
<u>Scales of Justice?" points out, for example, that lawyers have</u>   *Introduces First*
<u>begun to make increasing use of psychological experts to help</u>   *Illustration of*

them both select and sway members of juries. Under the guidance
of such experts, lawyers are able to interpret appearance, gesture,
and clothing in order to learn more about a juror's personality
and probable verdict. In some cases, lawyers have even used
psychologists to select what is called a "shadow jury." Shadow
jurors have the same backgrounds, personalities, and habits as the
real jurors. Thus a lawyer can use them to discover the feelings
and attitudes of the people he must ultimately persuade.

*Controlling Idea:
Psychological Experts
Who Sway Jury
Members*

Along similar lines, Lori B. Andrews, in "Exhibit A: Language,"
argues that how something is said may be almost as important as
the actual evidence. During a trial, both prosecution and defense
consciously choose words designed to influence jurors' reactions.
In rape cases, for example, the attorneys for the defense may use
words that suggest flirtation and romance to imply that the victim
is responsible for the rape. In direct contrast, lawyers for the
prosecution counter with the language of pure force and
aggression. According to Andrews, "A lawyer's linguistic style can
mean the difference between winning and losing a case."

*Topic Sentence
Reaffirms Controlling
Idea from Perspective
of Language*

Impossible as it sounds, not even eyewitness testimony can
always be counted on to guide a jury to the correct decision. As
the title of Elizabeth F. Loftus's article "Eyewitnesses: Essential but
Unreliable" suggests even eyewitnesses can lead a jury astray
without realizing it. Influenced by factors like the questions they
are asked, the photos they are shown, and the composition of the
lineup, eyewitnesses have been known to identify the wrong
person.

*Topic Sentence Affirms
Controlling Idea from
Perspective of the Eye-
witness Testimony*

Although television may make trial by jury seem an infallible
process wherein justice always triumphs, these three articles
suggest just the opposite: Subject to the influence of attorneys and
the errors of witnesses, jurors can make tragic mistakes.

*Conclusion Restates
Controlling Idea*

Now that you have studied the model synthesis, read through the
following articles on the subject of computers and write a synthesis of
your own.

Technology Alone Is Not Enough
People provide the missing link between
the disabled and computers.

TERIAN TYRE

1   The combination of computers and the handicapped creates an interesting
alchemy which often produces golden results. By using microcomputers
as manipulators, processors, controllers or all three, the technology now
exists to eliminate many of the functional disabilities plaguing human
beings.

2   The one vital ingredient usually overlooked in this mix, however, is
also the most elusive — that quirky human touch. People must provide
the knowledge, time, and above all, energy necessary to pull all the pieces
together. Fortunately, a new source of exactly this type of human support
is emerging from computer clubs, users groups, and even high-tech
manufacturers.

3   What seems to be happening are some unexpected (but not unwelcome)
side effects from the general public's growing interest in computers. The
mental chemistry which occurs when a human meets a computer generates
a literal whirlwind of ideas and speculations. Some wonderful creations
are being born from these tempests. Some of these ideas are hardware-
oriented, such as optical scanning devices and customized keyboards, and
some take software form, like text-to-braille translators. And some are both.

4   Minspeak is an excellent example of just what is meant by "both."
Recently created by Bruce Baker, linguist and artificial-language expert,
Minspeak is a phrase/sentence recall system. It uses a special keyboard
with just sixty keys, but their meanings change according to the order in
which they are depressed. Thousands of spoken sentences can be made
in this manner with fewer than seven strokes. Minspeak combines hardware
(new keyboard) and software (a meaning) to overcome the problem of the
slower speed at which information is communicated by some of the more
severely disabled.

5   None of these technological marvels can help anyone if they aren't
present in their everyday life. That's where other people come in. To
place a system in a home takes experience with both hardware and
software, knowledge of the special needs of the disabled, and the resources
to get the equipment in the first place.

6   DIGSIG, the Disabled Interest Group of the San Diego Computer
Society, is one group of people proving that 200 heads are infinitely more
productive than one.

7   DIGSIG was started in April 1982 by Milton Blackstone just after portable computers emerged. He's an able-bodied and enthusiastic man, a real dynamo, who believes that the disabled, more so than other people, need the flexibility of portable computers.

8   DIGSIG's membership includes all levels of expertise, from the curious novice to those working within the computer industry. Able and disabled are equally represented; each member is fueled by private motivations. Some people are stimulated by the human engineering challenges in getting systems physically adapted for use. Others have relatives they'd like to help. Still others want to help themselves by hands-on practice. As a whole, the group agrees that its main purpose is to assist all its members in reaching their personal goals.

9   The organization meets monthly at the Community Service Center for the Disabled in San Diego and usually invites a speaker. Every third month is Show and Tell, where new developments are demonstrated. The real action, however, isn't in the meetings. It's in the programs and projects they sponsor.

Computers

LINDSY VAN GELDER

1   Technophobia. They tend to regard my microcomputer as both boring and spooky.

2   It's hard for me to convey how wrong they are, and part of the problem is language. I sometimes think computer jargon is the Revenge of the Techno-Nerds — all those slide-ruley types you wouldn't have been caught dead talking to in high school. But new concepts do, in fact, require new words. (Do you really want to call a 747 a big silver bird?) The real problem is emotional resistance. I know; I never would have discovered computers if I hadn't been forced to use a word processor when I was working for a daily newspaper. I am a person who doesn't even drive a car, and I vaguely associated computers with a bunch of things I didn't particularly like: Progress with a capital P, higher mathematics, Big Brother, the aforementioned nerds, machines.

3   Well, it's not a machine. More and more, it's — dare I say it in a national magazine? — an extension of me. Let me tell you how it works.

4   If I were typing this article on a typewriter, I'd already have a mountain of paper on the floor. On my computer, when I make a mistake, I simply delete it electronically. If I want to stick in an idea I've just thought of,

I electronically insert it. I can move whole chunks of texts to other parts of the piece with the press of a few buttons. In a matter of seconds, I can shuffle to any part of a 30-page article. If I realize at the end of my article that I've consistently referred to someone I've interviewed by the wrong title, I can tell my word-processing program to find all the wrong references and replace them.

5   That's only the beginning. I can also choose to run a thesaurus program which will, any time I'm stumped for a synonym, instantly provide a half-dozen or more suggestions. Other programs will check my spelling, count the number of words in my article, tell me whether I've used certain words or phrases too frequently, and do automatic footnoting and indexing. With a box called a modem that connects my computer to my telephone lines, I can dial up various information utilities, allowing me to do library research via computer on numerous topics (or to check the latest stock prices, or play a few games, or do my banking, if I'm so inclined — or even just to hack around with other micro-owners on a computer version of CB radio.) When I'm finished writing, I press a few more buttons, and my printer spews out my article at less than a minute per page, with margins justified and pages numbered.

6   Once you get used to this sort of flexibility, the time gap between your original thought and its execution begins to narrow dramatically. Thinking begins to feel qualitatively different. Going back to a typewriter after using the newspaper word processor was a mental experience I can only liken to skinny-dipping in a suit of armor.

The Computer at the Wedding

GEORGE SWEETHAM

1   The bride and groom stand before the keyboard and cathode tube that constitute their interface with the machine. The groom, who has been coached, types in the command, RUN WED, and the screen comes to life. "Hello, my name is Rev. Apple," it announces. "I'm the world's first ordained computer. (Press space bar to continue.)"

2   The bar is pressed, Rev. Apple poses the time-honored questions and the couple answers them appropriately on the keyboard. Exit by husband and wife.

3   Rev. Apple works with Rev. Ron Jaenisch, of the Universal Life Church in Modesto, California. Jaenisch himself, who has been called "the Marryin' Sam of Silicon Valley," operates out of Sunnyvale, in the heartland of California's computer industry. So far he's wed only six couples with

Rev. Apple, but he has plans to jazz up his assistant and then, he says, "We can really give people a show."

4   Not many computers have jobs as happy as Rev. Apple's, but in diverse sizes and styles they are beginning to appear in all walks of life, confronting business people, professionals and consumers with a blizzard of information — and simultaneously helping them cope with it.

5   The problems computers now handle stretch far beyond the mathematical kind they have traditionally solved. Today, they enable architects to "walk through" unbuilt buildings, allow supermarkets to keep shelves stocked without needing inspection and offer couples saucy suggestions for an evening's entertainment.

6   Jaenisch says he makes use of this last function in his ministry for what he calls sex counseling. A home computer program known as Interlude, produced by Syntonics Software Corporation of Houston, asks couples a series of questions to determine their usual preferences and their present mood and then offers suggestions for engaging activities.

7   Computers are learning to listen. One surgeon has developed a system that allows him to manipulate some of his equipment by voice commands. And computers are learning to talk. The voice on the telephone informing you that a number has been changed may well be the product of a single silicon chip, with the speech of a human "digitized" in the circuitry it carries.

8   Computer-aided building design makes it possible for architects to revise blueprints again and again with the computer working out the consequences of each change in terms of plumbing, wiring and structural integrity. Today, it isn't unusual for an architectural firm designing a large building to have 100 different computer programs working out the details, according to Charles Eastman, an architect, computer scientist and urban planner at Carnegie–Mellon University.

9   Already, Eastman points out, the computer can save time by storing one three-dimensional model of a building, eliminating the need for separate drawings to show different perspectives. On some computers, Eastman adds, the perspective shown on a screen can be changed continuously. With a design stored in such a computer, he says, "You can walk through it; you can fly over it; you can even go underneath it."

10   Businesses can benefit from a new computer program that literally puts an understandable face on complex financial data. Developed by marketing expert David Huff of the University of Texas and colleagues, the program shows a cartoon face whose features change size and shape, making the face appear happy or sad depending on the strength of standard indicators such as return on assets, cash flow and capitalization.

Suggestions for
Your Writer's Notebook

SUGGESTION 1

Think about the writing you did for this chapter's final assignment. What part of the writing process seemed easy? What part seemed difficult? Can you explain that difference?

SUGGESTION 2

As you know from a previous entry in your notebook, metaphors and similes use comparison to bring unexpected connections to light. But at this point you are probably used to thinking of them as devices that appear in a sentence or two and then disappear, never to be seen again. Yet that is not always the case. In both poetry and prose, many writers make use of what are called "extended" metaphors or similes. After introducing the metaphor or simile, they continue to refer to it throughout the passage or poem. Here, as an illustration, is one student's paragraph. It begins with a simile. But the simile does not end with a single sentence. Instead Laura refers to it throughout her paragraph.

Laura Kruper

For more than forty years, my grandfather functioned like a well-oiled machine. No matter what his mood, no matter what the weather, he got up at six and went to work at exactly 7:15. But then one day, nobody knows why, the machine ground to a halt. It was broken and nobody knew how to fix it. My grandfather just lay in bed and stared at the wall. It didn't matter anymore what time it was. He just didn't care. The connections were broken, the circuits were dead, and the lights were all out. My grandfather had decided not to live anymore and nothing would change his mind.

Write a paragraph that uses an extended metaphor or simile.

SUGGESTION 3

Write several different sentences summing up your ideas about interpersonal relationships. Three examples follow.

Married couples should never live with their parents.

Friendship always takes a back seat to love.

There has to be a generation gap between parents and
their children.

Choose one and develop it into a short paragraph that explains what you
mean by the statement. Then give the same sentence you developed to
a friend. Ask him or her to write a paragraph explaining the same idea.
Compare the paragraphs. Did your friend develop your idea in the way
you expected, or did he or she take it in a completely different direction?

SUGGESTION 4

Can you create a context or a situation so that seemingly nonsensical
sets of events make sense? For an illustration, look at the way one student
has made sense out of a sentence that seems, at first, to make no sense
at all.

Example:

Laughing with delight she stared in the mirror at her
twisted and distorted form.

`Laughing with delight at her image in the fun house`
`mirror, she stared at her twisted and distorted form.`

1. Reaching the bottom of the stairs, his body turned an automatic
   somersault and he touched ground with his hands instead of his feet.
   Everything was going according to plan.
2. Screaming she clutched at the rail, sure that her life was over. Five
   minutes later, she told her mother she had never had a better time
   in her life.
3. He couldn't eat. He couldn't sleep. He couldn't concentrate. He had
   never been happier.
4. Sitting on her bed in her nightgown, she looked out the window and
   saw the tail of a long and slippery eel glide through the waves.
5. As he walked away, the man carelessly let fall the dollar bills he had
   just been given. He paid no attention as the wind scattered them out
   of reach forever.

SUGGESTION 5

You can learn a lot about the use of language simply by copying down and studying dialog or conversations between two people. Once you copy them down, look at the way in which one response elicits or brings forth another. For example, consider the following brief conversation.

> "Those pants used to fit you last year."
> "They still do."
> "Yeah, if you don't button them."
> "Don't worry. I'm going to start cutting down."

In this passage, each piece of dialog brings about both an explicit and an implicit response. If you analyzed the language in terms of explicit and implicit responses, it would look something like this:

> "Those pants used to fit you last year." (You are getting fat.)
> "They still do." (I am not.)
> "Yeah, if you don't button them." (Yes you are.)
> "Don't worry. I'm going to start cutting down." (I give in.
> You're right. I'm going to lose weight.)

SUGGESTION 6

Try inventing your own conversations between famous people. You might try imagining conversations that could have occurred at crucial moments in history. When Washington crossed the Delaware, for example, what were he and his men talking about? In the following illustration, one student imagines a very funny conversation between Christopher Columbus and the king and queen of Spain.

On Christopher's Visit to
Isabella and Ferdinand   David Etkin

Columbus paced nervously outside the throne room. At last he would have the audience with Isabella and Ferdinand promised to him so many months ago! The herald approached, and Columbus knew that his time had come.

This was it! His big chance to prove to royalty that his short sea route to the Indies was worth financing. He readjusted his ruff for the nth time, licked his lips, smoothed back his hair, and ran through his "sales pitch" once more.

"I'm as ready as I'll ever be," he muttered under his breath.

The Queen and King were so totally different from what he had expected that he almost walked out of the room. First the King. Christopher had expected him to be six feet tall and full of muscles. After all, what can you expect from a person who conquered the Moors after ten years of war? Instead, he saw a rather small, pudgy man with a snuff box in one hand and a pair of gold spectacles in the other. The Queen he expected to be soft and beautiful. Well, she may have been beautiful once, but her years were catching up and he couldn't help noticing a few lines around her eyes and hastily covered up wart on her neck. Her air reminded Christopher of a bully he had once fought; he knew who was in charge all right.

"Dear majesties," he began. No, that sounded too formal.

"Great rulers." No, that made it sound as if they were measuring sticks.

"Great majesties." Perfect. "As you know, I have come here to discuss a matter of great importance, both politically and financially. Financially because of the supplies to be saved; the sailors' wages will be smaller and finally . . ."

"Out with it!" the Queen bellowed.

Now he really knew who was in charge.

"A shorter route to India."

"Wonderous!" the King exclaimed.

"What are you asking?" the Queen demanded.

"Well, as some people have proved, the world is round, so — "

"Is it?" You-know-who demanded again.

"Yes, your grace, it is. Anyway, because no one knows where Africa ends, it is impossible to tell how long it will take to go down and around Africa going east, but I believe going west would be a straight, sure route since there is no land to get in our way."

"Pure genius," the King murmured, as though the thought had only partly penetrated his mind.

"Not bad," the Queen admitted, "but how much are you asking?"

"Well, considering that this is a breakthrough, that we must brave the Sea of Darkness, and that the natives on an island off Japan might think me a god . . ."

"I repeat, how much?"

"Three ships equipped and maintained at your expense, the governorship of any lands I discover, the title of Admiral, and noble rank. Also these privileges are to be passed on to my sons."

"We'll have to think it over," stated the Queen.

"Think who a god?" Ferdinand asked. Christopher's opinion of the King was getting lower by the minute.

"Hush! Now Sir Christopher, we would be delighted to take your offer, wouldn't we Ferdinand?" She gave the King a nudge with her elbow.

"Yes dear, whatever you say," he mumbled vaguely.

"Well then Sir Christopher, go along now," she said rather hurriedly, "I'm sure you're a very busy man."

"Yes. Thank you, your Highnesses. Good day."

When he was out of sight, Christopher sank to his knees, happy because he had finally gotten what he dreamed of and because the nerve-wracking meeting was over.

Combining Sentences

You have already worked with appositives. However, this exercise introduces you to a particular kind of appositive, one that comes at the very end of sentence after a colon. Withholding the appositive until the very end of the sentence is a way of creating emphasis.

Example:

1. ∧ He found the key ∧ ∧ .

> He had *it in a very short time.*
>
> The key was *to her heart.*
>
> [:] The key was *chocolate.*

In a very short time, he had found the key to her heart: chocolate.

But the appositive coming at the end of the sentence after a colon does not have to be just one word. It can also consist of several words or phrases.

Example:

2. He wrote about his experiences in prison ∧ .

> [:]
>
> He wrote about *the filth.* [,]
>
> He wrote about *the degradation.* [,]
>
> He wrote about *the despair.* [and]

He wrote about his experiences in prison: the filth, the degradation, and the despair.

Complete this exercise, inserting words, phrases, and punctuation as indicated. **EXERCISE**

1. ∧ She had never learned one ∧ thing ∧ .

> This was *despite her* ∧ *education.* [,]
>
> She had *years of* education.
>
> It was an *important* thing.
>
> [:]
>
> It was *how to laugh.*

_____
_____

2.   ∧ You will need two things ∧ .
         You decide to live in New York. [if,]
         [:]
         One is *money.*
         One is *courage.* [and]

_____
_____

3.   He summed up his ∧ enemy ∧∧ .
         His enemy was the *worst.*
         He did it *in one word.*
         [:]
         The word was *cocaine.*

_____
_____

4.   They studied ∧ writers ∧ .
         There was ∧ *a variety of* them.
             It was *wide.*
         [:]
         They studied *Marcel Proust.* [,]
         They studied *James Joyce.* [,]
         They studied *Raymond Chandler.* [and]

_____
_____

5.   There is only one antidote ∧∧ .
         The antidote is *for failure.*
         [:]
         The antidote is *success.*

_____
_____

6. The alley was filled ∧ ∧ ∧ .
        It was filled *with trash*.
        It was *of all kinds*.
        [:]
        There was *garbage*. [,]
        There were ∧ *beer cans*. [,]
            The cans were *empty*.
        There were ∧ *whiskey bottles*. [and]
            The bottles were *broken*.

    _____

    _____

7. Movies ∧ must attract one ∧ group ∧ .
        They are to make money. [,if,]
        The group is a *particular* one.
        [:]
        They are *teen-agers*.

    _____

    _____

8. ∧ England listened to the voice ∧ ∧ .
        This was *during World War II*. [,]
        It was the voice *of one man*.
        [:]
        The man was *Winston Churchill*.

    _____

    _____

9. ∧ He has only one goal ∧ .
        This is *despite his denials*. [,]
        [:]
        This is *the acquisition of power*.

    _____

    _____

10. I cannot call it a truly great western.

[;]

It lacked one $_\wedge$ ingredient $_\wedge$.

   The ingredient was *essential*.

   [:]

   The ingredient was *Indians*.

PATTERN 10

In patterns 2 and 4, you used coordinate conjunctions (*and, but, or, nor,* etc.) and conjunctive adverbs (*however, because, nevertheless,* etc.) to combine separate sentences. Pattern 10 focuses on yet another way of doing the same thing. The following pairs of words are called "correlative conjunctions," and they too function to connect independent clauses or sentences:

□ neither . . . nor

□ either . . . or

□ not only . . . but also

Like coordinate conjunctions and conjunctive adverbs, correlative conjunctions serve to emphasize the equality of ideas. For example,

1. The lifeguard rescued the boy.

   He rescued him *from the lake*.

   [not only . . . but also]

   He gave him artificial respiration.

   Not only did the lifeguard rescue the boy from the lake, but he also gave him artificial respiration.

As you can see from this example, to combine sentences through the use of correlative conjunctions, you will sometimes have to adjust both the form and order of the words provided. But this should be no problem if you read the combinations aloud and choose the one which sounds most natural to you.

You can use the same method to decide where to put the correlative conjunctions since they do not invariably appear at the beginning of sentences. The above sentence, for example, could have been written like this:

> The lifeguard not only rescued the boy from the lake, but he
> also gave him artificial respiration.

Again, reading your combinations aloud will usually tell you where correlative conjunctions can and cannot be placed.

Like coordinate conjunctions, correlative conjunctions do not necessarily join whole sentences. They can also serve to combine sentence parts. Note: When combining just parts of sentences you can also use another set of correlative conjunctions, "both . . . and."

> His father refuses to attend the graduation.
> His mother refuses to attend the graduation. [both . . . and]
>> *He is graduating magna cum laude.* [even though]
> Both his father and his mother refuse to attend the graduation
> even though he is graduating magna cum laude.

Complete the remaining exercise.

1. They will win the ∧ game.
>   The game is the *final* one.
    [either . . . or]
    They will forfeit the tournament ∧ .
>   *They have tried so hard to win* the tournament. [that]

_____

_____

2. The bride ∧ did not cry.
>   *The groom* did not cry. [neither . . . nor]
    [,but]
    Their parents cried ∧ .
>   They did it *all the way through the ceremony.*

_____

_____

3. They are tough.
    [not only . . . but also]
    They are smart.

[, and]
That gives them the edge.

———————————————————————————

———————————————————————————

4.   Someone must adopt that ∧ cat.
          The cat is a *stray*.
     [either . . . or]
     It will be taken ∧ .
          It will go *to the pound*.

———————————————————————————

———————————————————————————

5.   The group played ∧ rock and roll.
          It was *old-time* rock and roll.
     [not only . . . but also]
     They played ∧ music.
          It was *punk and new wave*.

———————————————————————————

———————————————————————————

6.   The book did not sell well.
     [neither . . . nor]
     Its author did not make a profit.

———————————————————————————

———————————————————————————

7.   She had to give him up.
     [either . . . or]
     She had to marry him.

———————————————————————————

———————————————————————————

8.   His actions ∧ did not improve the situation.
          His *attitude* did not improve. [neither . . . nor]
     [; however,]
     They hoped for the best ∧ .

They could only tolerate him ∧ . [if]
This was for one more day.

_____

_____

9.   She should apologize.
     [either . . . or]
     He should forget her.
     [;]
     She just isn't worth all that trouble.

     _____

     _____

10. His mother ∧ criticized the film.
          His father criticized the film. [both . . . and]
     [, but]
     He enjoyed it anyway.

     _____

     _____

Write five sentences using correlative conjunctions.   EXERCISE

1. _____

   _____

2. _____

   _____

3. _____

   _____

4. _____

   _____

5. _____

   _____

CHAPTER 7

The Writer's Voice

As you learned in Chapter 3, the term *voice* refers to the way in which writers use language to express their relationship to both their audience and their material. It is through the voice you create in your paper that you indicate to your readers your attitude toward both them and your thesis.

Your readers, in turn, respond to the attitude or *tone* they hear in your voice, and a great deal depends on that response. If you explain your thesis in a tone that is reasonable and direct, you encourage your readers to respond with interest and attention. But if your voice speaks in a tone that is overbearing and demanding, you increase the chance that your readers will put down your paper in annoyance.

In short, the language you use to communicate the message of your paper influences the way it is received. This means you have to do as much as you can to ensure that the voice you use has the appropriate effect on your readers. This chapter has been designed to help you do precisely that.

A Range of Voices

As you probably know from your reading, there are a wide range of voices that a writer can use when addressing a reader. What you may not know is precisely *how* writers create those different voices. The following illustrations should give you some idea of what goes into the making of a writer's voice.

PSYCHOLOGY AND THE HOMELESS (BY M. BREWSTER SMITH)

[1]The homeless, the "street people," are an acute embarrassment to us ordinary middle-class or blue collar types. [2]I am still uneasy as I remember how I felt about the street person, seemingly an alcoholic schizophrenic in his 30s, who was sleeping in the entryway of our upper East Side walk-up in Manhattan last winter — until the other tenants insisted on a new lock on the outside door. [3]It is disturbing to have to step over such a stinking person, and it is more disturbing to feel utterly baffled about how to help. [4]Back in Santa Cruz, I see many more street people, who are attracted by a mostly benign climate and by a civic culture that is very tolerant, for the time being, but is strained almost to the breaking point by the desire of the conservative business community to roust the unwelcome visitors out of town. [5]The situation is getting humanly intolerable.

In this excerpt the author uses a very personal and familiar tone, one that narrows the distance between herself and her readers. Not only is she very much present in the word *I*, but she also knows exactly how her readers respond to the situation she describes: "The homeless, the 'street people,' are an acute embarrassment to us ordinary middle-class or blue collar types." In this sentence, note how the phrase *blue collar types* serves to emphasize the author's familiar tone. Such a phrase is typical of colloquial or conversational English, but it is much less typical of formal, expository prose. Along the same lines, note the quotation marks around the phrase *street people*. This is the author's way of acknowledging that the phrase is not traditionally used in a written context.

In effect, those quotation marks signal that the author does not want her tone to become too casual; that might interfere with the way she treats her thesis. However casual the writer might be in her relationship with her audience, she still takes her thesis seriously, and she communicates that seriousness through the language she uses. The growing number of street people is not described as bad, difficult, or unpleasant. It is "humanly intolerable." In using the phrase *humanly intolerable*, the author suggests that the situation has to be remedied or it will become dangerous to human welfare. However, informal or casual her voice may be in addressing her audience, the author's tone still emphasizes the seriousness of her subject.

Now compare a second example.

HYPNOSIS ON TRIAL (BY ELIZABETH STARK)

[1]In a San Francisco case involving the kidnapping and rape of two young girls, the criminal was caught after one of the girls remembered, under hypnosis, distinguishing rust spots on the car and the location of a service station where the abductor had stopped to have car-repair work done.

[2]These and similar successes have made hypnosis a very popular investigative tool. [3]But there have been equally striking incidents in which witnesses were wrong. [4]In 1975, a sailor at the Philadelphia Naval Base was shot but not seriously wounded. [5]The police had a suspect, but the sailor could not positively identify him as the assailant. [6]During hypnosis, however, he said that the suspect was definitely the man who had shot him. [7]He remained positive of the defendant's guilt even after two people cleared the accused man by confirming his alibi.

[8]Because of such failures and because recent research suggests that some memories retrieved under hypnosis may be inaccurate, many states are re-evaluating the use of eyewitness testimony obtained by hypnosis.

In this excerpt the author speaks with a voice that is more distant and more formal. The word *I* does not appear, and her language is devoid of colloquial expressions. Distant from her readers, the author remains somewhat distant from her thesis as well. Her tone is cool and objective, without emotional involvement. It is not she who criticizes the use of hypnosis. Instead "research suggests that some memories retrieved under hypnosis may be inaccurate."

In the next excerpt, the author once again makes his presence felt in the pronoun *I*. But he is not quite so familiar with his readers as the author of the first excerpt.

CLEVER ANIMALS (BY LEWIS THOMAS)

[1]The risks are especially high when the scientist is engaged in training the animal to so something or other and must bank his professional reputation on the integrity of his experimental subject. [2]The most famous case in point is that of Clever Hans, the turn-of-the century German horse now immortalized in the lexicon of behavioral science by the technical term the "Clever Hans Error." [3]The horse, owned and trained by Herr von Osten, could not only solve complex arithmetical problems, but even read the instructions on the black board and tap out infallibly, with one hoof, the right answer. [4]What is more, he could perform the same computations when total strangers posed questions to him, with his trainer nowhere nearby. [5]For several years Clever Hans was studied intensively by groups of puzzled scientists and taken seriously as a horse with something very like a human brain, quite possibly even better than human. [6]But finally in 1911, it was discovered by Professor O. Pfungst that Hans was not really doing arithmetic at all; he was simply observing the behavior of the human experimenter. [7]Subtle, unconscious gestures — nods of the head, the hold of breath, the cessation of nodding when the current count was reached — were accurately read by the horse as cues to stop tapping.

[8]Whenever I read about that phenomenon, usually recounted as the exposure of a sort of unconscious fraud on the part of

either the experimenter or the horse or both, I wish Clever Hans could be given more credit than he generally gets. [9]To be sure, the horse couldn't really do arithmetic, but the record shows that he was considerably better at observing human beings and interpreting their behavior than humans are at comprehending horses or, for that matter, other human beings.

The voice in this excerpt strikes a nice balance. Words such as *immortalized, lexicon,* and *cessation* are not typical of everyday conversation and they serve to create a formal and learned tone. But that tone never becomes pompous or stuffy. At no time does the author overload his prose with learned words designed more to impress than to explain.

That the author is not trying to awe his readers with his learning is clear from the way in which he quickly moves from a general statement to a specific illustration. The opening sentence is a topic sentence outlining, in general terms, the problems of working with animal subjects, but the remainder of the paragraph quickly brings that generalization down to a more specific level. You can almost hear the author saying, "Let me show you what I mean by that statement." Such specificity reveals the author's respect for both his material and his audience. He considers what he has to say important enough to be carefully and precisely explained. And he values his audience enough to do everything possible to be sure they understand what he has in mind.

In addition to speaking clearly, the author speaks with humor as well. In the second paragraph he talks about "Clever Hans" as though he were a human being who should get more credit for his accomplishments. That kind of humor gives the author's voice an informal and direct quality that nicely balances the effect of the very learned vocabulary. No author who is willing to praise horse sense over human sense can be considered pompous or stuffy!

Humor is the primary characteristic of the following excerpt, where the author uses the language of scientific discovery to explore the habits of shellfish eaters.

Eating Shellfish

[1]If a research team systematically interviewed serious shellfish eaters about their most memorable shellfish experience, I suspect that the unifying theme of the testimony would be messiness. [2]Ask anyone who truly loves shellfish about the best he ever had, and the answer tends to be a story ending with the table being

hosed down after the meal or mountains of shells being shoveled into trash bins. [3]It is apparent to serious shellfish eaters that in the great evolutionary scheme of things crustaceans developed shells to protect them from knives and forks. [4]Extracting fish from a shell tends to be time-consuming, but shellfish eaters are, as a group, patient. [5]In fact, the most pedantic among them — those amateur professors of shelling who loiter around Chesapeake Bay — sometimes seem more interested in extracting crabmeat with finesse than in eating it.[*]

Here the author's voice speaks with mock seriousness. He creates that tone largely by using very big words to talk about a very small topic. Imagining a situation wherein a "research team" would "systematically interview serious shellfish eaters," he insists that "messiness" would be the "unifying theme." The contrast between the importance of the language and the relative unimportance of the topic is what creates the humorous tone. The author also makes effective use of exaggeration. The table he describes is not wiped off; it is "hosed down." After the meal, there aren't piles of shells on the table; there are "mountains" that are "shoveled" into trash bins. In addition, he has a talent for saying the ridiculous in a very solemn and serious way, as when he claims that crustaceans developed shells to protect themselves from knives and forks.

Although the author of this excerpt does not openly try to narrow the distance between himself and his readers in the way the author of excerpt 1 does, his consistently humorous tone tends to put writer and audience on a familiar footing. In addition, the use of the first-person pronoun intensifies the teasing, friendly, and familiar tone.

The author of the following excerpt also injects humor into her voice, but she does it to a different end. She is not interested in making fun of herself, but she is interested in making fun of her topic.

CAN YOU TRUST A SOAP OPERA DIAGNOSIS? (BY SUSAN DWORKIN)
[1]One analysis found that of 844 conversations on soap operas, the most frequent topic was health and that two out of the four favored soap interiors that were medical: the doctor's office and the hospital room. [2]Annenberg researchers Gerbner, Morgan,

[*] Calvin Trillin, *Alice, Let's Eat* (New York: Vintage, 1979) 89–90.

and Signorielli concluded that "It may well be that daytime serials provide the most prolific single source of medical advice in America."

[3]Guess who is giving this advice? [4]Right. [5]Nine out of 10 prime-time television doctors are male, white, and young or middle-aged, and Morgan surmises the statistics don't vary for daytime TV. [6]Nearly all the nurses are female and young or middle-aged, and nine out of ten are white. [7]Is their advice accurate? It is now, but apparently it wasn't back in the days of Ben Casey and Marcus Welby. [8]Casey would mispronounce technical words; Welby had personal relationships with many of his patients and made *housecalls* at a time when real doctors were united in their efforts to send the house call the way of the unamplified guitar.

This author's tone in addressing the reader is very chatty and familiar. At times it sounds as though she were in actual conversation with her readers: "Guess who is giving this advice? Right." Clearly this author is not interested in maintaining any distance between herself and her audience.

Like the author of excerpt 4, she too treats her topic with a certain breezy humor. But whereas the author of the previous excerpt used humor to describe an imaginary situation (the study of serious shellfish eaters), this author uses humor to suggest the absurdity of a real situation, one in which people get their medical advice from soap operas. It is her way of indicating that this state of affairs is slightly ridiculous.

At this point, having examined five different authorial voices and having learned something about how they are created, you are ready to do some analysis of your own.

Read through each of the following excerpts. After reading each one, characterize its voice. Once you have characterized the voice, identify some of the elements in the passage that convey it. Following is an example:

EXERCISE 1

THE ANDROGYNOUS MAN (BY NOEL PERRIN)

The summer I was 16, I took a train from New York to Steamboat Springs, Colorado, where I was going to be assistant horse wrangler at a camp. The trip took three days, and since I was much too shy to talk to strangers, I had quite a lot of time for reading. I read all of "Gone With the Wind." I read all the interesting articles in a couple of magazines I had, and then I went back and read all the dull stuff. I also took all the quizzes, a thing of which magazines were even fuller then than now.

The one that held my undivided attention was called "How Masculine/Feminine Are You?" It consisted of a large number of inkblots. The reader was supposed to decide which of four objects each blot most resembled. The choices might be a cloud, a steam engine, a caterpillar and a sofa.

When I finished the test, I was shocked to find that I was barely masculine at all. On a scale of 1 to 10, I was about 1.2. Me, the horse wrangler? (And not just wrangler, either. That summer, I had to skin a couple of horses that died — the camp owner wanted the hides.)

The results of that test were so terrifying to me that for the first time in my life I did a piece of original analysis. Having unlimited time on the train, I looked at the "masculine" answers over and over, trying to find what it was that distinguished real men from people like me — and eventually discovered two very simple patterns. It was "masculine" to think the blots looked like man-made objects, and "feminine" to think they looked like natural objects. It was masculine to think they looked like things capable of causing harm, and feminine to think of innocent things.

Even at 16, I had the sense to see that the compilers of the test were using rather limited criteria — maleness and femaleness are both more complicated than that — and I breathed a huge sigh of relief. I wasn't necessarily a wimp, after all.

The writer speaks in a very personal and familiar voice. He is not interested in appearing cool and objective. In part, he creates the effect by giving a number of very specific details of what he felt and did. "I was much too shy to talk to strangers"; "I read all of 'Gone with the Wind.'" He also uses language more typical of conversation than prose. "I wasn't necessarily a wimp, after all." And he tries very hard to convey his emotional reactions to the audience through words like "shocked" and "terrifying."

1. Twenty-two years ago, Dwayne Lee Gosso was born into the custody of New York State, the son of a prison inmate who did not want him.

For two decades he was a child of the state bureaucracy, living in foundling and foster homes, mental hospitals and rehabilitation centers.

Along the way, according to his lawyer, he was diagnosed as mildly retarded and troubled with behavioral problems. Eventually, he turned 21 and left to live on his own. He did not make it. His odyssey has now come full circle. He is back where he started life, in jail.

"I was born in jail and I can't take much more of it," Mr. Gosso, a lanky youth with dirty-blond hair and a gap where his front teeth were lost in a fight, said the other day.

According to social workers, lawyers, judges, experts on the rehabilitation of troubled young people, state legislators and others, Mr. Gosso's story illustrates the failings of a foster-care system that has custody of thousands of young wards of the state.[1]

_____

_____

_____

_____

_____

2. My mother, Anne America Dempsey Watts, loved life too much to relish planning for her own end. But after losing two brothers, she was motivated to get her affairs in order. When Mama died recently at the age of 67, she managed to "go in style." She hadn't done everything by the book, but she had taken sufficient steps so that her surviving children could manage closing her affairs. Her example prompted me to write this article.

If there are people in your life that you love — or people that you emphatically don't love, and would prefer to keep at a distance even when you die — you need to complete certain plans and actions so that your preferences are clearly stated to your survivors, and are also legally binding. Consider the following keys to "going in style" through the pearly gates.[2]

_____

_____

[1]Sam Roberts, "The Troubled, 21 Year Long Odyssey of a New York Child of Bureaucracy," *New York Times* 17 October 1983: 12.
[2]Emily Card, "Writing Your Will," *Ms.* (July 1984): 88.

_____

_____

_____

_____

3.   It is possible to gather a great deal of knowledge about human consciousness simply from the careful observance of physical behavior. Such observation can reveal certain contradictory messages that the subject himself might not verbally acknowledge. One need only think of the guest lecturer who speaks with authority while nervously pulling his tie or adjusting his spectacles. Clearly, gestures of this sort reveal an underlying tension and anxiety not obviously manifested in verbal expression. Similarly, the corporate executive who claims not to feel the pressure of his occupation may reveal his internal fears by an inordinately erect posture, accompanied by a certain stiffness of facial expression.

_____

_____

_____

_____

_____

4.   What I yearned for was to be published, to be read, "to be great, to be known" (in the words of a poem by Stephen Spender which I have never forgotten), to open communication with an audience, to exist for others; utterly alien others, bound to me — unlike family and friends — only after the fact of having read me.

How hypothetical that audience, those alien others, might remain, and consequently how unreal, how impalpable the recognition, honor and love, I did not at first realize. To be sure, like other writers, even at the beginning of my career, I received reviews in the press, plus after a while, as happens to almost anyone who lives long enough, testimonials and ceremonies of recognition. But for a long time, money (the one fiction of universal currency) is the only, and indeed always remains the most reliable, token that one has touched, moved, shared one's most private fantasies with the faceless, nameless "you" to whom the writers all-too-familiar "I" longs to be joined in mutual pleasure.[3]

[3]Leslie Fiedler, *What Was Literature?* (New York: Simon & Schuster, 1982) 23–24.

_____

_____

_____

_____

_____

_____

To get some idea of the range of authorial voices at your disposal, sit   EXERCISE 2
down and compose two different letters of introduction. First write a letter
introducing one good friend to another. Then write another that introduces
the same friend to a potential employer. After you are finished, read both
letters and try to identify the changes that took place in your voice as
you changed audiences.

The Appropriate Academic Voice

The previous section used five different excerpts to indicate the range
of authorial voices a writer can assume. But here, I want to use them
to make an additional point as well: Though all five excerpts speak with
voices appropriate to the pages of popular magazines, the same five voices
would not necessarily be appropriate in an academic setting. For example,
some instructors would respond negatively to the voices that speak in
the Perrin and Fiedler excerpts. They might be too personal and too
familiar for academic readers who are accustomed to a more distant and
impersonal tone. For that matter, even the voice in excerpt 3 has its
limitations in an academic setting, where, for the most part, you are
expected to take your subject seriously. The point is this: When you write
in an academic setting, the range of voices you have to choose from is
more limited than it would be if you were writing for the pages of a
popular magazine.

Having said that, however, I have to admit that there are no rigid rules
for creating the appropriate academic voice. To a large extent, each time
you sit down to write a paper, you have to discover your particular voice
— one appropriate for your thesis and suitable for an academic audience.
In addition, you have to remember that different instructors have different
expectations about the appropriate voice. Those expectations are a product

of their particular training and discipline. Some may believe, for example, that a student does not have to maintain a great distance between himself and his audience. These instructors may not be put off by the writer's use of pronouns such as *I* and *you*. But others might be. As a student writer, it is your responsiblity to discover those expectations and modify your voice accordingly.

The following guidelines will help you decide how to create an effective academic voice that encourages your readers to be both attentive and interested.

1. Voice is a creation of the drafting process. It is not a fixed and final characteristic of the first draft.

There will be times when you know immediately what voice you want to adopt in your paper. But at other times you will know *what* you want to say but not exactly *how* you want to say it. This is not a cause for despair. Usually, as you draft and the message of your paper becomes clearer in your mind, your voice will emerge of its own accord.

Although your voice may vary in your drafts, that is not a problem either. You can always refine it for consistency and appropriateness before you turn the paper in to your instructor.

2. Extend your authority over your material rather than your audience. The voice you create should indicate your respect for your audience's intelligence.

Although you want to supply the specific details that will explain your thesis statement, you do not want to tell your readers what to think. That is, you want to avoid the overbearing and bullying tone of the following sentences: "Without question, the individual who is arrested for drunk driving is a disgraceful human being. It is impossible for a sensible person to have any sympathy for someone who threatens the lives of others through the careless use of alcohol."

Certainly you can be forceful, even passionate, about what you want to say to your readers. But you can do that without insisting that they share your attitude. "Given the number of terrible, even fatal, accidents that have been caused by people who drink while driving, I can feel no sympathy for anyone arrested for that crime."

3. Do not feel you have to qualify everything you say.

I do not know precisely how it happens, but many student writers
become nervous about saying what they think, simply and directly. Instead
they try to qualify every statement. Unfortunately, the resulting voice
sounds weak and indecisive. "Although some people believe that employers
have no right to monitor employee phone calls, this would seem to be
a rather sensible practice, at least if the employer believes that excessive
use of the telephone is interfering with productivity." In this example,
the words *it would seem* and *rather* work to undermine the author's voice.
She seems unsure and indecisive about what she has to say. Given the
voice in this excerpt, it would be easy for her readers to distrust or ignore
her message. The passage needs to be rewritten so that the author speaks
with more assurance. "Some people believe that employers have no right
to monitor employee phone calls. Nevertheless, it's a sensible practice,
particularly if the employer believes that excessive use of the telephone
interferes with productivity."

> 4. Try to create a voice that speaks with simplicity and di-
> rectness. Always ask yourself this key question: "How can I
> make what I want to say as clear as possible for my readers?"

Many student writers believe an academic voice should sound pompous
and self-important. They mistakenly assume that they have to speak in
a way that will dazzle their readers. It is this assumption that makes them
choose such words as *obtain* and *utilize* rather than *get* and *use*. Guided
by that mistaken assumption, students produce prose that sounds stuffy
and pretentious. Yet to be truly effective, an academic voice should speak
with simplicity and directness. If you think of language as an instrument
of clarification rather than display, you will have a better chance of
creating the appropriate academic voice.

> 5. Remember to avoid words that are considered more ap-
> propriate for conversation than for writing.

As you revise, be conscious of the way colloquial diction (word choice)
can make your tone of voice waver. Consider the following: "Hamlet
feels betrayed by his mother and consequently detests all women. Furious
at the female sex, he even feels contempt for his girl friend Ophelia and
treats her like dirt."
In this example, the phrases *girl friend* and *treats her like dirt* create
an odd, contradictory effect. This is the kind of language you might well

hear in casual conversations, but it doesn't usually appear in written prose. In this particular example, it clashes with the rest of the passage. At one breath, the writer seems to be addressing a group of scholars and explaining an idea he takes quite seriously. But in the next, he seems to be talking to old friends and treating his material casually, even flippantly.

> 6. Revise to make the voice in your paper consistent. Be wary of creating not one voice, but contradictory voices.

The following paragraphs illustrate this point. In the first paragraph the voices clash. At first it seems that the writer thinks a mania for chocolate is amusing and funny. But suddenly, without warning, he grows serious and grave.

1   Chocolate mania is a familiar addiction. People of all ages suffer from it, and they need chocolate in huge quantities to get them through the day. In their desperate hands, a two-pound box of chocolates does not have a chance of surviving more than twenty-four hours. This craving for chocolate can actually be an indicator of a vitamin deficiency, and anyone who craves chocolate on a regular basis should see a doctor for a check-up. The need to eat chocolate might well be the body's way of demanding a better balanced diet."

In the next example, the foregoing paragraph has been revised to create a more consistent voice. Note how the author uses the word *tend* to suggest, from the very beginning, that an addiction to chocolate should not be taken lightly. He has also eliminated the verbal exaggeration that contributed to the previous passage's initially humorous tone: "In their desperate hands. . . ." In addition, he has added a transitional sentence that prepares the reader for the increasing seriousness of his voice.

2   We tend to laugh at people with a mania for chocolate, particularly when those people are adults, and we smile good-naturedly at their need to consume huge quantities of chocolate. *But, in fact, a need to eat chocolate may not be a laughing matter.* This craving for chocolate can actually be an indicator of a vitamin deficiency, and anyone who craves chocolate on a regular basis should see a doctor for a check-up. The need to eat chocolate

might well be the body's way of demanding a better balanced diet.

7. Use personal pronouns with care.

There was a time when most college teachers discouraged the use of personal pronouns in academic essays. But that is no longer true. In fact, some of your instructors may actually encourage the use of *I* or *we* as a way of creating a direct and confident tone of voice.

However, that does not mean you should sprinkle personal pronouns throughout your paper, using them when they are unnecessary. If you do, you may stop sounding confident and start sounding self-centered. Generally, when you put words down on paper, your readers know they represent your thoughts. Thus *I believe* and *I think* are usually needless. For the most part, use *I* sparingly and precisely. You can use it effectively, for example, to show the way in which your point of view differs from the traditional one. "Although many believe that eyewitness testimony is infallible, I believe that just the opposite is true."

Use of the pronoun *we* can be an effective way of expressing your belief that certain ideas are generally accepted or affirmed. "We all like to believe that suffering has a reason or a purpose." But be careful how you use *we*, for it can incite reader rebellion. Some will not like your assumption that you know how they respond or think. It is advisable to use *we* only when you are positive that your readers will share your sentiments. "After the horror of war, we all want to believe that such a tragedy will never happen again."

Read through one of your previous papers. Decide what voice you hear. Then give that same paper to a classmate. Ask her or him to characterize the voice she or he hears. Is it timid or confident? Is it formal or informal? Is it casual or serious?   EXERCISE   3

Collect three examples of authorial voices you admire. Write a paragraph on each, describing what it is you like about each voice you hear.   EXERCISE   4

Try to describe in a paragraph the expectations you think your instructor has for *your* academic voice. Turn that paragraph in to see how accurately you have assessed your instructor's expectations.   EXERCISE   5

Using the passages from Exercise 1, try to decide whether different instructors would have different responses to the voices in those passages.   EXERCISE   6

For example, you might predict the following responses to the example excerpt on pages 216–217.

> My composition instructor would respond favorably to the voice in this excerpt. He prefers a voice that is relaxed and personal.
>
> My history professor would hate it. He thinks that student writers should speak with a voice that is very formal, cool, and distant. He would especially hate all those "I's."

Read through the following excerpts from essays written for college composition courses. On the basis of the guidelines given on the foregoing pages, explain what aspects of the voice in each passage need revision. Then rewrite the passages, making whatever changes you think are necessary.

EXERCISE 7

Example:

> It appears that eating disorders may be a growing affliction. These disorders, like bulimia (overeating and then purging) and anorexia (the refusal to eat), seem to strike primarily teen-age girls, who may, for some unknown reason, be particularly susceptible to these rather strange illnesses. Because the number of victims appears to be growing or increasing, high schools and colleges have started treatment programs. It is hoped that these programs will be successful and perhaps help alleviate needless suffering.

> Eating disorders like bulima (overeating and then purging) and anorexia (the refusal to eat) are on the rise. Victims of these disorders are primarily teen-age girls, who seem to be particularly susceptible. Because the number of victims is increasing, high schools and colleges have started treatment programs. With time and luck, we can hope these programs will be successful and eliminate needless suffering.

This rewrite eliminates the writer's tendency to qualify everything: *it appears, it seems, rather strange.* Such continual qualification reduces the sense of authority that the writer would like to convey. Use of *we hope* (in place of the vague *it is hoped*) makes the voice of the writer more forceful and indicates a shared set of attitudes between writer and reader.

Complete the remaining paragraphs in the same fashion.

1.   At one well-known university, chimpanzees are partially blinded by having a chemical solution of lye injected into their eyes. At another, mice die a terrible death when they are forced to undergo repeated and painful electric shocks. In point of fact, these examples represent only a small portion of the larger whole. Every day, I believe thousands of laboratory animals undergo similar horrible experiments, experiments that leave them deformed or dead.

Yet, I think, many laboratory animals might be spared much of their misery and pain. For one thing, analgesics or pain killers could be used far more frequently than they are. Requiring a relatively small investment in time and money, the use of pain killers could probably relieve laboratory animals of much suffering.

_____

_____

_____

_____

_____

2.   For years critics have argued about the play "Oedipus Rex." Some have argued, for example, that Oedipus knows nothing of his guilt until the end of the play, when it is revealed that he himself is the murderer of his father. However, others have insisted that Oedipus knows all along that he is the guilty one. From this point of view Oedipus, the brilliant solver of riddles, could not possibly have ignored the mounting evidence that he was the murderer of the king.

Just how or why this debate has raged for so many years completely eludes me. The correct interpretation is so obvious. Oedipus knows from the beginning that he is guilty and he just pretends his ignorance. For example, when a servant tells the story of the king's murder, he uses the word *bandits*. But when Oedipus repeats the story, he utilizes the singular form *bandit*. Clearly Sophocles uses clues such as this one to spell out, even for the very blind, Oedipus's knowledge of his crime.

_____

_____

_____

---

3. It is essential that every public building in this country be made accessible to the handicapped. Architects who do not keep in mind the problems of the handicapped should be shot on sight. After all, how would you feel if you had to sit helplessly outside a building that you needed to enter but could not because of your wheelchair. Without question you would feel frustrated and furious.

Fury is, of course, exactly what handicapped men and women feel when they are confronted with such flagrant examples of public irresponsibility. But by themselves, they cannot possibly influence the government officials who can effectively remediate this horrendous situation. They need public support from those who are not handicapped. Only then will their voices be heard by those incompetents in the city council.

---

4. In many states where capital punishment is still in force, lethal injection has begun to replace the electric chair as the method of public execution. Quick and painless, the injections avoid the suffering frequently caused by electric chairs that malfunction. In addition, lethal injection does not deform or distort the body in any way. Electrocution does, causing even more pain to the relatives of the diseased. As the benefits of lethal injection are discussed and analyzed, it will probably become the uniform method of execution in this country. All I can say is "It's about time!"

Choose a movie or book that you particularly liked (or disliked), and write a paper explaining the sources of your admiration (or dislike). Distribute copies of the paper to classmates who have not read or seen the work you describe.

GETTING STARTED

In very general terms, you already know the thesis or controlling idea of this paper. You want to tell your audience how good (or bad) a particular book, play, or movie is, from your point of view. If you are like most people, what made you like or dislike something you saw or read can be hard to figure out. But, having some questions to ask of the work can help. Although each individual work suggests its own set of questions and answers, many writers find it useful to ask the following questions. In one way or another, they can always be adapted to the particular work at hand.

1. Who wrote or directed it? Do you know anything about the purpose of her work in general, about what she usually tries to do with words or images? Have you seen or read anything else by her? Was it similar or dissimilar to this work? Is what she does similar or dissimilar to the work of other people writing at this time?

2. Who are the major actors or characters? What is their relationship to one another? Does that relationship stay the same throughout or does it change? What causes that change?

3. What actions (mental or physical) do the characters perform? Why do they act this way? What is their objective? What motivates them? What methods do they use to achieve their goal? Are their actions or objectives consistent or do they seem to contradict one another?

4. Against what background or setting do these people perform? How does the setting affect them?

5. Are you familiar with any books or films similar to this one? Are they more successful or less? What makes them succeed where this one fails, or vice versa?

The answers to these questions can help you isolate and evaluate the individual elements of a work, providing you with the material for your final paper.

The following paragraphs illustrate how one student's answers to some of the foregoing questions began to show a pattern. They helped him realize that nothing in the movie *Flashdance* consistently made sense to him, and that was one of the reasons why he ended up more annoyed than delighted with the film.

Who are the major actors or characters? What is their relationship to one another? Does it change? The major character is Alex, a beautiful young girl who is a welder by day and a dancer by night. She dances in a bar with a bunch of other girls. But she wants to be a ballerina and enter a school of dance. When she gets home from work she practices ballet, and she has taught herself to be an accomplished ballerina by watching television. The other major character is Nick, her boss. He owns the construction company Alex works for in the daytime. But at night he also seems to lead a double life, for he appears at charity balls and has a socialite for a wife. They fall in love, though at the end its not clear what's going to happen when Alex gets into school and prepares to devote herself to dance.

What actions do they perform? Why do they do what they do? Primarily Alex practices her ballet or dances on the stage while a bunch of drunks scream their enjoyment. But she gets really upset when her best friend, who wants to be a skater, starts dancing in a strip joint. When this happens, Alex gets furious and drags her out. Exactly why Alex gets so upset is not clear, because where she works is not much better. Maybe it is because she is supposed to be religious; at one point, she is shown making a confession to a priest. But the rest of the time she doesn't seem very religious, particularly when she starts swearing and using four-letter words. It is also not clear how Alex got interested in being a ballerina. She doesn't seem to have any parents. There's only some old woman who was once a prima ballerina. Alex sees her once in a while, and this woman encourages her to continue dancing. But who she is or where she came from is never made clear. In the end she dies, and how she dies (or of what) is also unclear.

What is the background of the characters? Against what kind of setting do they move or perform? Background is really mysterious in Flashdance. Alex lives in Pittsburgh, but she seems to come from nowhere. Although money is supposed to be a problem — that's why she works as a welder — she lives in a beautiful

apartment and wears what seem to be designer clothes. At one
point she says she dances to forget, but what she's trying to forget
is never clear. It sounds like she is unhappy about something, but
she looks as if she has everything.

SUGGESTIONS FOR ORGANIZATION

Usually, unless your instructor says otherwise, you should not assume
that your audience has read or seen the work in question. However, that
does not mean you want to give your readers a detailed summary. Just
briefly summarize the plot of the work, telling who the actors are, what
they do, and where they do it. Above all, don't make the mistake of
replacing evaluation with summary. Limit your summary to no more
than one page.

The major portion of your paper (at least two-thirds of it) should be
devoted to your evaluation. As you grow more experienced with critical
papers, the papers themselves will grow longer and allow you to deal
with several different questions about the text or film. But for this assignment,
limit yourself to answering only two or three questions. The following
sample paper may help you organize your own.

Joe Kelley

The music in Flashdance is wonderful, particularly the title song
"What a Feeling." But even the music could not save the picture,
and in the end it was mindless and silly, a bad picture with a good
sound track.

Absolutely nothing in the movie made any sense. It was as if the
director had several different films in mind, and in each scene
decided to start all over again with a new movie. For example,
Alex, the heroine of Flashdance, is a welder by day and a dancer
by night. Trying to earn enough money to study ballet, she dances
half naked in a run-down bar where drunken men cheer her
performance.

But when a friend decides to become a stripper, Alex is horrified.
Suddenly she behaves as if she herself were a grammar school
teacher. Dragging her friend off the stage, she lectures the girl
about losing her self-respect. That lecture would make a lot more
sense coming from someone who didn't finish her own

performance by dousing herself with water so that the audience could see through her costume.

Similarly, there are hints that Alex has a tragic past, that she dances to forget. But exactly what she wants to forget remains a mystery. The only person who gives any clue to her past is her ballet teacher, a mysterious foreign lady, who was apparently once a great ballerina. But just how she came into contact with a young girl who welds for a living is never explained. Like everything else in the film, she is just there — at least until the end, when she mysteriously dies.

Equally implausible are Alex's talents. It is never explained, for example, how she learned, at the age of nineteen, to be a welder. Even stranger are her talents as a ballerina. Supposedly she learned how to dance from watching television and reading books, but that explanation seems slightly ridiculous, given the complicated routines she performs.

In the end, "ridiculous" may just be the key word for describing this film. It is as if the director decided the music was so good that the script didn't have to make any sense at all.

REVISING

When you revise, pay particular attention to the tone of voice you want to assume for your readers. Even if you really liked or really hated the work you are talking about, use a little restraint. It will make your opinion seem more trustworthy. If you begin by saying "This book is a piece of trash that no respectable reader would pay good money for," you appear so disgusted and angered by the book that it will be difficult for your audience to take you seriously. You seem so biased or prejudiced against the book that your audience will assume you could not see any virtues in it even if they did exist.

In presenting yourself to your readers, try to maintain a delicate balance. Yes, you have a definite opinion about the subject at hand. But you are not so enthusiastic or so disgusted that you cannot maintain a degree of objectivity. That is, you are still able to view your subject with a certain distance and control. Don't let your audience think you are so overwhelmed (positively or negatively) that you cannot acknowledge something good in a work you disliked or something bad in a work you adored.

Suggestions for Your Writer's Notebook

SUGGESTION 1

What would you say is the most difficult aspect of creating an authorial voice?

SUGGESTION 2

If you were writing for readers who had never met you, you would, in effect, be introducing yourself through your prose. Your readers would imagine a person behind the words. Describe the kind of person you would like your readers to discover in your writing.

SUGGESTION 3

From your reading, select an author whom you would like to imitate. Write a paragraph analyzing what you think is good about this author's style. Look at word choice, sentence length, kind of punctuation, use of description, degree of explanation, and the like. Here is one student's analysis of the following paragraph from *The Art of Eating* by M. F. K. Fisher.

Bill Williams

The only stew I ever heard of made without either cream or milk was from three gentle sisters. They spoke sadly at first, and then with that kind of quiet inner mirth that rises always in members of a family who have lived together for several decades, when they begin unexpectedly to remember things. These three sisters sat in the hot California sunlight under a eucalyptus tree, and laughed at last in spite of all the things in between, as they recalled the way they always ate oyster stew when they were children in New Hampshire. (M. F. K. Fisher, The Art of Eating).

I would like to write like M. F. K. Fisher because she sounds smart but doesn't sound like she's showing off. Even though I have to look up some of the words she uses, like "mirth," I don't have to read her with a dictionary in my hand. And I like the way she describes things. She always tells you just enough so that you can really understand what she's talking about. I know exactly what she means when she talks about how families start remembering things they have done in the past. She knows how to describe things just enough so that you can see them. But she never sounds fancy. I hate when a writer sounds fancy, like he was showing you how many adjectives he could use in one sentence.

SUGGESTION 4

Now see whether you can *imitate* the author of your choice. Begin by picking out three or four characteristics of your author. Then draft a paragraph on a similar subject. Once you have a draft, revise it to include the characteristics you have chosen to imitate. Here is Bill's imitation of M. F. K. Fisher.

My grandmother is so tiny and so frail, it's hard to believe she was ever young. But every Sunday, she still cooks a big meal for the entire family and lays it all out on a white, cotton tablecloth that never has a spot on it. She always cooks exactly the same thing, but I never get tired of it. The first course is a thick, brown stew with potato dumplings. The dumplings are wonderful. They look heavy, but they are light as air and go down just as easily. Then comes a crisp, flaky chicken, spiced with some secret herb my grandmother will never talk about. My mother always asks her what it is, but she just smiles this little smile and shakes her head. Dessert is rich chocolate pudding, with homemade whipped cream that you can put on yourself, as much as you want. At the end of the meal, everyone finds a place to sleep and the house is very still.

SUGGESTION 5

Think about the question "Who Am I?" For most of us, the answer to that question changes when the circumstances change. It all depends on where you are and who you are with. Many of us feel different in private than we do in public, or else we appear to be one person on the outside and feel like another on the inside. For most of us, that odd creature we call "the self" is a very contradictory being. In your notebook, try writing two paragraphs that sum up those contradictions. Once you have written these paragraphs, think about which "self" you reveal in your writing.

Melissa Muñoz

One side of me seems very quiet and reserved. She is innocent, never daring to get into trouble. Her idea of a good time is going to a movie with one of her friends or spending the night at a friend's house. She is always trying to please others; she pleases her parents by doing well in school, she pleases her boss at the snack bar in the hospital by always keeping busy, making sure she does not do anything wrong. She's honest, never lying to her parents, her friends, or her teachers. She's always nice to everyone. If someone makes a crack about her, she ignores it and will compliment her on something.

But there's another side of me that's anything but quiet and reserved. Only her friends see this side often. She is noisy in the library on purpose, so a teacher will kick her out. In Spanish, she'll constantly talk to her friends so Mrs. Schaeffer will get mad and separate them. She'll go to the tech fair at Carnegie—Mellon and scream her lungs off on a ride. Every once in a while she won't do anything on a school night except watch TV or maybe play football with her next-door neighbors. Sometimes she'll continuously make fun of someone behind their back and enjoy every moment of it. Yes, there are two sides of my personality, the perfect me and the wild, the crazy, and the unkind me. But these are the extremes of my personality; what most people see is a balance between the two.

Combining Sentences

Pattern 11 will give you practice with *participles*. These are words which look like verbs but function like adjectives. In the following sentence, for example, the word "running" is a participle modifying the subject, "he."

Running, he felt his heart beat faster and faster.

Participles, however, can also appear as part of a phrase. In the next sentence, for example, the words "flapping in the wind" would be considered a participial phrase:

The house was barren and old, with shingles flapping in the wind.

Participles not only have different forms; they can also express different relationships to time. For example, "driven" and "riddled" in the following sentences are called *past participles*. (The third principle form of a verb is always the past participle: *drive, drove, driven*).

Driven by ambition, the politician neglected his family.

The body, riddled with holes, was found in Gorky Park.

And in the following sentence, "having made" is called a *present perfect participle* (have + past participle)

Having made the decision, he could finally rest easily

In addition, to making your writing more vivid, participles can also indicate relationships in time. Compare for example these two sentences:

1. I hoisted the rifle to my shoulder. I marched to the front of the line.
2. *Hoisting the rifle to my shoulder*, I marched to the front of the line.

Through the use of a participial phrase, the second sentence more clearly indicates the relationship between two separate actions.

The following exercise will give you practice using both past and present   EXERCISE
participles. Directions about which form of the participle to use will
appear in brackets, as they do in the following example:

1.   ∧ The ∧ dog limped away ∧ .
         He *held up his paw.* [ing]
         He was *injured.*
         He limped *away from the pack.*
     Holding up his paw, the injured dog limped away from the pack.

Complete the remaining sentences.

1.   ∧ The posse rode for miles.
         They *stopped only occasionally* ∧ . [ing,]
         They stopped *for a brief rest.*

     _____

     _____

2.   ∧ The child cried ∧ .
         He was *frightened by his mother's absence.* [,]
         He cried *for hours.*

     _____

     _____

3.   ∧ The ∧ woman hid from the social worker.
         She *had been terrified by the robbery.* [having,]
         The woman was *elderly.*

     _____

     _____

4.   The marriage ∧ no longer interfered with Henry the Eighth's desires.
         It *had been annulled.* [, having,]

     _____

     _____

5.   ∧ He kept his mouth shut ∧ .
         He *waited for disaster to strike.* [ing,]

He *hoped the situation would disappear*. [, ing]

_____

_____

6. ∧∧∧ The monkeys behaved just like human children.
        They *climbed trees*. [ing,]
        They *screeched at one another*. [ing,]
        They *threw things*. [and ing,]

_____

_____

7. ∧ Sam Spade looked ∧ at the criminal ∧ .
        Sam Spade *lit a match*. [having,]
        He looked *long and hard*.
        The criminal *cringed before him*. [ing]

_____

_____

8. ∧ The cyclist hit ∧ the boy.
        The cyclist *hurtled down the street*. [ing,]
        The boy was *little*.

_____

_____

9. Sugar Ray Leonard ∧ punished his opponent ∧ ∧ .
        He did it *cruelly*.
        He *pushed him against the ropes*. [, ing]
        He *beat him to the mat*. [and ing]

_____

_____

10. ∧ He had an exotic view of life ∧ .
        He *grew up in the tropics*. [having + grown,]
        It was *drawn from his* ∧ *experiences as a child*. [,]
            Those experiences were *strange*.

_____

_____

Write five sentences using a participle or participial phrase.   EXERCISE

1. _____

_____

2. _____

_____

3. _____

_____

4. _____

_____

5. _____

_____

PATTERN 12

Pattern 11 focused on the participle, a verb form used like an adjective. The pattern discussed here uses a verb form called a *gerund*. Although it resembles the participle, it functions differently: It is used as a noun rather than an adjective. In the following sentences, for example, the word "distorting" is a gerund used as a noun:

His *distorting* the facts did not help the situation. (subject of a sentence)

He was accused of *distorting* the news for his own benefit. (object of a preposition)

Sometimes, the word preceding the gerund needs an apostrophe. As   EXERCISE
usual, in the following exercise, that information will appear in parentheses:

1. The president could not accept _____ ∧ .
      The committee dismissed his plan. ['s + dismissing]
      They did it *after only an hour's deliberation.*
    The president could not accept the committee's dismissing his plan after only an hour's deliberation.

Finish the remaining exercise.

1. ∧ His father could not understand ———.
       This was *despite his explanations*. [,]
       He cheated on the exam. [his + cheating]

———————————————————————

———————————————————————

2. ——— was his dream ∧ .
       He hoped to *write the great American novel*. [ing]
       This was *for many years*. [,]
[, but]
He finally gave it up ∧ .
       This was *after too many rejections*.

———————————————————————

———————————————————————

3. ∧ ——— is not very good.
       He was not born in this country. [because,]
       He doesn't *understand English*. [his + understanding + of]

———————————————————————

———————————————————————

4. ——— kept us awake.
       The woman moaned. ['s + moaning]
[, but]
We did not complain.
[;]
She was obviously in a great deal of pain.

———————————————————————

———————————————————————

5. ∧ ——— is the best part of writing.
       You don't believe it right now. [even if,]
       This part is *revision*. [revising]

———————————————————————

———————————————————————

6. ——— left him exhausted ∧ .

He *laughed hysterically.* [his + laughing]
He was *happy.* [but]

_____

_____

7. The women enjoyed _____.
    They *played* poker. [ing]
[, but]
Their husbands disliked the game ∧ .
    They *wouldn't play.* [and]

_____

_____

8. _____ can help you sleep ∧ .
    It helps to *count sheep.* [ing].
    You suffer from insomnia. [if]

_____

_____

9. _____ is the best revenge.
    You should *live well.* [ing]

_____

_____

10. Her fear of _____ wasted a lot of time.
    She could not *fly.* [flying]
[; however,]
She could not overcome it.

_____

_____

Write five sentences using a gerund. Try to make the gerund fulfill   EXERCISE
different functions, e.g., as subject or object of the sentence.

1. _____

_____

2. _____

_____

3. _____

_____

4. _____

_____

5. _____

_____

CHAPTER 8

Writing to Persuade

Up until now, the chapters in this text have concentrated on expository essays written to explain and develop a thesis statement. But in this chapter, I want to stress that some of your assignments will expect you to do more than explain your thesis. If, for example, you are asked to write an essay *in favor of* or *against* the use of nuclear weapons, you are being asked to expand or enlarge the purpose of your essay. You are being asked, in effect, to make persuasion as important as exposition. This means that your paper should do more than explain your thesis. It should also encourage your readers to share it. You want them to finish reading your paper and say, "Yes, I see what you mean. And, as a result of reading your essay, I am beginning to see things your way."

To a large extent, writing to persuade utilizes everything you have learned so far about expository essays. But a persuasive essay has some additional requirements as well, and the objective of Chapter 8 is to introduce them.

Developing a Debatable Thesis

Sometimes the thesis for a persuasive essay will be assigned, but that is not always the case. You may well be given more open-ended assignments such as "Write an essay that will convince your readers to accept your position on some aspect of educational reform." Here you have nothing more than the general topic. It is up to you to develop the thesis you want your readers to share.

In developing your thesis, you have to consider the expanded purpose of your essay. You must be aware that not every thesis is appropriate for an essay written to persuade. A thesis statement like the following would not be appropriate for a persuasive essay: "Suicide is a growing problem among teen-agers." It would not be appropriate because no one would disagree with the fact that statistics show teen-age suicide to be on the increase. That lack of disagreement makes this statement unsuitable for a persuasive essay. When you are assigned a persuasive essay, your instructor wants to test your powers of persuasion. If you develop a thesis that no one needs to be persuaded to agree with, you defeat the objective of the assignment.

When you are assigned nothing more than a general topic for a persuasive essay, you have to be sure that the thesis you develop is in some way arguable or debatable. One very efficient way to discover such a thesis is to think in terms of a problem that needs to be solved.

Let us say you had decided on the following tentative thesis statement: "Boating accidents should be prevented." But after thinking about that statement for a few minutes, you realized that it did not express a debatable or disputable thesis. No one would disagree, so this thesis statement is not appropriate for an essay that has persuasion as its aim. To make it more appropriate, you would have to rewrite it. At this point you might consider changing your thesis statement to "Boating accidents could be reduced if every single person using a boat were required to take intensive classes in safety, management, and maintenance." Presented with this thesis statement, some people would insist that they have been boating since they were children and therefore do not need any classes. Others might claim that such classes are a waste of time because it is only on the water that real learning takes place. Still others might insist that with the little leisure time they have, they do not want to waste it in a classroom. In short, this thesis statement generates disagreement. Therefore, it is suitable for a persuasive essay.

When you write to persuade, you have to be sure that there are two sides to the problem or issue you describe. Your goal or purpose in writing, then, is to encourage your readers to move from one side to the other.

Read the following thesis statements and put a check next to those you consider inappropriate for a persuasive essay.   EXERCISE   1

1. In the last ten years, a number of different studies have confirmed the link between cigarette smoking and lung cancer. ✓

2. More publicity should be given to the fact that repeated studies have confirmed the link between cigarette smoking and lung cancer.

3. More should be done to increase public awareness about the physical and emotional devastation caused by Alzheimer's disease.

4. Cindi Lauper and Madonna have very different performing styles.

5. Some universities do not see to it that their star athletes maintain respectable academic averages.

6. Cindi Lauper is a truly original presence in rock music, whereas Madonna relies on nothing more than the stereotypical image of woman as sex object.

7. In the twenties, a group of young artists made Harlem the intellectual and cultural capital of black America, and that era has come to be known as the "Harlem Renaissance."

8. No athlete should be allowed to participate in sports unless he or she maintains a "B" average.

9. Every survey course in modern American literature must address, in detail, the extraordinary cultural explosion known as the "Harlem Renaissance."

10. Until quite recently, very little was known about Alzheimer's disease.

Using the topic of educational reform, develop a tentative thesis statement suitable for a persuasive essay of two or three pages. The following are some sample thesis statements: **EXERCISE 2**

1. Final exams should be eliminated in favor of final papers.

2. Grammatical correctness should not be a criterion for grading papers.

3. Teachers should receive training in giving effective lectures.

Building an Argument

Once you have a tentative thesis statement and know what conclusion you want your readers to share, you need to consider another important question: "How can I convince my readers to agree?" Yet, if you consider for a moment what you do when you want someone to act or behave in a certain way, I think you'll know the answer to that question. Imagine, for purposes of comparison, that you wanted a friend to stop relying on tranquilizers to relax. To convince him, you might say that the tranquilizers can be addictive and that they can cause serious side effects. In other words, you would give him an argument. And that is precisely what you have to do in an essay written to persuade. In its simplest form an argument consists of two essential elements, a conclusion and the premise or premises it is based on. Here, in one sentence, are the premise and the conclusion of an argument.

Smoking in all public places should be strictly forbidden, because it is becoming increasingly clear that nonsmokers are affected by the smoke they are forced to inhale.

PREMISE: Nonsmokers are affected by the smoke they are forced to inhale.

CONCLUSION: Smoking in all public places should be strictly forbidden.

Once you have your tentative thesis statement, you already have the conclusion of your argument. But a conclusion without a premise is not an argument. It is an assertion. When you present your readers with nothing more than an assertion, you tell them *what* they should think without telling them *why*, and the only people who will be convinced are those who already agreed with you in the first place. To convince those readers who do not agree with you to begin with, you have to provide the premise or premises on which your conclusion is based. Here are the tentative thesis statement and thesis paragraph that one student developed upon being assigned to select a topic in the general area of educational reform.

Ed Rosenthal
    Students too often believe they can do nothing about the instruction they receive. They think their only option is to sit passively in class and complain about their instructors when no one is around. But instead of complaining privately, what students should do is to develop a system for rating their instructors. Those ratings would cover everything from knowledge about the subject to frequency of office hours, and the results would be published and distributed schoolwide.

The foregoing thesis paragraph offers a very clear statement of the conclusion Ed wants his readers to accept: "Students should rate their instructors and publish the results." What he has to do now is decide what reasons he could offer for affirming that conclusion. He has to ask himself such questions as "Why do I believe that?" and "How have I arrived at that conclusion?" In response to those questions, Ed outlined the following argument:

<u>Conclusion</u>: Students should develop a system for rating the performance of their instructors and publish those ratings school-wide.

    <u>Premise 1</u>: Public ratings can guide students toward good teachers and away from poor ones.

    <u>Premise 2</u>: Public ratings can discourage bad teaching.

At the point when you have a skeleton argument like this one, you are ready to think about the next step in drafting your essay, which is analyzing your argument. But before you do that, complete the following exercise.

Using the tentative thesis statement you developed in Exercise 2; write out, in skeletal form, the argument you intend to offer your readers in your persuasive essay.

EXERCISE   3

Analyzing Your Argument

As you know from ordinary conversations, there are effective arguments and there are ineffective arguments. There are those that convince and those that do not. Obviously you want your paper to be based on an argument that convinces. That means that you should do more than outline your argument before your write. You should also analyze it, looking for errors in reasoning that might reduce its effectiveness. The following are some of the criteria you can use.

1.   Your premise or conclusion should not be based on an over-generalization.

PREMISE: The present safety regulations designed to protect boxers from harm are absolutely useless.

CONCLUSION: The boxing commission has to institute a new set of rules for boxers' safety.

If this were your argument, you would have to be sure that none of the current safety regulations were in any way effective. If some were, your argument would lose credibility, and you would look as though you did not know what you were talking about. Once you revise to eliminate overgeneralization in your premise, you will probably discover that you have to limit the generalization of your conclusion as well.

> PREMISE: The present safety regulations do not adequately protect boxers from serious head injuries.

> CONCLUSION: The boxing commission must introduce rules that will make headgear for boxers mandatory.

2. Make sure your premise is relevant to the conclusion.

> PREMISE: Smoking causes premature wrinkling.

> CONCLUSION: Smoking should be forbidden in public places where nonsmokers are present.

Although there is evidence that smoking contributes to the skin's aging, in this case that premise is not relevant to the conclusion. Here the author has to explain not why smoking is bad for the individual who smokes but why it should be forbidden when nonsmokers are present. Revised to contain a premise that is relevant to the conclusion, the foregoing argument would look something like this:

> PREMISE: A growing body of research suggests that non-smokers are affected by the smoke they are forced to inhale.

> CONCLUSION: Smoking should be forbidden in public places where nonsmokers are present.

3. Your premise should be based on accurate information.

> PREMISE: If Americans don't master a foreign language, they won't be able to travel abroad.

> CONCLUSION: American students should learn at least one foreign language.

Here the premise is relevant to the conclusion, but unfortunately it is not true. In many European countries, the people who live there speak English, and it is not at all difficult for Americans traveling abroad to communicate. Here again, the argument needs to be revised.

> PREMISE: A great deal is lost from the original work when
>   a book is translated into another language.
>
> CONCLUSION: American students should learn at least one
>   foreign language so they can read some of
>   the European classics in the original.

4.   Your premise should not just restate your conclusion in different words.

> PREMISE: It is not fair that, in some states, people who
>   are adopted cannot have access to their adoption
>   files.
>
> CONCLUSION: Adopted children need to have access to
>   their files.

Here the premise does not give a reason for arriving at the conclusion; it just repeats it in different words. Thus the argument needs to be revised.

> PREMISE: Without knowing the medical background of
>   their biological parents, people who have been
>   adopted cannot adequately safeguard their own
>   health.
>
> CONCLUSION: Adopted children need to have access to
>   their files.

Once you have analyzed the argument you plan to present in your paper, there is still one more step to complete before you begin drafting. You have to anticipate the objections to your argument that might be raised. But before considering that step, complete the following exercise.

Analyze the argument you intend to develop in your paper.   EXERCISE   4

Anticipating the Opposition

The purpose of a persuasive essay is not to convince people who already agree with you but to win over those people who don't. Among those who do not agree, there are probably a few who will not be convinced no matter what you say. But the majority are open to persuasion in the sense that they are willing to listen to new arguments and reconsider their position. It is these people whom your instructor will try to represent when he reads a persuasive essay. No matter what his personal opinion, he will read your paper as someone who is open to persuasion but still ready to object. This is his way of testing your powers of persuasion.

In response to the role your instructor will assume, you have to anticipate and answer objections he might raise. So first of all, you must define what groups might object and decide what they might say. One way to do that is to think about the kinds of people who would be most acutely affected by what you say in your thesis statement. These are the people who are most likely to raise objections. In Ed Rosenthal's case, for example, college students and teachers were the two groups who might object to his thesis.

Once you have defined the group or groups that could raise objections, your next step is to decide what they might say. One good way to do this it to ask your classmates to role-play the group or groups you need to address. For example, when Ed Rosenthal presented his argument in favor of rating instructors, he asked his classmates to respond to his argument twice — first as themselves and then as their instructors. Here are the responses he received.

Students

1. Ratings aren't going to discourage bad teaching. What difference will they make?
2. Other universities don't have such rating systems.
3. Teachers don't care what students think of their work.
4. Teachers will retaliate if they get bad ratings.

Teachers

1. Students will use low ratings to get even for bad grades.

2. Students don't know how to judge a teacher's performance.
  It will be a popularity contest.

This kind of group role-playing can give you a good sense of the potential objections you should answer. But it is still up to you to decide which ones are most relevant to your thesis. In Ed's case, he did not think it was important to answer the objection about other universities not having such a system. He knew of other universities that *did* have such rating systems, and furthermore, he did not think there was anything wrong with being the first.

From Ed's point of view there were two more crucial objections to be answered. Students reading his essay would object that the ratings would not discourage poor teaching, and teachers would object that the ratings would not adequately reflect performance. Given the fact that these two objections appeared more than once, Ed was convinced that they were issues he should address in his paper.

The First Draft

When you know what argument you want to present and what objections that argument might raise, you are ready to start drafting. Here, for example, is Ed's first rough draft.

1   Students at this university too often behave like a bunch of sheep. They act like they have no control over the instruction they receive. They seem to think that their only option is to sit passively in class and complain about their instructors. But instead of complaining in private, they should develop a system for rating their instructors and publish the results. The ratings would cover everything from knowledge about the subject to frequency of office hours, and the results would be published and distributed schoolwide.

2   Such a rating system would serve to guide students in the selection of courses. Most of the time students, particularly new ones, are totally in the dark about which instructors to choose for which courses. Not knowing that Professor X doesn't keep office hours or return papers, they mistakenly choose his course instead of Professor Y's, who meets with students every week and returns every paper. If these students were informed about Professor Y's

strengths as well as about Professor X's drawbacks, they would be in a better position to get the most out of their classes.

3   Such a rating system would have long-range effects as well. It would force teachers to present their material in stimulating and interesting ways. The ratings could also provide a basis for merit raises, allowing good teachers to be rewarded for their hard work and dedication. At the university level, good teaching is too often ignored and too rarely rewarded. Admittedly, a public rating system has some problems, but none that couldn't be solved.

4   Some students would use the system just to get even: giving low grades to those teachers who had given them low grades. But if the results of the ratings were analyzed and broken down into percentages, it would be obvious where the majority had been favorably impressed even if a few were not satisfied. Thus a teacher whose rating in lecture skills was 75% "very satisfied" would not be hurt if 2% criticized him simply because he had given them low grades.

5   Too, a rating system could be devised that would emphasize teaching ability more than personality. The inclusion of categories like "interest in student questions," "attendance at office hours," and "willingness to accept challenges" would force students to consider professional and intellectual capability.

Having completed this first rough draft, Ed's next step was to "step back" and pause for a few hours, so that he could return later and reassess what he had written.

Write the first draft of your essay.   EXERCISE 5

ANALYZING THE FIRST DRAFT

For the most part, revising a persuasive essay is much like revising an expository one. That means you still have to consider questions such as those listed on page 58. However, there are some additional points you should also think about as you revise:

1.   Does my thesis statement clearly define the way I want my readers to think or act?

When the purpose of your essay is to bring about a change in opinion or behavior, you should use your thesis statement and thesis paragraph to explain precisely the conclusion you want your readers to come to after reading your paper.

2.   Have I adequately developed the premises on which my conclusion is based?

Outlining your argument is one thing, but fully developing it is another. Not only should the conclusion of your argument be clearly explained in your thesis paragraph, but your supporting paragraphs should develop each premise with specificity and precision.

3.   Have I adequately anticipated and answered potential objections?

You may very well not be able to totally contradict or defeat objections to your argument. But you should respond to them fully enough to show your readers that such objections do not totally undermine or defeat your position. By responding to potential objections, you tell your readers that you can be trusted — that you are not so blinded by your own convictions you cannot see the other side.

4.   Does my voice express the appropriate attitude toward my readers?

Not surprisingly, writing to persuade can profoundly affect a writer's voice. Intent on convincing your readers, you can easily lapse into a tone that is overbearing or demanding. But remember: You do not want to *insist* that your readers think as you do, you want to *persuade* them to see things your way. There is a difference. Although you will be able to shape and revise your voice as your draft, it is still a good idea to keep in mind, from the very beginning, the need to create a voice that consistently announces your respect for your readers' potential opposition. When you write to explain, a tone of voice that is somewhat overbearing does not necessarily defeat the purpose of your paper — to explain your thesis. But when you write to persuade, you are much more dependent on your readers good will. The surest way to lose that good will is to assume a voice that demands they see things your way.

For an illustration of how you might use these questions, let us analyze Ed's draft, paragraph by paragraph:

1   Students at this university too often behave like a bunch of
     sheep. They act like they have no control over the instruction
     they receive. They seem to think that their only option is to
     sit passively in class and complain about their instructors.
     But instead of complaining in private, they should develop a
     system for rating their instructors and publish the results.
     The ratings would cover everything from knowledge about

What about the tone here?

Is this a clear statement of my message?

the subject to frequency of office hours, and the results would be published and distributed schoolwide.

what questions would readers have?

What is good about this paragraph is that the thesis statement clearly and precisely sets forth the conclusion Ed wants his readers to share. Less effective, however, is the voice of the paragraph, which seems to express contempt for students who do not act to improve their lot: "Students at this university too often behave like a bunch of sheep." Ed wants to win over students who are skeptical about their ability to control their education, but this kind of language could defeat his purpose.

2   Such a rating system would serve to guide students in the selection of courses. Most of the time students, particularly new ones, are totally in the dark about which instructors to choose for which courses. Not knowing that Professor X doesn't keep office hours or return papers, they mistakenly choose his course instead of Professor Y's, who meets with students every week and returns every paper. If these students were informed about Professor Y's strengths as well as about Professor X's drawbacks, they would be in a better position to get the most out of their classes.

Have I made my first premise clear?

At this point, Ed is clearly following the original argument he outlined, and this paragraph introduces the first reason why students should do as he suggests. Although there are some grammatical errors, the paragraph does adequately develop his first premise, and is therefore successful as a first draft.

3   Such a rating system would have long-range effects as well. It would force teachers to present their material in stimulating and interesting ways. The ratings could also provide a sound basis for merit raises, allowing good teachers to be rewarded for their hard work and dedication. At the university level, good teaching is too often ignored and too rarely rewarded. Admittedly, a public rating system has some problems, but none that couldn't be solved.

Explain

Do I want to make all three points? Can I make all three in one paragraph?

This paragraph introduces a premise not in the original outline of Ed's argument: The use of a rating system could provide an effective basis for giving merit raises. There is nothing wrong with that. It is very possible that you will discover a new premise as you draft — one not indicated on your original outline. The real problem with this paragraph is that it does not fully develop any one premise. Instead it touches on several, and none is adequately discussed: (1) The ratings could be used as a basis for merit raises. (2) The present merit system does not adequately reward good teaching. (3) The rating system would make teachers present their material in stimulating ways.

4   Some students would use the system just to get even: giving low grades to those teachers who had given them low grades. But if the results of the ratings were analyzed and broken down into percentages, it would be obvious where the majority had been favorably impressed even if a few were not satisfied. A teacher whose rating in lecture skills was 75% "very satisfied" would not be hurt if 2% criticized him simply because he had given them low grades.

Does this really answer the objection?

Here you see Ed answering the objection that the rating system would not adequately reflect a teacher's performance but would instead reflect a student's anger at receiving low grades.

5   Too, a rating system could be devised that would emphasize teaching ability more than personality. The inclusion of categories like "interest in student questions," "attendance at office hours," and "willingness to accept challenges" would force students to consider professional and intellectual capability.

What about objection concerning quality?

In this paragraph Ed continues to meet the objection that the rating system could not adequately reflect teacher performance. In fact, Ed has gotten so caught up with this objection that he has forgotten the need to answer the other major objection: A rating system will not change the quality of instruction. Although he touches on this issue briefly in paragraph 3, it is never fully addressed. And it should be, because his readers will need more than one premise to be convinced.

Using the questions for revision introduced in Chapter 3 (p. 58), as well as the ones introduced here, analyze your first draft in preparation for writing your second draft.

EXERCISE   6

The Second Draft

As Ed's second draft illustrates, he was able to resolve the problems discovered in analyzing his first draft.

1   For some reason, many students believe they cannot control the quality of instruction at their university. They act as though their only option were to sit passively in class and complain where no one can hear them. But instead of complaining privately, students should make their discontent more public. They should develop a system for rating their instructors and publish the results. Teachers would be rated in categories ranging from "frequency of office hours" to "knowledge of subject matter," and every student would receive a copy of those ratings.

Here in this draft, Ed has begun to modify the harsh tone of his first draft. There is no mention of students behaving like sheep.

2   Such a rating system would serve to guide students in the selection of their courses. For the most part, students, particularly new students, have no idea who does the most effective job teaching a particular subject. Thus if Professor X doesn't keep office hours and doesn't return papers, students still file dutifully into his class simply because they don't know any better. They don't know, for example, that Professor Y, who teaches the same subject, is meticulous about keeping his office hours and returning every paper. If they did, Professor X's enrollment would decrease and Professor Y's would increase.

Ed was satisfied with paragraph 2. But now he has linked paragraphs 2 and 3 more carefully. Paragraph 2 ends with a transitional sentence that paves the way for the topic sentence of paragraph 3.

3   That increasing or decreasing enrollment would also work to produce long-term change as well. In effect, instructors who had decreasing enrollments would have to ponder why students were not signing up for their courses, and they would have to consider making changes in their methods of

instruction. I can think of few professors who, year after
year, would willingly accept low ratings of their performance,
particularly if those ratings were made public. Given
consistently poor ratings from their students, most
instructors would be too embarrassed not to pay more
attention to the quality of their teaching.

In paragraph 3, Ed is trying to develop the second premise of his argument:
Using a public rating system would discourage inadequate teaching. In
the previous draft he tended to give this premise a rather superficial
treatment. But in this draft he is addressing it with much more specificity.
At this point he has developed his second premise fully enough to answer
one of the basic objections he had identified prior to writing: The ratings
would not change anything. Although he might be better off in the third
draft dividing this paragraph in two (in order to highlight the two different
ways in which ratings would discourage poor teaching — decreasing
enrollments and public embarrassment), the basic revision is still very
effective.

4   Admittedly, to be successful, this kind of public rating
       system would have to be carefully devised. In particular, the
       categories by which a teacher is evaluated would have to be
       precisely defined so that students would be encouraged to
       judge performance rather than personality. This means the
       questionnaire would have to focus on very specific questions,
       such as "Does your instructor try to make his generalizations
       clear by providing many specific examples?" Questions like
       these would force students to think more deliberately about
       what actually makes a good instructor. In addition, the
       responses to the evaluations would have to be further
       analyzed and broken down into percentages. In the end, each
       instructor would receive a rating like the following: "The
       instructor always allows time for student questions: 75%
       very satisfied, 20% satisfied, and 5% dissatisfied." If the
       individual responses are translated into percentages, students
       who want to use the ratings as an expression of their anger
       will not have much effect.

Here Ed answers in very specific detail, the objection that the ratings
would not adequately reflect performance. The only real problem with

this paragraph is that it could easily overburden the reader with information and should therefore be divided into one major and one minor supporting paragraph. Note, too, that Ed has eliminated the original discussion of merit raises. Because he was unable to develop that premise adequately, Ed felt it would detract from the power of his argument.

At this point, Ed's paper was ready to be revised into a final draft.

Write the second draft of your essay.   EXERCISE   7

The Final Draft

Once you finish your second draft, you may well be ready to write the final version of your paper. But before doing that, you should review the questions for revision given on pages 66–68 in Chapter 3, as well as the questions for revision on pages 251–252 of this chapter. If you can answer "yes" to those questions, you are ready for final editing. Here, as an illustration of what your finished paper should look like, is the final draft of Ed's persuasive essay.

Grading Teachers   Ed Rosenthal

1   Unfortunately, many students believe they cannot control the quality of instruction they receive at their university. They think that their only option is to complain privately but say nothing in public. There is, however, an alternative to being silently miserable and dissatisfied. Students would have a lot more control over the quality of their instruction if they would consider using a public rating system for their professors. With such a system, teachers would be rated on everything from willingness to hold office hours to clarity of lectures, and the results would be published and distributed schoolwide.

2   On an immediate level, such a rating system could serve to guide students in the selection of courses. For the most part, students, particularly new students, have no idea who does the most effective job teaching a particular subject. They do not know, for example, that Professor X does not keep office hours or return papers, and they register for his course. Equally important, they do not know that Professor Y, who teaches the same subject, returns

every paper and meets with students every week. If they did, they
would probably have the good sense to choose his course over
Professor X's.

3   Such a system of public ratings would have long-term effects as
well. Professors who could not infer from their decreasing
enrollment that their methods were not adequate would still have
to face the results of the public ratings. Given consistently
negative evaluations, the majority of instructors would seek to
change their methods of instruction. It is hard to imagine an
instructor who would receive low ratings year after year and still
continue to do exactly the same thing he did before.

4   Admittedly, such a rating system for instructors could be abused,
and some students might use it to retaliate against instructors
who had given them low grades. But that problem could easily be
solved by analyzing all the responses and breaking them down
into percentages, to give each instructor a rating like the

following: "Encourages students' questions: 75% very satisfied, 20% satisfied, and 5% dissatisfied." With this method, the few students wishing to use the rating system for retaliation could do little harm.

5   Far too often, students in college feel that the only way they can respond to inadequate instruction is to withdraw from the course and lose the credits. But in the end, that does not solve the problem of inadequate or incompetent instruction. The teacher does not learn anything — and neither does the student. A better solution is for students to speak out. By adopting the method of rating and evaluation described in this paper, students can do just that.

Writing a
Persuasive
Essay

Write an essay in which you try to convince your readers to share your conclusion about solving, fully or partially, some current social problem. Before writing your own paper, read through the model paper that begins on page 261, where a student, Gabriel Geier, addresses the problem of closed adoption files.

GETTING STARTED

The following is a list of general topics. You can select one of them or think of your own. The important thing to remember here is that your thesis should generate some controversy. Therefore, you do not want a thesis that cannot be disputed, such as "Every year countless numbers of animals are used for scientific experimentation." Instead you want to discover one that could generate opposition: "The use of animals for scientific experimentation must be much more rigidly and carefully controlled than it is at present."

1. Eating disorders
2. Teen-age athletes
3. Teen-age suicide
4. Medical malpractice
5. Unemployment
6. Animal rights
7. Religion in the schools
8. Rape
9. Alcoholism
10. Compulsive gambling

ORGANIZING

This is the time to make a preliminary outline of both your argument and the potential objections it might raise. Think about which group or groups would be most deeply affected by what you have to say, and ask your classmates to role-play the audience you want to address.

REVISING

Before turning in your paper, it is a good idea to let some of the students who played your audience read it. Ask them to concentrate on answering two questions: (1) Have I clearly presented my argument? (2) Have I effectively answered objections to it?

Opening Adoption Files   Gabriel Geier

In many states, people who have been adopted are not allowed to
have access to their files. They have no idea who their real
parents are or why they were put up for adoption in the first
place, and all their attempts to discover this information are met
by firm bureaucratic resistance. In short, adoption officials will tell
them nothing.

However, in the last decade many adoptees have publicly
protested this state of affairs, and some states have begun to
change their policies. What I want to argue here is that this
change in adoption policy should take place nationwide. Adopted
children need to know about both their parents and their past,
and those who do not care can simply refuse all access to their
files.

What people do not realize is that restrictions against opening
adoption files do not, for the most part, deter those adoptees who
want to discover who their parents really are. Those men and
women who want to find their biological parents will, if they can
afford it, hire a detective to find out what they want to know. If
they cannot afford it, some are willing to devote all their time and
energy to learning more about their origins. What this should
show is just how important it is to adoptees to recover their past.

It is important because, by and large, adoptees feel guilty because
they were put up for adoption. In some part of their mind, they
always assume that they did something that made them unlovable,
that made their parents give them up. To counteract such feelings,
they need to know the real causes for their adoption. It helps the
adoptee to know, for example, that his mother gave him up for
adoption because she was too young to support him, not because
she didn't love him. This knowledge helps relieve the painful
burden of guilt many adoptees carry around all their lives.

There are also physical — rather than psychological — reasons
why adoptees need access to their files. To take proper care of
their health, they need to know what diseases they might be prone
to because of inheritance. In more extreme cases, knowledge about
the biological parents can make the difference between life and
death. Sometimes an individual needs to have an organ that comes
from a natural relative, but if all his relatives remain unknown,

the adoptee is at a terrible disadvantage — one that may cost him his life.

Many parents who have given up their children for adoption resent the idea of opening up the files. They feel that their right to privacy will be threatened. Yet this objection is based on the assumption that adopted children want to hunt down their parents and intrude upon their lives. But at the most, what they want is to know who their parents are. In some cases they may even want to meet them, but they do not want to push their way into the lives of people who will not accept them. Giving the adopted person access to his files does not mean that the parent or parents forsake all rights to privacy. It only means that the adopted child can attempt to make contact if he or she wishes, and the parents can refuse or accept.

When adoption authorities refuse to give adoptees access to their files, they cite the parents' right to privacy as a major reason for their refusal. Yet, this objection, if looked at closely, seems to be based on a very unfair attitude — the assumption that the feelings of the parents are more important than those of the children.

Many parents try to forget the adoption because they feel guilty about having to give up their children, and the state helps them in their attempt to forget their past. But why should the adoption authorities assume that the parents have all the rights in this matter? Shrouding the past in mystery may make them feel better, but it makes the children feel worse. It is not right to simply assume that the parents' feelings should be spared and the children's forgotten.

Suggestions for
Your Writer's Notebook

SUGGESTION 1

How would you interpret the following quotation? In particular, explain why you think the author has emphasized the two words *being* and *seeming*.

> Most of the time we persuade by being reasonable — and also by seeming so. The *being* is clear thinking; the *seeming* is tone.[1]

SUGGESTION 2

What do you think is the biggest difference between writing to explain and writing to persuade?

SUGGESTION 3

According to the poet Ezra Pound, "The meaning of a word is not a set, cut-off thing like the move of a knight or pawn on a chess board. It comes up with roots, with associations." You can test the truth of Pound's statement by reading the following list of words to different people and asking them to "free associate." That is, they should simply respond to the word with whatever thought comes into their minds.

1. Water
2. Parent
3. Home
4. School
5. Strength
6. Power
7. Woman
8. Man
9. Love
10. Hatred

SUGGESTION 4

List pairs of words that say much the same thing but call up different associations, such as *slender–skinny*, *fussy–discriminating*, *work–drudgery*, and *disturbed–crazy*.

[1]Donald Hall, *Writing Well* (Boston: Little, Brown, 1973) 239.

SUGGESTION 5

In a book called *The New Diary*, Tristine Rainer offers an interesting suggestion on how to deal with people who intimidate or scare you. She suggests writing a letter that will remain unsent but that articulates your feelings about that person. If you want to, you can always send the letter, but that's not important. What is important is that you use the letter to discover for yourself why you feel nervous or inadequate when you deal with this particular person. Try writing an "unsent letter" to a someone who, for unknown reasons, makes you feel uneasy. Just sit down and write whatever you would like to say to or about that person.

SUGGESTION 6

Try following the advice that Kenneth Koch gives in a book called *Sleeping on the Wing*: "Turn on some music (preferably without words) and write whatever the music makes you think or see."[2]

[2]Kenneth Koch, *Sleeping on the Wing* (New York: Vintage, 1981) 22.

Combining Sentences

This pattern emphasizes the many different roles infinitives can play within sentences. Verb forms that are usually introduced by the word *to*, infinitives can function as nouns and appear as the subject of a sentence.

Example:

1. _____ is the sign of a true winner.

        It is *to give up gracefully*.

    To give up gracefully is the sign of a true winner.

They can also appear as direct objects.

Example:

2. He wanted _____ .

        It was *to give up gracefully*.

    [, but]

    He didn't know how ∧ .

        He had never done it before. [because]

    He wanted to give up gracefully, but he didn't know how because he had never done it before.

They can play the role of adjectives.

Example:

3. The lecture gave him something ∧ .

        It was *to think about*.

    The lecture gave him something to think about.

And they can be adverbs expressing intention or purpose.

Example:

4. The man was desperate ∧ .

        He had *to have a job*.

    The man was desperate to have a job.

When you are revising, think about using infinitives to make your sentences more compact.

Example:

    She hopes that she can sail next week.

    She hopes *to sail* next week.

You can also use infinitives to express more clearly the relationship between ideas.

Example:

    You want to live longer. You should eat nutritious foods.

    To live longer, you should eat nutritious foods.

Finish the following exercise.   EXERCISE

1.   ∧ They need a ∧ map.

        They want *to drive to Florida*. [,]

        It should be a *good* one.

  [; unfortunately,]

  They can't find one.

  _____

  _____

2.   He has several decisions ∧ ∧ .

        He wants *to make* them.

        He can take a vacation. [before]

  _____

  _____

3.   She taught her sons ∧ .

        They learned *to be self-reliant*.

  [, and]

  They thanked her for it ∧ .

        They grew up. [when]

  _____

  _____

4.   Helen needs help ∧ .

She wants *to graduate*.
[, but]
She can't admit it.

_____

_____

5. The prisoner was crazy ∧ ∧ .
        He wanted *to take the chance*.
        He tried to *threaten a guard*. [and]

_____

_____

6. He will have _____ ∧ .
        It is *to fight hard*.
        He hopes *to win the election*.

_____

_____

7. He came to the funeral ∧ .
        It was *to see his ex-wife*.
    [, but]
    She refused _____ .
        She didn't want *to talk to him*.

_____

_____

8. ∧ He decided _____ .
        He was fighting for his political life. [because]
        It was *to tell the truth about the scandal*.

_____

_____

9. _____ would be difficult.
        It was *to leave his job*.
    [; however,]
    He truly had no other choice.

_____

_____

10. The doctor ∧ is away ∧ .
       She is the one *to notify in an emergency.*
       This is *for the entire summer.*
   [, but]
  She calls in ∧ .
       She does it *at least twice a day.*

_____

_____

   Write five sentences using infinitives. Be sure to make the infinitives   **EXERCISE**
fulfill different functions in each of your sentences.

1. _____

_____

2. _____

_____

3. _____

_____

4. _____

_____

5. _____

_____

PATTERN 14

   Pattern 14 concentrates on noun clauses introduced by such words as
who, whoever, which, where, whether, when, and *why.* Previously, many
of these words introduced clauses functioning as adjectives:

   The man *who brags about his achievements* probably has an
   inferiority complex.

or as adverbs:

   When the dog is housebroken, it can stay inside.

That is not their function here, however. In this pattern, words such as
who, why, and *which* introduce clauses functioning as nouns.

Example:
1. The question is ———— ∧ .

    He will divorce her. [whether]

    She has supported him for years. [after]

    The question is whether he will divorce her after she has supported
    him for years.

2. ———— is obvious ∧ .

    Who will win the election?

    It is obvious *to anyone with experience.*

    Who will win the election is obvious to anyone with experience.

Complete the following exercise.   EXERCISE

1. I do not know ———— .

    He received a suspended sentence. [why]
    [, but]
    He did.
    [and]
    It isn't fair.

    _____

    _____

2. ———— will be sorry.

    Whoever said that?

    _____

    _____

3. ∧ I do not know ———— .

    He doesn't get another one soon. [if,]

    He will survive the loss of his job. [how]

    _____

    _____

4. ———— is anyone's guess.

    Where will he go from here?

————————————————————————

————————————————————————

5. Diane did not know ———— ∧ .
    She could raise the question. [when]
    This was *without inviting trouble.*

————————————————————————

————————————————————————

6. The police know ———— .
    They can find the burglar ∧ . [where]
        The burglar *robbed every house on the block.* [who]

————————————————————————

————————————————————————

7. His smile told her ———— .
    She wanted to know ∧ . [what]
        This was *about his situation at home.*

————————————————————————

————————————————————————

8. David wondered ———— .
    He could recoup his gambling losses. [how]

————————————————————————

————————————————————————

9. ———— remained a mystery to everyone ∧ .
    They survived the blast. [how]
    Everyone *saw the shattered building.* [who]

————————————————————————

————————————————————————

10. ———— probably needs ∧ ∧ .
    Someone *wants to join a cult.* [whoever]
    It is *to see a psychiatrist.*
    This should come *before making that decision.*

————————————————————————

————————————————————————

Write five sentences using a noun clause introduced by any one of the   EXERCISE
words listed in Pattern 14. Be sure that the clauses play different roles
in each of your sentences.

1. _____

_____

2. _____

_____

3. _____

_____

4. _____

_____

5. _____

_____

CHAPTER 9

Research and Writing

Most of the assignments in this text have not required you to use outside sources. But as you may already know, some of your instructors will ask you to write a research or "term" paper. In order to fulfill such assignments, you will have to collect, analyze, and use the work of other writers. However, using outside sources does not mean you are writing a paper that is totally different from the ones you normally write. In fact, everything you have learned so far applies when you write a research paper.

Let us approach the preparation of the research paper by thinking of the persuasive essay you wrote for Chapter 8 as an "exploratory" or "working" paper. At this moment your paper presents what you consider an effective solution to a current social problem. But it has not yet been tested through reference to outside sources. This is the time, then, to use your research as a way of enlarging, enchancing, or even contradicting your original ideas. To illustrate how you can use your exploratory essay to develop a research paper, Chapter 9 traces one student's progress as he moved from a persuasive essay to a final research paper.

As you will discover in your college career, research can take many different forms—interviews, laboratory observation, and case studies, for example. However, this chapter has been written primarily for the beginning or novice researcher. Because most research done at this level takes place in the library, the chapter focuses on exploring and using material available in your campus library.

The Function of the Exploratory Essay

The exploratory essay that follows was written by a student named Pat Fresa. In this essay, Pat argues that parental violence can be better controlled if the public will make an effort to understand rather than condemn such behavior. To write the essay, Pat drew only on what he already knew and had concluded about his topic from watching television and hearing people talk. That paper, then, became the stimulus for his research. It was a "stimulus" because it generated a series of questions that Pat could answer only by consulting outside sources:

1. Do other writers support my conclusion that we have to understand rather than condemn abusive parents?
2. If they agree with that conclusion, do they present the same premises in support of it? Or do they present others?
3. Do other writers disagree with my conclusion? What premises do they present in favor of their own conclusion?

What these questions suggest is that a research paper is not an exercise in simple information gathering, where you begin with a thesis and then amass support. At its best, research forces a writer to rethink, re-evaluate, and revise his or her original ideas. Thus you should use your exploratory paper as a starting point for the development of your thoughts; what you said in it may differ dramatically from what you say in your research paper.

Exploratory Essay   Pat Fresa

Given the sensational publicity surrounding the most horrible cases of child abuse, it is easy enough to view all abusive parents as monsters, as people undeserving of our pity or understanding. Better to punish them in some way, to hurt them as they have hurt their children. But such a reaction offers little hope for any positive solution to the problem of child abuse.

A better solution begins with a clearer understanding of the abusive parent's psychology. We have to understand, for example, that in the majority of cases, abusive parents are victims too.

Understanding that, we can begin to heal the parent and save the child.

In numerous cases, abusive parents were once abused children who learned two painful lessons. They learned, first of all, that violence was a natural and acceptable part of life. Second, they learned to hate themselves, to see themselves as worthless and evil human beings. As a result, they grew up and continued the same vicious cycle: They beat their children as they themselves were once beaten.

It is not that they consciously want to continue the cycle. But they cannot control their behavior. Filled with years of pent-up anger and frustration, they are like walking sticks of dynamite, ready to explode at a moment's notice.

In part, too, they see their children as a mirror of themselves. Like them, the children are bad and worthless beings who must be punished in order to become good. From this point of view, striking out at the children becomes yet another way for the parents to punish themselves.

Desperate to control behavior they consider despicable and disgusting, many abusive parents have begun to seek help. They have begun to make use of such associations as "Parents Anonymous" and "Parents United." Through a mixture of therapy and counseling, these associations help abusive parents control their violent impulses. Talking to a volunteer--often a volunteer with a similar history--these parents learn to wait out the dangerous moments and protect their children.

However, the parents' willingness to seek help and admit their crime depends a lot on their sense of being understood rather than insulted. If abusive parents feel they will only be treated with hatred and contempt, they will never admit their behavior. They will not seek the help they need. Emotionally satisfying as it may be to label the parents "monsters" who deserve to be punished, it does not help the abused child. It only serves to drive the parents underground and make them even more unwilling to tell the truth.

Similarly, solutions to child abuse that focus only on imprisoning the parents and separating them from their children do not effectively attack the problem. Instead, such solutions create a new set of problems. Imprisoning the parents frequently leaves the children wards of the state, free from abuse but lonely and isolated.

Although prison may be the only answer for the most severe cases of child abuse, it should not be used in all cases. A better solution is to provide the abusive parent with a source of therapy, counseling, and control. For it is only by healing the parents that we can offer the children any future at all.

Read over the essay you wrote in response to the assignment on page 260, and jot down two or three questions you hope to answer through your research.

EXERCISE 1

The Card Catalog

Unless your thesis concerns a topic so new that there has been little time for books about it to be published, the place to start is the card catalog of your school library. This is where you will begin what is called a "working bibliography," a collection of sources you will look at in order to decide what you will finally use. However, when you go to the card catalog, you should be aware that there are both an efficient way and an inefficient way to use it.

With the inefficient method, it is easy to get drowned in a sea of sources, write down every reference no matter how irrelevant, make repeated trips back and forth to the catalog, and quickly become so depressed you never want to hear the word *research* again.

Luckily there is a more efficient method as well. With this method, you do not even approach the catalog until you have a precise subject heading through which to locate your topic. For example, Pat was careful to use a specific subject heading such as "child abuse" rather than a general one such as "children" or "punishment."

Although you can simply use the specific topic of your paper as your subject heading much of the time, you might also check the *Library of Congress List of Subject Headings* or the *Sears List of Subject Headings* (depending on the classification system used by your library). Located in the reference section of the library, this resource will give you the headings used in the card catalog, along with appropriate cross references.

An efficient researcher knows full well that, most of the time, the card catalog contains more information than he will ever need for one research paper, particularly if the paper is to be written within a month or less.

Therefore, from the very beginning, he tries to sift out the essential sources from the less crucial ones. He tries to select only those titles that seem most relevant to his thesis. To use the card catalog effectively, a researcher should try to get an overview of the texts and authors considered essential in his field of research. There are several ways to discover that information.

1.   One way is to ask your instructor whether she knows one or two names of authors who have established themselves as experts in your area of research. You can also draw on other departments by asking professors or students who are knowledgeable in the area you are studying whether there are any established "classics" you should read. In this case "classics" are those books that are considered essential reading for a particular subject. They are the books to read if you want to begin with the most respected and well-known point of view.

2.   Of course, you do not want to look at the established classics only. You also want to have some idea of what has been published recently in your area of interest. *The Subject Guide to Books in Print* will give you that information. With this text as your guide, you will have a good idea of the most recent titles of texts that might help you in your research, and you will be able to look for them in the card catalog or order them through interlibrary loan.

3.   The index cards in the card catalog will alert you if a book contains a bibliography of sources cited or consulted. Look for at least two books that have such bibliographies. Find those books and leaf through their bibliographies. Look for names that appear more than once. Such repetition usually signifies that these are experts in the field, and you should record both their names and the titles of their works. Some books even contain what are called "annotated" bibliographies. These are bibliographies that briefly describe each source. Finding and reading one of them can give you a good idea about what books are particularly relevant to your thesis.

4.   Use the specialized encyclopedias contained in the reference section of the library. *The Encyclopedia of World Art, The Encyclopedia of the Social Sciences, The Encyclopedia of Education Research*—these are all examples of specialized encyclopedias containing articles on a wide range of topics. At the end of each article, you will usually find a bibliography listing classic sources on the subject.

5.   Be aware too that there may be book-length bibliographies you can use. Such bibliographies list the standard sources a researcher should consult when dealing with a particular topic. Usually they are listed in the card catalog, but you can also double-check with the librarian.

Obviously, having a tentative thesis based on the essay you have already written will also help you sift out the relevant from the irrelevant sources. For example, Pat knew he was looking for information about what causes parents to become abusive. Therefore he could safely ignore those titles that seemed too far away from his thesis. For example, he did not bother to write down titles that seemed specifically concerned with state laws attempting to control child abuse.

Here again, however, you should be prepared for the possibility that your thesis might change dramatically as you do your research. You may find out that what you originally thought about a subject simply does not hold up once you have more facts at your disposal.

For example, one student, Eva Fasano, wrote a very interesting essay about Joe Hill, an early labor leader who was tried, convicted, and executed for the crimes of robbery and murder. In her essay she argued that Hill had been unfairly treated. She had seen a movie to that effect, and she firmly believed that a great injustice had been done. Thus her research began with this tentative thesis: "Joe Hill was not executed for being a thief. He was executed because he was a dangerous and very effective labor organizer." But, after looking through the information available, she wrote a research paper that expressed a very different point of view: "The legend of Joe Hill as a martyr, like most legends, doesn't hold up very well under close examination."

MAKING NOTE CARDS

Once you finish going through the card catalog, what you should have in your hand is a collection of note cards or slips of paper with the names and titles of the books you need. Separate cards or slips have two important advantages over a continuous list:

1. Your final research paper must contain a list of sources you cited or consulted. That list must be in alphabetical order. When the time comes to make up your final list, you can easily alphabetize your note cards.
2. You can bring individual cards to the library to check sources.

That collection should also contain at least twice the number of books you will actually be able to read in the time allotted for your assignment. Having more titles in the beginning will save time in the end. Chances are that several of the books you have selected will not have information that you need. Therefore having more than you need to begin with will save you from repeated and unnecessary trips back to the catalog.

Here is the information from one of Pat Fresa's note cards:

362.7 D66 Dolan, Edward F. Child Abuse
New York, London and Toronto: Franklin Watts, 1980

As you can see, this information is quite detailed.

1. It lists a "call" number (362.7 D66). This number (or series of letters) is what you need to find where the book is located in the library.
2. It contains all the information about author, title, place, and year of publication.

Even at this stage of the bibliography, it is a good idea to get this information down accurately. Not only will you be sure to have all the information you need for your final bibliography of sources, but if you cannot find an important book and want the library to trace (search for a missing book) or recall (request another borrower to return a particular book), you will already have the information you need. You will not have to return to the card catalog.

In addition, if you compare the foregoing card with the list of sources accompanying Pat's research paper, you will see that the format is the same. Giving your note cards the correct format at this stage can save you time later on when you compile the final list of references. You can just eliminate those cards you didn't use, put the ones you did use into alphabetical order, and type up your bibliography from the cards. At the tentative bibliography stage, it is tempting just to scribble down, in any order, the bare essentials you need to find the book (the title and call number). But time spent here will save you time later.

SURVEYING SOURCES

Once you have a collection of note cards, your next step is to discover which books will actually be of use to you. Using the call numbers written on your cards, track each book down and survey it to determine whether it covers material relevant to your paper. In general, your survey should consist of the following steps:

1. Read the table of contents.
2. Read the preface or introduction.

3. Using some key words from your tentative thesis, check the index to see how many pages are devoted to your subject. In general, abandon books that devote only a page or two to your topic. However, be sure to try several versions of your topic. For example, Pat did not always find information listed under the title "children, abuse of." Sometimes he found what he needed under entries like "children, violence against" or "parental abuse." Again, the Library of Congress Subject Headings List will give you some alternative words or phrases.
4. If there is a bibliography, look through the titles cited to see if any of them focus on your area of research.

Use the card catalog of your library to find a selection of books you might be able to use in your research. Write down all the necessary information on 3-by-5 note cards.   **EXERCISE 2**

Find and survey the books you have selected. Remember to check with the librarian if the book you want is listed in the catalog but does not appear on the shelves. You can always trace or recall the book you are looking for. And if the book cannot be found, you can make use of interlibrary loan. That means your library can request to borrow the book you need from another library. So don't despair when a book you consider essential does not turn up. There are always ways of obtaining the book you need—provided you don't put off your research until the last minute.   **EXERCISE 3**

Using your survey, decide which books you will actually read. However, do not throw away the cards you think will be of no use. You might have a use for them later. Your ideas might change as you read, and the sources you do not want today may be the very ones you will need tomorrow. Put them aside for future reference.

Indexes for Periodicals

Once you have a list of books, the next step is to look at the indexes of periodicals available in your library. Indexes are books that list articles published about different subjects. Without an index, researchers would have to thumb through magazines issue by issue to find when and where their subject was discussed. Luckily, there is no reason for you to do that. Almost all established periodicals have been indexed.

As a novice researcher, the first index you should consult is the *Reader's*

Guide to Periodical Literature. Published by H.W. Wilson Company, the *Reader's Guide* lists articles written for the general public. The articles listed do not assume any specialized knowledge on the reader's part, and they can give you the information you will need to understand the more specialized journals that assume an audience with considerable background knowledge about the subjects they discuss.

The *Reader's Guide* is organized alphabetically, and you can unlock its secrets only if you have a specific subject heading in mind. For his research, Pat used the same heading he had used for the card catalog. Here are some of the titles he found:

Child abuse
>   *See also*
>   Child molesting
>   Shaken child syndrome

The child beaters and their critics [views of M. Disend on Moral Majority resistance to child abuse laws] *Natl Rev* 34:449 Ap 16 '82.

Clients who refer themselves to child protective services [Voluntary Intervention and Treatment Program in Erie, Pa.] D. DePanfilis, il *Child Today* 11:21–5 Mr/Ap '82.

The evolution of child abuse [behavior in humans and primates] W. Herbert. il *Sci News* 122:24–6 Jl 10 '82.

Fouling up [child abuse charges against California state senator J. Schmitz] pors *Time* 120:19 Ag 2 '82.

Help for the youngest victims [Crisis Nursery at Presbyterian Hospital, N.Y.] J. L. Lippert. *Health* 14:22 Mr '82.

Incidence of child abuse [study by the National Center on Child Abuse and Neglect] *Child Today* 11:27 Ja/F '82.

Kansas and the Children's Trust Fund. J. Glenn. il *Child Today* 11:21–2 My/Je '82.

Little house on the prairie [R. Luyendyk charged with child abuse in Cremona, Atla.] G. Legge. il por *Macleans* 95:18 D 20 '82.

Locating abused and neglected children in Israel. H. Zimrin. il *Child Today* 11:20–4 S/O '82.

Not guilty because of PMS? [Brooklyn, N.Y. case] A. Press. il *Newsweek* 100:111 N8 '82.

Our neglected kids. A. P. Sanoff. il *U.S. News World Rep.* 93:54–8, Ag 9 '82.

Although it may not look like it at first, each item in that list gives you all the information you need to find the article you want. Each item gives you the title of the article, the author, the place where it was published, the volume in which it appears, and the pages where it can be found:

Our neglected kids.	explicit or assumed title of the piece
A. P. Sanoff	author
il	the magazine is illustrated
U.S. News World Re.	an abbreviated title
93:	volume
54–8	pages
Ag 9 '82	year and month published

The entries in the *Reader's Guide* contain all the information you will need in order to find the article you want, so take that information down carefully. (The key to all abbreviations is in the opening pages of the *Reader's Guide*.)

That does not mean, however, that you should take down every entry you find under the appropriate heading. Even at this point in your research, you should be trying to sift out the essential from the nonessential. Although it is a good idea to start with more sources than you can use, there is no point in copying information that is obviously unrelated to your paper. It is difficult at this stage to be sure about what you need and what you do not, but you can use your exploratory essay to make some decisions.

For example, Pat's essay focused on child abuse in the United States. Therefore there was no point in copying down the reference about children in Israel, "Locating abused and neglected children in Israel."

For more specialized material, Pat looked next in the *Social Science Index*, again using the heading "child abuse." Set up much like the *Reader's Guide*, the *Social Science Index* differs primarily in the kind of material it covers. As you can see from the entries, the periodicals you will find here have been written for a more specialized audience.

Child abuse

Aggression, emotional maladjustment, and empathy in the abused child. G. Straker and R. S. Jacobson. bibl *Devel Psychol* 17:762–5 N '81.

Body-image of physically abused and normal adolescents. C. W.
    Hjorth and M. Harway. bibl *J Clin Psychol* 37:863–6 O '81.
Child abuse and neglect statutes: legal and clinical implications.
    M. J. Guyer. bibl *Am J Orthopsych* 52:73–81 Ja '82.
Child maltreatment: an overview with suggestions for intervention
    and research. H. D. Watkins and M. R. Bradbard. bibl *Fam
    Relat* 31:323–22 Jl '82.
Competency-based parent training program for child abusers.
    D. A. Wolfe and others. bibl *J Consult & Clin Psychol* 49:633–
    40 O '81.
Developmental approach to helping families at risk. J. B. Ruger
    and R. H. Wooten. *Soc Casework* 63:3–14 Ja '82.
Economic antecedents of child abuse and neglect. L. D. Steinberg
    and others. bibl *Child Devel* 52"975;85 S '81.
Empathy and stress: how they affect parental aggression. C. Le-
    tournear. *Soc Work* 26:383–9 S '81.
Experiencing child abuse: effects on emotional adjustment. E. M.
    Kinard. bibl *Am J Orthopsych* 52:82–91 Ja '82.
Familial correlates of selected types of child abuse and neglect.
    M. J. Martin and J. Walters. bibl *J Marr & Fam* 44:267–76
    My '82.
Family discipline, intimacy, and children's rights [dialog]. *Center
    Mag* 14:35–9 N/D '81.
Maternal personality and attitude in disturbances of child rearing.
    D. Brunnquell and others. bibl *Am J Orthopsych* 51:680–91
    O '81.
Social-cognitive development of abused children. R. M. Barahal
    and others. bibl *J. Consult & Clin Psychol* 49:508–16 Ag '81.
Treatment of child abuse: a review of the behavioral interventions.
    C. D. Isaacs. *J App Behav Anal* 15:273–9 Summ '82.

Like the *Reader's Guide*, the *Social Science Index* provides all the information
you need to locate an article in a journal. In addition, it notes which
articles include bibliographies (bibl).

Specialized indexes have certain limitations for anyone who is not an
expert in the particular field. But even here it is possible to do some
educated guessing to figure out which journals might be appropriate and
which might not. For example, Pat avoided journals where he could not
even decipher the titles, such as *The American Journal of Orthopsychiatry*.
Instead he chose journals with simpler titles like *Child Welfare* and *Family
Relations*.

Although you probably need to read some encyclopedia articles as well as some articles from the *Reader's Guide* before approaching the more specialized indexes, you will find this extra effort well worth your while. The indexes for the various disciplines will be invaluable tools in your research.

Using the periodical indexes available in your library, make cards for five to ten articles you think could be sources for your paper. Here is just a brief list of some of the indexes you can use to track down useful periodicals. If this list does not apply to you and you need more information, ask your librarian for help.

EXERCISE 4

1. *Art Index*
2. *Biography Index*
3. *Biological and Agricultural Index*
4. *Business Periodicals Index*
5. *Education Index*
6. *General Science Index*
7. *Index to Children's Poetry*
8. *Index to Fairy Tales*
9. *Index to Legal Periodicals*
10. *Index to Literature on the American Indian*
11. *Music Index*
12. *Short Story Index*
13. *Subject Index to Children's Magazines*

Indexes for Newspapers

You should also know that newspapers can be fruitful sources for research. And, like periodicals, they are organized into indexes. Fewer in number than indexes of periodicals, newspaper indexes can still help you find the articles you need quickly and efficiently. You might want to look at the *Wall Street Journal Index* or the *Subject Index of the Christian Science Monitor* as well, but *The New York Times Index* is often the most rewarding. It is widely distributed in libraries and has been indexed since 1851, when some of the entries were written by hand. Important, too, is the fact that entries contain story summaries. And you can usually tell whether the article will be useful to you just by reading the summary. Here, for example, is what Pat found under the heading "child abuse."

>   Susan S. Turner article reviews problem of child sexual abuse, particularly incest (M), Ap 5, XXII, 26:1
>
>   National Conference on Child Abuse and Neglect convenes, Milwaukee; child-care professionals charge Reagan Adm's proposed $1.2 billion cut in social-service programs will sharpy curtail fight against abuse; Anne Harris Cohn warns that states which have not developed specific programs will not be able to do so; James A. Harrel doubts future of Center on Child Abuse and Neglect, which he heads; his portrait (M), Ap 8, III, 1:3
>
>   Texas court rules evangelist Lester Roloff is not required to submit his church-run child-care homes to state inspection because he has now transferred ownership to his People's Baptist Church; 2-year-old dispute raised church-state issues (S), Ap 18, 6:6
>
>   Tech Sgt John Raaen 3d and his wife Jantee are found guilty of trying to sell their 7-month-old daughter for $2,000 last Nov (S), My 1, 12:5
>
>   Bran and Robbin Nisen of Moretown, VT, are charged with abusing NYC girl, Iona Brasier, who stayed with them in summer of '80 through Fresh Air Fund (S), My 14, 11, 11:1
>
>   Westchester County, NY, Domestic Violence Prosecution Unit has become national model as program which counsels perpetrators and victims of family violence; stress is on stopping patterns of abuse (M), My 17, XXII, 1:1

In addition to the summary of each story, entries in the *NYT Index* give you everything you need to know in order to locate the article you want. F 25,1:1, for example, means the story appeared on February 25 on page 1 and in column 1 of *The New York Times*.

Using the newspaper indexes available in your library, see whether you can find at least five newspaper articles pertinent to your research.   EXERCISE   5

Find and survey the articles you have selected for tentative research. For articles in periodicals, use the following steps: EXERCISE   6

1. Read the title and the subtitle.
2. Read the first two paragraphs.

3. Read all headings and skim any material that has been emphasized via italics, underlining, or illustration.
4. Read the first sentence of four or five paragraphs.
5. Read the last two paragraphs.

For articles in newspapers, read only the first two or three paragraphs. Articles in newspapers are set up so that the most essential information comes first. Therefore the first two or three paragraphs should tell you whether you can use the article.

Even though you have not yet thoroughly read any of the material you plan to use, you should still take a few minutes and ask yourself whether you have begun to find any information that confirms or contradicts your original thesis and your support for it. Read over your exploratory essay. In the margins write down any thought or fact you think might lead you to expand, revise, or eliminate your original statements. Remember: Research can prove that you were right all along. But it can just as easily prove you were wrong.

EXERCISE 7

Additional Library Resources

You should also be aware of some of the additional library resources that Pat did not use but that could prove useful in your research. For example, you might want to make use of sources that have been put into microform (reduced in size and put on pieces of film). Over the past forty years, a variety of newspapers, manuscripts, books, and letters have been put into some kind of microform, such as micro cards and microfilm. To find out what is available in microform, you can consult a number of different reference works, including the *Guide to Microforms in Print* and *Readex Microprint Publications*. Although materials in microform have to be read with special machines that enlarge the print, those machines are easy to use, and you should not be intimidated if you discover that some of the sources you want are in microform.

An increasing number of libraries have begun to use computers for the storage and retrieval of information, and you may even discover that the card catalog is "on line." What this means is that the contents of the catalog have been put into a data base. This is a collection of information compiled so that it can be searched by a computer. Instead of your going through the catalog card by card, the computer searches its data base and produces a list of books and periodicals containing the title, topic, or author you ask for.

Although the computerized catalog is a remarkable time-saving device, it is still in the early stages of development, and that can cause some minor problems. For example, the data base may not be complete, and some of the books that are actually in the library may not appear on the computer's screen.

You should also be aware that some libraries may have access to computerized versions of the major indexes, and you can use the computer to do a quick search of such reference works as *Resources in Education* and *Psychological Abstracts*. To use them, you have to give the computer a set of "descriptors" that identify key words in your tentative thesis. Using these descriptors, the computer searches the data base looking for articles containing those words. If your library does have an index or indexes in a data base, it will also have a listing of descriptors in current use. To get a better idea of what is available to you in this area, you may want to consult either the *Directory of Online Databases* or *Computer–Readable Databases—A Directory and Data Source Book*.

Taking
Notes

Once you have your sources, the next step is to start reading and taking notes. Again, there is an efficient and an inefficient way to do this. An inefficient student sits down with a book and reads and takes notes at the same time, jotting notes down on a pad of paper without any organization. After hours of work, he usually ends up with piles of notes that leave him more confused than anything else. To avoid such frustrating results, you should consider a more efficient method.

First get yourself several packages of index cards, approximately five by eight. However, do not start taking notes until you have finished reading either one entire article or one complete chapter. Without an overview of the article or chapter you are reading, you cannot reliably distinguish between major and minor points in the text. If you try to save time by taking notes at the same time you read, you are more than likely to write down points that are essential neither to the text nor to your paper. Once you have finished reading and have a grasp of the writer's controlling idea and the way he or she supports it, you can tell what is relevant to your paper and what is not.

When you are ready to take notes, use the following method of organization:

1. In the left-hand corner of a card, write down an abbreviated version of your source: Dolan, "Child Abuse," p. 46. When you look at the information on that card a week or a month later, you want to know where you got it.

2. In the right-hand corner, put a subject heading. Those subject headings should be developed from your original exploratory essay as well as from what you have learned through your research. Pat used these headings to organize his note cards:

--Distinctions among abusive parents

--Causes of abusive behavior

--Public attitude toward

--Rehabilitation of

--Media coverage of

--Case studies

--The cycle of abuse

3. Use one card to write a summary of the entire article or chapter. Remember, your goal is to reduce the material to about one quarter of its original length. As an illustration, here is the information from one of Pat's note cards. It summarizes a two-page article on child abuse.

Magnuson, "Child Abuse"   The Cycle of Abuse
Time, pp. 20–21.

   The article claims that child abuse is on the rise. In 1976 the American Humane Association reported 413,000 cases. This is compared with the 1981 figure of 851,000 cases.

   As the statistics rise, however, more is becoming known about the problem, and it has become clearer that there is a cycle involved: Abused children often become abusive adults. Still, the problem remains that the parents, despite their own past, do not know or cannot admit that they need help. And experts cannot agree about how to treat offenders.

You may also want to record some direct quotations. These should go on a second card. Giving quotations their own card takes some extra time. But it is usually worth it. The quotations will be easier to locate later on, and you will not overlook them because they are hidden on the back of a summary card. Like your summaries, the quotations should appear under the appropriate heading. In addition, it is a good idea to indicate where you think the quotation might be useful.

Although your research papers should not rely too heavily on direct quotations, it is sometimes necessary to use the author's exact words, and you do want to have them on file. For example:

> Magnuson, "Child Abuse"   Parent's Self-Hatred
>
> <u>Time</u>, p. 20
>
> "When you abuse your child, it seems like you're watching someone else. There is guilt, horror, and pain. Society need not hate us. We hate ourselves. No one hates an abusing parent more than the abusing parent." The words belong to a woman who had been an abused child and had become an abusive parent. Use for section on parental guilt and self-hatred.

No one can really tell you how to take notes. Everyone has his own individual system. However, the following guidelines may be helpful.

1. Summarize and condense the information you find. Do not rewrite the article or chapter.
2. Do not just record information. Use your notes to have a "dialog" with what you read. Ask yourself whether the author's ideas conform to what you have learned previously and whether they are well supported and documented. In particular, ask yourself whether your own ideas are being challenged or confirmed. Use your notes to take stock of what you are learning as you go along.
3. Give everything you record a specific source. You do not want to have the perfect quote for your paper but have to eliminate it because you have no idea where it came from.
4. Develop categories for all the information you gather.
5. Have a system for ordering your material so that you know which notes came from the same sources.

To be sure you are taking efficient notes, summarize one of the articles you are using for your research. Make a xerographic copy of the article and hand it in to your instructor along with your summary.

EXERCISE 8

Making Use of the Research

The previous section emphasized the importance of giving each note card a subject heading. These headings will allow you to sort and classify your notes into individual groups. It then becomes much easier to compare what you have learned from your research with what you originally said in your exploratory essay.

For example, using his essay on child abuse, Pat outlined what he initially thought on the subject. Then he went through his note cards point by point, jotting down differences and similarities between what he thought before doing his research and what he thought after. When he was finished, he could see clearly what sections of his paper needed to be changed, expanded, revised, or eliminated altogether. Here is his outline.

Exploratory Essay

1. To solve the problem of child abuse, we have to understand more about the parents' background and use that understanding to keep abuse from happening.

2. There are differences among parents.

3. Parents are abusive because they were victimized.

4. Contempt and disgust on the part of the public only aggravate an already dangerous situation.

5. Abusive parents want and need help.

Re-evaluation

1. With one exception, the experts agree.

2. Make distinctions more precise: "hard core," "malignant."

3. Enlarge definition of victimization; include isolation, deprivation as causes. Use Gil.

4. On this point, almost everyone agrees.

5. Revise. Some do, but the majority cannot admit they have a problem. Hard to treat them. Fontana argues that they don't admit it because of social stigma. (use)

Once you can make a rough outline of what you thought before beginning your research and what you think after conducting it, you can note those potential revisions on your original essay and start drafting your research paper. And you can do it piece by piece, section by section.

For example, as Pat's outline shows, his research gave him more precise ways to talk about the differences among abusive parents. Thus it was important that he revise the section where he discussed those differences. Here is a first rough draft of that section.

Americans may ... (keep as is). Unfortunately, when stories about child abuse make the papers, they are always the most monstrous and inexplicable kind, and we read about parents who hurt, torture, maim, even kill their own children. Given those stories, the ones that make headlines and sell papers, it is easy enough to react (look, view?) with disgust and hatred at abusive parents, to argue that they should be separated from their children and from society as well. But the media have not adequately represented the case of abusive parents. Failed to explain or spell out what most experts know: the fact that there are distinctions among abusive parents, important distinctions that cannot be ignored if we are ever to have insight into this terrifying social problem. Use direct quote from Gil here: "Physical abuse of children does not seem to be a 'major killer and maimer' of children, as it is claimed to be in sensational publicity in the mass media of communication. Such exaggerated claims reflect an emotional response to this destructive phenomenon which, understandably, touches sensitive spots." Follow here with Chase on severe and moderate abuse. Severe abuse is repeated and leaves visible results. Moderate abuse occurs when parents hurt children under stress. Severe abusers cannot be helped. Along the same lines, the psychiatrist P. D. Scott has argued against seeing all abusive parents as the same because, in his words, all other forms of deviant behavior have a "small hard core of subjects who are difficult to treat" and a much larger number who are "only peripherally involved with the behavior." For Scott, the crucial point is the need to distinguish between the two in order to separate the "malignant" cases from those that are less dangerous and

more readily treatable. End discussion of distinctions by
introducing thesis.

Working section by section like this through an exploratory essay to
expand, revise, or eliminate altogether what you first said is a very efficient
way of doing research. What you end up with are the pieces of a rough
draft that can be revised, shifted around, or discarded as new ideas occur
to you. Being able to shift the "pieces" is especially valuable. You will
be surprised at how readily connections between the separate parts come
to you as you arrange and rearrange them.

Make a list of the ideas you covered in your exploratory essay. Be sure   EXERCISE   9
to include not just the elements of your argument but your response to
objections as well. After you have organized your note cards into separate
piles based on your subject headings, read over each group. Make a list
of similarities and differences between your ideas before and after research.
Note: It is a very good idea to put those lists in parallel columns as Pat
did.

Read over your exploratory essay. Make notes in the margin indicating   EXERCISE   10
changes you need to make. Before you make your own notes, look at
the jottings Pat made on his paper.

Exploratory Essay

Given the sensational publicity surrounding the most horrible
cases of child abuse, it is easy enough to view all abusive parents
as monsters, as people undeserving of our pity or understanding.
Better to punish them in some way, to hurt them as they have
hurt their children. But such a reaction offers little hope for any
positive solution to the problem of child abuse.

> *Make distinctions
> clearer.*
>
> *Use terms like
> "hard core".*
>
> *Expand.*

A better solution begins with a clearer understanding of the
abusive parent's psychology. We have to understand, for example,
that in the majority of cases, abusive parents are (victims) too.
Understanding that, we can begin to heal the parent and save the
child.

> *Explain other kinds
> of victimization.*
>
> *Use for conclusion.*

In numerous cases, abusive parents were once abused children
who learned two painful lessons. They learned, first of all, that
violence was a natural and acceptable part of life. Second, they

> *give actual examples
> from case studies.*

learned to hate themselves, to see themselves as worthless and evil
human beings. As a result, they grew up and continued the same
vicious cycle: They beat their children as they themselves were   *Expand.*
once beaten.

It is not that they consciously want to continue the cycle. But
they cannot control their behavior. Filled with years of pent-up
anger and frustration, they are like walking sticks of dynamite,
ready to explode at a moment's notice.

In part, too, they see their children as a mirror of themselves.   *Explain more.*
Like them, the children are bad and worthless beings who must be
punished in order to become good. From this point of view,   *Use quotations to
striking out at the children becomes yet another way for the   illustrate.*
parents to punish themselves.   *add section on external problems,
                                                                          sickness, unemployment.*
Desperate to control behavior they consider despicable and
disgusting, many abusive parents have begun to seek help. They   *Revise: not true —
have begun to make use of such associations as "Parents   can't admit it.*
Anonymous" and "Parents United." Through a mixture of therapy
and counseling, these associations help abusive parents control
their violent impulses. Talking to a volunteer--often a volunteer
with a similar history--these parents learn to wait out the
dangerous moments and protect their children.   *add material about Colorado
                                                                          experiment.*
However, the parents' willingness to seek out help and admit
their crime depends a lot on their sense of being understood   *Quote expert opinion
rather than insulted. If abusive parents feel they will only be   in support.*
treated with hatred and contempt, they will never admit their
behavior. They will not seek the help they need. Emotionally   *Use Fontana's
satisfying as it may be to label the parents "monsters" who   story.*
deserve to be punished, it does not help the abused child. It only
serves to drive the parents underground and make them even
more unwilling to tell the truth.

Similarly, solutions to child abuse that focus only on
imprisoning the parents and separating them from their children
do not effectively attack the problem. Instead, such solutions create
a new set of problems. Imprisoning the parents frequently leaves
the children wards of the state, free from abuse but lonely and
isolated.

Although prison may be the only answer for the most severe
cases of child abuse, it should not be used in all cases. A better
solution is to provide the abusive parent with a source of therapy,
counseling, and control. For it is only by healing the parents that
we can offer the children any future at all.

Take the section of your essay that introduces your thesis. Rewrite it according to the findings that emerged from your research. Then systematically work through the supporting paragraphs. Enlarge, revise, or eliminate the ideas they contain. At this point do not spend time worrying about how the pieces fit together. You can figure that out by shifting them around as you draft.

You need not worry about including the exact text of your quotations either. Just indicate where they should go, as Pat did in his rough draft on pages 290–291.

EXERCISE   11

Make a rough outline of the way you think you want to present your thesis and support. Then assemble the pieces of your research paper on a desk or table, spreading them out horizontally. Read the sections through in that order, making notes in the margins about possible changes. When you are finished with the first reading, rearrange the pieces to reflect the changes mentioned in your notes. But don't reread the paper yet. Take a break for at least two hours—even an entire day. Then go back and read the paper again. When you find an order you like, cut and paste together a rough draft that you can hand in to your instructor.

EXERCISE   12

Paraphrasing and Quoting

For the most part, when you write a research paper you want to show your readers how your ideas affirm or contradict the ideas of others working in the same field. Consequently, you have no choice but to refer to the works of others. Unfortunately this creates a problem for some students, because they incorrectly assume that the only way to make such references is through direct quotation, and they produce a paper that looks as though they had done nothing more than cut out and paste together passages from the writings of other people.

To avoid giving this impression, a researcher has to learn the art of careful paraphrasing. When you paraphrase material, you try to restructure the sentences and change the language of the original version without altering the content. Paraphrasing allows you to refer to the work of others without turning your paper into a collection of unconnected quotations and competing voices.

For example, in this excerpt from his research paper, Pat has carefully paraphrased an idea taken from the work of David Gil, an expert in the field of child abuse. Although he cites Gil as his source, Pat has not chosen to use the author's exact words. Instead he has chosen to paraphrase.

> As David Gil has pointed out, abuse most frequently occurs
> where the parent has no other individual or authority figure
> available. By and large, abusive parents are without
> supporting friends or relatives who might help them control
> their behavior (28).

Here Pat is drawing on the following direct quotation: "The deterrent power of grandparents, religious or social authorities as an antidote is seldom available to the abusive parent." He chose to paraphrase rather than to quote his source because he did not want to overload his paper with too many direct quotations. However, as you can see, paraphrasing does not free a researcher from the responsibility of attribution. If you use another person's ideas, you must give him or her credit, even though you have changed the language in which the thought is expressed.

To become skillful at paraphrasing, you need to think about how you can change the language of your original quotation without altering its meaning. To do that, you should first consider where you can substitute synonyms or other verbal equivalents for the author's exact words. Second, see whether it is possible to divide or combine sentences. Finally, see whether you can reorder the sequence of thoughts without destroying their meaning. The following two passages are a good illustration. The first one is the original, the second one the paraphrased version.

> Politicians, real-estate agents, used-car salesmen, and advertising
> copy writers are expected to stretch facts in self-serving directions,
> but scientists who falsify their results are regarded by their peers
> as committing an inexcusable crime. Yet the sad fact is that the
> history of science swarms with cases of outright fakery and instances
> of scientists who unconsciously distorted their work by seeing it
> through the lens of passionately held beliefs.[1]

> For members of the scientific community, the distortion of
> research results is a crime. Although scientists, like most of
> us, may casually accept the idea that people in such fields as
> politics, advertising, and sales use the facts to serve their

---

[1] Martin Gardner, *Science: Good, Bad and Bogus* (New York: Avon Books, 1981) 123.

own self-interest, that acceptance does not extend to their
peers, who are expected to remain objective. However, despite
the threat of peer criticism and censure, the history of
science is filled with examples of scientists who have, both
consciously and unconsciously, forced their results to fit their
theoretical convictions.

In the second passage, words have been changed and sentences have
been restructured and reordered, but the essential message remains the
same: Like a host of other people, scientists have found it difficult simply
to report the facts without any distortion.

In general, when you write your research paper, you should rely more
on paraphrase than on direct quotation. Save your quotations for those
citations where the exact words are necessary—where your argument
depends not just on what was said but also on *how* it was said. As he
wrote the following passage, for example, Pat was convinced that a direct
quotation was absolutely essential to establishing the truth of his claim
that abusive parents punish their children as a means of punishing
themselves.

The cycle continues, too, because abusive parents find it
difficult to separate their own identity from that of their
child's. For many of them, the child is a mirror image of
themselves (Dolan 80). From this perspective, it is not
surprising that an abusive parent will be most harsh with
the child who bears a strong physical or emotional
resemblance. As one abusing mother expressed it, "He has all
my faults, and I have tried to beat all his other phobias and
problems out of him. I know it is not sensible, but I can't
control myself. I think he must be me, and I'm a combination
of my mother and father" (Brandt, 79).

Used sparingly, direct quotations are an important part of a research
paper. But the key word in that sentence is *sparingly*. When the pages
of your paper consist of little more than a collection of direct quotations,
your readers are bound to question how well you have really understood
the material you have collected.

Paraphrase the quoted material that appears in each item of this exercise.   EXERCISE   13
The first one has been done as an example.

ORIGINAL

George Orwell, in his essay, "Politics and the English Language," written shortly after the Second World War, observed that the whole tendency of modern prose was away from concreteness (and also in our time most political speech was the defense of the indefensible). Orwell's genius was for interpreting portents and what he foresaw was perhaps to grow even worse in America than in England.[2]

PARAPHRASE

George Orwell had a gift for predicting the future. Shortly after the Second World War, he pointed out that modern prose seemed to be shifting away from the concrete and specific and moving toward the vague and the abstract. (He also suggested that most political speech was used in the service of the indefensible.) That prediction has proved correct, and the tendency to avoid the concrete in favor of the abstract appears to have beome even more popular in America than it is in England.

1. Most of us, when we think about our memory, do so chiefly in a negative context. If memory works well, we take it for granted, as we do breathing; we notice it only when it fails us. But the attitude of most cognitive scientists is very different: they are deeply impressed by, and respectful of, what they have been discovering about both the size and the efficiency of the human memory system.[3]

2. Because of the strong kinship bonds of gorilla families, the capture of the young gorilla may involve the slaying of many of its familial groups, and certainly not every animal collected from the wild reaches its destination alive. Moreover, three times more gorillas have been taken from the wild than have been born in captivity, and gorilla deaths in confinement continue to outnumber gorilla births.[4]

3. The first and for a long time the only slave songs known to a wider public were the spirituals. This fact gives rise on occasion to the hastily drawn conclusion that the Negro was unusually religious. But the

[2] J. R. Pole, "The Language of American Presidents" *The State of the Language*, ed. Leonard Michaels and Christopher Ricks (Berkeley: U of California P, 1980) 425.
[3] Morton Hunt, *The Universe Within* (New York: Simon & Schuster, 1982) 85.
[4] Diane Fossey, *Gorillas in the Mist* (Boston: Houghton Mifflin, 1983) xvii.

religion of the African, which was based on the ancestor cult, represented for him something quite unlike the role allotted to religion by Western man. It was inseparable from his daily life, affecting and giving meaning to its every gesture. Thus the spirituals are not exclusively religious songs but must be considered as a body of documents dealing with slave life, just as the African chants often constituted historical narratives handed down by oral tradition.[5]

Documentation

Whenever you use outside sources in your writing, you need documentation. That is, you must tell your readers where you got your information.

HOW TO DOCUMENT

At one time the *MLA Handbook for Writers of Research Papers*, the standard reference manual used in composition and literature courses, specified a format for a within-text reference that looked like this:

> In *The Theatre and Its Double,* Antonin Artaud outlined his program for the theater of the future.[1]

with an endnote reference like this:

> [1]Antonin Artaud, *The Theatre and Its Double* (New York: Grove Press, Inc., 1958), p. 89.

However, that format has recently been revised. For the most part, sources are identified directly in the text. In what are called "parenthetical references," the author's name and the appropriate page number are incorporated into the text itself.:

> In *The Theatre and Its Double,* Antonin Artaud outlined his program for the theater of the future (89).

Here information about the source—author, title, and page number—appears within the text, and more complete bibliographical information

[5] Jean Wagner, *Black Poets* (Urbana: U of Illinois P, 1973) 26.

appears at the end of the paper under the heading "Works Cited" or "Works Consulted":

> Artaud, Antonin. *The Theatre and Its Double*. New York: Grove
>   Press, 1958.

The information you give at the end of your paper should provide your readers with the information they need to find the book or article for themselves. When you title your list "Work Cited," you list only the material explicitly mentioned in your paper. When you title it "Works Consulted," you list all the sources you looked at, even if you did not use them in your paper.

Although the research paper at the end of this chapter gives a detailed example of how to set up a final list of sources, you should know the three main divisions necessary. Whenever possible, you should include the author, the title, and the publication information, and you should separate each item by two spaces and a period:

> Berthoff, Warner. *The Ferment of Realism: American Literature,*
>   *1884–1919.* New York: Free Press, 1965.

In general it is a good idea to draw up your list of works cited just as you are ready to write your final draft. That way, as you include information from outside sources in your paper, you will have everything you need for the parenthetical references.

There is one important point you need to remember about the new MLA format: Whatever appears in the actual text of your paper does *not* have to appear in the parentheses also. Compare, for example, the following examples:

> The idea was not new; Sarah Orne Jewett had used it years
> before in *Country of the Pointed Firs* (135–140).

> The idea was not new; it had appeared years before in a little-
> known book called *Country of the Pointed Firs* (Jewett 135–140).

Endnotes have not completely disappeared, however. You can still use them to offer explanation or information that simply cannot be included in the text. When you read the sample research paper at the end of this chapter, you will see that Pat uses endnotes to cite a group of experts who share the same opinion. It would have been too complicated to try to cite more than one author within the text itself. But in general, you should rely as much as possible on parenthetical references.

WHAT TO DOCUMENT

Although the correct form for documentation is important, it is even more important to be able to answer two key questions: "What should you document?" and "Why?"

"Direct quotations" is the most obvious answer to the first question, and almost everyone knows that if you use someone's exact words, you need to acknowledge that fact. You must tell the reader that the words you are using are not your own. But paraphrased information also has to be documented. Putting ideas into your own words does not make them yours. You still have to identify the source of those ideas. Even tables, diagrams, and charts taken from outside sources have to be documented. They too are the product of somebody else's work.

However, you do not have to document information that is considered common knowledge. A difficult term to define adequately, *common knowledge* refers to facts about a subject that appear in a number of different sources and are widely available to a general audience through dictionaries and encyclopedias. Generally, biographical information such as a person's place of birth, number of years in school, and choice of occupation are considered common knowledge. Similarly, the dates and places of important historical events do not require documentation.

Much of the time, you can decide what facts or ideas can be treated as common knowledge simply by referring to some of your research sources. If several books or articles introduce the same facts in the same way without documentation, you can usually do the same. But if you have doubts about whether a fact or idea should be considered common knowledge, you would do well to provide the appropriate documentation.

It will be easier to decide what to document if you consider for a moment why you document. Basically, there are two reasons. The obvious one, of course, is that you do not want to plagiarize—to take credit for words or ideas that are not your own. But good documentation does not have to be seen simply as avoidance of plagiarism. It is a way of sharing ideas and telling your instructor or your fellow classmates where they can look if they are interested in pursuing the ideas presented in your paper.

Prepare your list of works cited or consulted and hand it in to your instructor so that he or she can see whether you are using the appropriate format.

EXERCISE   14

Revising the Research Paper

For the most part, you already know the questions you need to ask in order to revise your research paper. They are the same ones you used to revise the previous essays that you have written. However, preparing a paper written with the help of outside sources does force you to consider some additional points as you revise.

1.   The longer your paper is, the more chance there is for your readers to lose sight of your thesis and forget what conclusion you want them to come to after reading your paper. To avoid this problem, you need to remind them of your thesis periodically. See the model research paper that begins on page 301 for examples of how you can do this without being clumsy.

2.   Whenever possible, interpret your quotations so that your readers understand why they are there. That is, show how the quotations you include are related to what you say in your paper. Do not expect your quotations to explain themselves. Look at how carefully Pat has prepared the way for a direct quotation:

> If, however, public understanding does not take the place of
> public outrage, chances are that abusive parents will
> continue to hide and deny their shameful secret. This point is
> well made by Vincent Fontana in his book Somewhere a
> Child Is Crying, where he writes of a woman who struggled
> alone to stop her abusive behavior: " ... "

3.   Introduce your quotations as smoothly as you possibly can. Here is a poor lead-in:

> In the book Gorillas in the Mist, Diane Fossey details her
> years spent observing the great apes. "I deeply hope that I
> have done justice to the memories and observations
> accumulated over my years of research on what I consider to
> be the greatest of the great apes" (xviii).

Here is a better one:

> In her book <u>Gorillas in the Mist</u>, Diane Fossey details her
> years spent observing the great apes. Throughout the text
> one thing stands out: Fossey's respect and admiration for the
> object of her study. As she writes in the preface, "I deeply
> hope that I have done justice to the memories and
> observations accumulated over my years of research on what
> I consider to be the greatest of the great apes" (xviii).

4. Usually the use of outside sources further restricts the range of your voice. You are expected to maintain a certain distance between yourself and your readers. It is rare to find a writer who directly addresses her audience as "you" at the same time that she uses outside sources and footnotes.

When your first rough draft has been handed back to you, write a second draft that incorporates the revisions you and your instructor have decided on.

EXERCISE 15

When you think you are ready to hand in a final draft, use the points on pages 300 and 301 to help guide your revision.

EXERCISE 16

A Model
Research Paper

Read the following model research paper twice. The first time, ignore the explanatory notes. Read them the second time.

Pat Fresa
Professor Flemming
Composition 101
May 30, 1985

The Vicious Cycle of Child Abuse

1   Americans may deplore violent crimes, but they are seldom
shocked by them. Statistics on muggings and murders climb, and

we shake our heads in disgust rather than disbelief. One crime,
however, retains the capacity to shock and appall--the crime of
child abuse.

> Notice that your research paper does not require a separate title
> page, but your name, the instructor's name, the title, the date,
> and the name of the course should all appear on the first page.
> Your name should appear at the right, one inch from the top
> of the page, and you should double-space twice between the title
> and the first line of the paper. Do not put the title in quotation
> marks or underline it.

2   Public shock and outrage are understandable, however,
considering the stories that make headlines. They are always of
the most monstrous and inexplicable kind. And we read about
parents who hurt, torture, maim, and even kill their own children.
3   Given the stories that make headlines, it is easy enough to view
abusive parents with nothing more than repulsion and disgust, to
argue that they should be isolated from their children and from
society as well. Understandable as that response is, it is not
usually based on informed opinion. For the media have not always
adequately represented the parent's case.

> You should note here the way in which Pat has expanded the
> introduction to his thesis statement, to explain in more detail
> why the public feels such outrage about child abuse.

4   As most experts agree, important distinctions have to be made
among abusive parents. Very few are the murderous monsters of
newspaper headlines. If the public is ever to gain insight into this
terrifying social problem, we have to learn the difference between
the headlines and the reality. As David Gil argues in his book
Violence Against Children, which is considered a standard
reference work on the subject, the public must have a more
"balanced perspective" (134). That means we have to control our
outraged emotions and try to discover the facts behind the
sensational headlines. One such fact is that the majority of abusive
parents do not go so far as to maim or kill their children, no
matter what the headlines imply. As Gil writes:

Physical abuse of children does not seem to be a 'major killer
or maimer' of children as it is claimed to be in sensational
publicity in the mass media of communication. Such
exaggerated claims reflect an emotional response to this
destructive phenomenon which, understandably, touches
sensitive spots (138).

Unlike the first piece of quoted material, "balanced perspective,"
which can be integrated into the text, the second quotation must
be set off from the text. This is because it is more than four
typewritten lines long. Anything longer than four typewritten
lines must be set off from the text by triple-spacing. In addition,
it should be indented ten spaces from the left margin and double-
spaced. Such long quotations are usually introduced by a colon,
and they do not require any quotation marks.

Just as important as the form of the quotation is the reason for its existence in the first place. In other words, why did Pat choose to use a direct quotation in this paragraph? The answer is simple. Within the paragraph, Pat argues that expert opinion generally contradicts the sensational headlines. He claims that people who are knowledgeable about child abuse have not generally found the parents to be naturally vicious, insane, or murderous. To back up that statement, Pat identifies David Gil as a leading expert, and he gives Gil's qualifications: His book is a standard reference work. Then he cites Gil's exact words to confirm his own statements. Used this way, the quotation functions to persuade Pat's audience that his statements are both informed and accurate.

5   In a similar attempt to put the subject of abusive parents into a "balanced perspective," Naomi Feigelson Chase's book <u>A Child Is Being Beaten</u> emphasizes the need to distinguish between "severe" and "moderate" abuse. Moderate abuse occurs when a parent hurts a child under stress or duress. Severe abuse is consistent beating that leaves visible results. According to Chase, only the severe abusers cannot be helped, and they are not the majority (102–103).

Note here the way in which repetition of the phrase "balanced perspective" links this paragraph to the previous one.

6   Along the same lines, P. D. Scott, a psychiatrist specializing in the treatment of abusive parents, has argued against seeing all abusive parents as the same, because all other forms of deviant behavior have a "small hard core of subjects who are difficult to treat" and "a much larger number only peripherally involved with the behavior" (190). According to Scott, abusive parents can be divided between those only "peripherally involved" and those "malignant cases" that are all but untreatable (190).

Note here the transitional phrase *along the same lines*, which serves to link this paragraph with the previous one.

7   What expert opinion suggests, then, is that there are cases so "malignant" and "severe" that they cannot or will not be treated. But they are not the majority. The majority are those parents who never plan to hurt their children. They are parents whose actions

are not premeditated, and they are bitterly ashamed of what they do. Difficult as it may be to comprehend and accept, most abusive parents are victims too: They suffer from a past that has brutalized them either emotionally or physically, sometimes both. And in many cases, the present offers little improvement over the past. If we are ever to solve the problem of child abuse, we must understand its origins and learn to accept the fact that, in many cases, the parents are also victims.

> If you compare Pat's exploratory essay with his research paper, you will see that here he spends much more time making distinctions among abusive parents. This was one of the changes dictated by his research, because he discovered that almost every expert began by defining categories of abuse. He could not afford to dismiss their implicit suggestion that such distinctions had to be made. In addition, such careful distinctions help undercut the emotional response to child abuse, and clearly, to win over his audience, Pat needs to do precisely that. Note, too, how Pat develops his thesis. It has become far more specific and detailed than in the exploratory essay. He first gives a general statement of the thesis "Parents are victims too." Then he uses a colon to introduce a more specific version of the same idea, being careful to define what he means by the word *victims*. That restatement also tells the reader something about how the paper will develop: It will show how the parents suffer from both the past and the present. It is also important that this paragraph explains why the thesis is important: Increased understanding of the parents' victimization can help in the control of child abuse.

8   Although exact figures are not known, most experts in the field of child abuse consider the parents' own past a major source or origin for their abusive behavior.[1] In a very real way, they have been programmed to repeat on their children what they have learned from the adults who cared for them. This point is clearly made by the psychiatrist Brandt Steele in his article "Psychodynamic Factors in Child Abuse":

> Parents and others who maltreat the infants under their care are not haphazardly discharging destructive impulses in the form of abuse and neglect. They are following understandable

and predictable patterns of parent-child interactions that
have basically been determined by the way they themselves
were cared for in infancy (81–82).

Remember you can always use the old form of documentation
when you want to cite several different sources. This is what Pat
has done in order to document his claim that "most experts in
the field" consider the abusive parents' own unhappy past a source
of present violence.

9   In effect, then, the pattern learned in one generation repeats
itself in another as the abused child becomes the abusive adult.
This theme is stressed repeatedly in the literature on child abuse;
numerous case studies cite stories of abusive parents who were
themselves beaten or neglected as children. In one case study, a
father who had injured his baby daughter by slapping her too hard
had himself been severely beaten in childhood; his father had
disciplined him with pieces of lumber that amounted to wooden
clubs. In another, an abusive mother reported persistent and
severe beatings throughout her childhood. Over and over again, the
same pattern reappears with abusive parents doing to their
children what was earlier done to them.[2]

Here you see the same method of documentation used again,
as Pat tells his readers where they can find out more about the
"case studies" he cites.

10   Abusive parents continue the cycle not because they want to
punish their children but because they want to punish themselves.
Having learned as children that they were inadequate, no good,
even evil, they feel compelled to fulfill that prediction by doing
something they themselves consider contemptible and repulsive.
They hurt their own child. For example, one mother with a history
of child abuse reported how she felt when she hit her child: "I was
fulfilling my mother's predictions. I was no good, and I'd never be
any good." In her words, "No one hates an abusing parent more
than the abusing parent" (Magnuson 20).

Here the direct quotation provides proof that abusive parents do
feel the way Pat claims they do.

11   The cycle continues, too, because abusive parents find it difficult
to separate their own identity from that of their child. For many
of them, the child is a mirror image of themselves (Dolan 80).
From this perspective it is not surprising that an abusive parent
will be most harsh with the child that bears a strong physical or
emotional resemblance to him or her. As one abusing mother
explained it, "He has all my faults, and I have tried to beat all his
other phobias and problems out of him. I know it's not sensible,
but I can't control myself. I think he must be me, and I'm a
combination of my mother and father" (Brandt 79). As this
revealing remark suggests, abusing one's child can be seen as
another way to hurt and abuse oneself.

> Here is another case where a direct quotation offers proof of
> what has been said. Note too how Pat further interprets the quote
> for his readers.

12   But abusive parents are victimized by more than their past;
their present is frequently not much better. Perhaps more than
anything else, it is marked by profound isolation. As David Gil has
pointed out, abuse most often occurs where the parent has no
other individual or authority figure available (28–32). By and
large, abusive parents are without supportive friends or relatives.
They belong to no religious or social groups of any kind, and they
have no one to turn to when their behavior gets out of control.

> Note how this paragraph begins with a reference to the thesis.
> This kind of repetition is particularly important in a long paper
> where you should always remind the reader how new information
> supports your original point. This paragraph also illustrates why
> paraphrasing is essential to research.

13   The majority of abusive parents have no one to turn to for help
in facing stress that is external as well as internal. As Gil
explains in his study, child abuse appears to be linked to problems
such as prolonged unemployment, chronic illness, and substandard
housing (128). Poorly equipped to handle adult life in the first
place, abusive parents frequently face the additional stresses of
debt and disease. And they face them alone.

14   To argue, as I have done, that abusive parents are victims is not

to suggest that the shame of child abuse can be understood and
then dismissed or forgotten. On the contrary, to have any value at
all, such understanding of the parents' plight must have a larger
objective: It must help eliminate the crime of abuse. And, in fact,
understanding the parents' suffering can help in several ways.

> Here Pat has used *I* instead of *we*. The shift in pronouns is
> intentional. At first he used *we* to indicate a set of shared attitudes.
> But now Pat wants to emphasize that the conclusion of the paper
> is based on his individual research and interpretation. He is
> acknowledging that his audience may not be in immediate
> agreement.

15   First of all, public understanding can make it easier for abusive
parents to admit what they have done. For many such parents,
the admission that they have hurt their own children is all but
impossible to make. When accused of such behavior, they deny it
vehemently. Aware of how public opinion views their actions--as
monstrous and disgusting--they cannot admit, even to themselves,
what they have done.

> If you compare what Pat said in his original paper with what he
> says here, you will see a good example of how research has
> changed his mind. In his exploratory essay he claimed that abusive
> parents want and seek help. Here he says something quite different.

16   But if the public begins to understand the causes of most child
abuse, the parents involved may be more willing to seek help.
Aware that they are no longer branded as monsters but are viewed
as people suffering from an illness, they will find it easier to admit
what they have done. More will seek help and put a stop to their
abusive behavior. If public understanding does not take the place
of public outrage, however, the chances are that abusive parents
will continue to hide and deny their shameful secret.

17   This point is well made by Vincent Fontana in his book
<u>Somewhere a Child Is Crying</u>, where he writes of a woman who
struggled alone and in silence to stop her abusive behavior.
Fontana uses the woman's story to make two different points. He
is not only illustrating how desperately some parents struggle in
an effort to stop abusing their children. He is also showing how
afraid the woman was to admit the truth. Desperate to stop her

behavior, even to the point of thinking about suicide, she <u>still</u> couldn't tell anybody about it. As Fontana explains, her fear of public shame and stigma made her keep silent when she needed to speak: "Had we, those of us who cried out longest and loudest against the monstrosity of child abuse, branded her so deeply with her stigma that we had crowded her into her corner to be alone with her excessive shame?" (90).

18   As Fontana suggests, branding abusive parents does not encourage them to speak out about what they have done. If anything, it may encourage them to continue.

> Paragraphs 16, 17, and 18 are a good illustration of how one main idea can guide several paragraphs. The first of them introduces the idea that public understanding must replace public outrage. The second and third further develop the same point. This is a good example of the relationship between major and minor supporting paragraphs, which was discussed in Chapter 3.

19   The way in which an understanding of abusive parents' victimization can contribute to rehabilitation or cure is best illustrated by the work currently being done in a child abuse program at the University of Colorado. Here doctors Ray Helfer and Henry Kempe, who coined the term "battered child," have focused on the abusive parent's sense of being unloved and unlovable (Chase 108–109). To help alleviate that sense of self-hatred, the clinic provides "surrogate mothers." These are men and women available at all times to counsel and nurture abusive parents when they feel unable to cope. Believing that abusive parents suffer from the misery of their own childhood, Helfer and Kempe attempt, in part at least, to remake that childhood. To that end, "surrogate mothers" provide the support, respect, and care that was once denied.

> Note that the existence of such specialized clinics is documented. Compare this reference to the one that follows.

20   In addition to such clinics as the one sponsored by Helfer and Kempe in Colorado, the last ten years have seen the rise of more informal groups like "Parents Anonymous" and "Parents United." These groups offer the therapy and counseling that abusive parents need in order to control their violent impulses. Most

important, they provide telephone hotlines that parents can call
any time, day or night, when they feel out of control. Talking to a
volunteer--often a volunteer with a similarly abusive history--
parents can wait out the dangerous moments. They can protect
their children from any further harm.

> In this case Pat has not documented the existence of groups like
> "Parents Anonymous." He assumes that such groups have been
> advertised sufficiently and could be considered common knowledge.

21   But once again, the success of such groups or clinics depends on
the willingness of parents to ask for help. It depends, then, on a
public atmosphere that allows and encourages such admissions.
This atmosphere can exist only when the roots of abusive behavior
are better understood.

22   Solutions to child abuse that focus simply on isolating and
punishing the parents are short-sighted at best. They ignore the
fact that such methods often leave the children wards of the state,
free from the threat of abuse but still lonely and isolated. A better
solution is to focus on healing the parent along with the child.

Notes

[1] See Dolan: 80; Chase: 102–103; Scott: 195. For one of the few
opposing points of view, see Leishman: 22–25.

[2] See Silver, Dublin, and Lourie: 405–406. See also Steele: 51, 54,
and 62.

Works Consulted

Chase, Naomi Feigelson. A Child Is Being Beaten. New York: Holt,
    Rinehart and Winston, 1975.

> The authors' last names are listed flush with the left margin.
> When the entry takes more than one line, indent the second
> line five spaces. Double-space the entire list.

Curtis, G. C. "Violence Breeds Violence--Perhaps?" American
    Journal of Psychiatry 120 (1963):386–387.

> Remember to underline titles of periodicals, but use quotation
> marks for individual articles. If the article appears in a volume
> with continuous pagination, you do not need the issue number

of the individual journal. Just enter the number of the volume, the year, a colon, and the pages where the article can be found.

Dolan, Edward F. Child Abuse. New York, London and Toronto: Franklin Watts, 1980.

Fontana, Vincent. Somewhere a Child Is Crying. New York: Macmillan, 1973.

Gil, David G. Violence Against Children: Physical Child Abuse in the United States. Cambridge, Massachusetts: Harvard University Press, 1973.

Leishman, Katie. "Child Abuse: The Extent of the Damage." Atlantic Monthly (1983):22–32.

Magnuson, Ed. "Child Abuse: The Ultimate Betrayal." Time, 122 (1983):20–21.

Time is collected in volumes that are paged consecutively, so the number of the issue is not included.

Miller, Carolyn Clark. "Primary Prevention of Child Mistreatment: Meeting a National Need." Child Welfare, 60 No. 1 (1981): 11–23.

Here the articles are collected in the volume in separate issues and the pagination is not continuous. Therefore you need the issue number.

Schrier, Carol J. "Child Abuse--An Illness or a Crime? Child Welfare, 58, No. 4 (1979):237–244.

Scott, P. D. "The Psychiatrist's Viewpoint." In The Maltreatment of Children, ed. Selwyn M. Smith. Baltimore: University Park Press, 1978, 178–203.

Collections of articles require the name of the editor. If you use at least half of the articles in a collection, you can cite the entire book instead of the individual pieces.

Silver, Larry B., Dublin, Christina C., Lourie, Reginald S. "Does Violence Breed Violence? Contributions from a Study of the Child Abuse Syndrome." American Journal of Psychiatry, 126, (1969):404–407.

Steele, Brandt. "Psychodynamic Factors in Child Abuse." In The Battered Child (3rd edition), ed. C. Henry Kempe and Ray E. Helfer. Chicago: University of Chicago Press, 1980, 49–85.

In this assignment, you are to pick a famous or well-known person and write her or his biography. However, your paper should not become a simple list of dates and events. To make this paper successful, you must use the dates and events of your subject's life to illustrate a thesis.

For example, one student did a very interesting paper on the late Malcolm X. It was interesting because the student used the events of his subject's life to illustrate the following thesis:

Gene Coleman

In his biography, Malcolm X makes it clear that his visit to Mecca dramatically changed his ideas about how best to achieve racial equality. From that point on, Malcolm began to stress not the supremacy of one race over the other, but the equality of both.

Do not worry about being the only researcher to point out the significance of the particular events you describe in your paper. You probably will not be. But the way in which you select or eliminate details from the different accounts you read will give your paper your own original perspective.

GETTING STARTED

Write down the name of a famous person whose life you would like to know more about. That person can be from any field. Athlete or world leader, it does not matter. Whether the person is alive or dead does not matter either. However, you should make sure that you can find enough biographical information about your subject. You want, for example, to be able to read at least two different accounts of the same person's life. The following reference works should give you an idea of what has been written and should help you select an appropriate subject.

1. *Current Biography* contains fairly detailed biographical sketches as well as a short bibliography of further reading material.
2. *Biography Index* tells you where you can find biographical material in various periodicals.

3. *The McGraw-Hill Encyclopedia of World Biography* lists 5000 biographies along with bibliographies of materials.

4. *Encyclopaedia Britannica* concludes biographical articles with a bibliography of selected references.

5. Using your subject's name, you should also check the card catalog and the *Subject Guide to Books in Print*.

These references will give you more than the appropriate subject; they will also give you some idea of what names and titles to look for when you turn to the card catalog and appropriate indexes.

ORGANIZING

In the research paper you have already written for this chapter, you consulted outside sources in order to confirm or deny some idea you already had. This paper is slightly different in that you will probably begin reading equipped with little more than your admiration for the subject. But as you immerse yourself in that subject, ideas will come to you. It is important that you give yourself enough time to let that happen. Do not even *begin* thinking about your controlling idea until you have read at least one biography and several different articles. Only after you grasp the whole of a person's life can you begin to understand the significance of the parts.

Once you feel familiar with the details of your subject's life, you can start to look consciously for a focus. You might ask yourself, for example, whether your subject challenged or reversed traditional opinion or behavior in some way. One student used that question to produce this thesis:

Megan Donnelly

In his own unique way, Cole Porter made American music grow up. Intelligent, wealthy, and well-traveled, Porter refused to write the silly lyrics of his contemporaries. Instead, using the material of his life, he wrote lyrics that reflected his own wit, sophistication, and experience.

Or you might look for some crucial event or happening that changed your subject's life. This is obviously what another student did to discover the following thesis:

Jill Williams

For most of her youth, the nineteenth-century abolitionist
Harriet Tubman believed that slaveholders would some day
voluntarily give up the practice of slavery. But that belief
changed dramatically when she was injured by a blow to the
head. As she lay on her bed, half delirious and in pain, she
heard her owner demanding that she get up and go to work.
From that moment on, she lost all her illusions about
winning the hearts and minds of slaveholders. She knew that
if she got well, she was going to fight slavery, not wait for it
to end.

Once you have such a tentative thesis, you also have the key to organizing
your notes and drafting your paper. Your thesis tells you which parts of
your subject's life you want to emphasize or highlight.

REVISING

In addition to the suggestions for revision given throughout this chapter,
you should revise with the following point in mind: In this assignment,
you are interpreting a life, not recording it. You do not want to hand
in a paper that gives all dates and events equal emphasis. Instead you
want to select and stress those that illustrate or explain your thesis.

Suggestions for
Your Writer's Notebook

SUGGESTION 1

Write a paragraph explaining what you consider to be the hardest part of writing with outside sources.

SUGGESTION 2

Write a letter to someone famous whom you admire. To find the person's address, look in *The Address Book: How to Reach Anyone Who's Anyone* by Michael Levine. (Someone I know faithfully writes letters of appreciation to people of all kinds, and she almost always gets an answer. She even got a response from the lengendary actress Katherine Hepburn.)

SUGGESTION 3

If you have a taste for trivia, acquaint yourself with the many reference works available in your library and develop trivia questions to stump your friends. A few examples follow.

1. What is Pete Rose's nickname in the National League?
   (See *Current Biography*.)
2. Name three famous people who were born in 1882.
   (See *Who Was When*.)
3. Where did Geraldine Ferraro go to high school?
   (See *U.S. Congressional Directory*.)
4. When was Mickey Mouse born?
   (See *World Almanac and Book of Facts*.)
5. What *other* important things happened the day you were born?
   (See *The American Book of Days*.)

SUGGESTION 4

Pick some important current event and follow the way it is covered, for one week, in two different newspapers. Compare the two accounts each day, noting similarities and differences. At the end of the week, write your own account of the event, summing up the developments of seven days.

SUGGESTION 5

How would you interpret the following quotation from the writer Rudyard Kipling?

Words are, of course, the most powerful drug used by mankind.

SUGGESTION 6

According to an article in the *Writer's Digest* (March 1985, 24), the first hundred words of a novel are the most important: "From the first word of a story, you are on a countdown. If you haven't snared the reader by the time 100 words have passed, you lose the sale."

Read the first hundred words of two or three best-selling novels, and try to figure out *how* the authors have "snared" their readers.

Combining Sentences

This pattern will give you practice working with nominative absolutes. A nominative absolute consists of a noun or pronoun followed by a participle (occasionally by an adjective), and it modifies the sentence as a whole, rather than in part:

Example:

1. ∧ The referee announced their names ∧ .

> *The boxers* had *returned to their corners.* [~~had~~ + having + ,]
>
> He announced it *to the screaming crowd.*

The boxers having returned to their corners, the referee announced their names to the screaming crowds.

2. ∧ We were thoroughly exhausted ∧ .

> *Our trip* was *over.* [~~was~~ + ,]
>
> We were *crabby.* [and]

Our trip over, we were thoroughly exhausted and crabby.

Note: Nominative absolutes can appear anywhere in a sentence, but they should always be separated from the rest of the sentence by a comma.

Complete the following exercise. EXERCISE

1. ∧ The firemen left the house.

> *Their faces* were *lined with despair.* [~~were~~ + ,]
>
> [;] They had been unable to stop the blaze from spreading.

_____

_____

2. The woman sat at her desk ∧ ∧ .

> This was *until two o'clock in the morning.*
>
> *Her head* was *bowed over the pile of papers*
> *on her lap.* [~~was~~ + ,]

_____

_____

3. ∧ The doctors thought _____ ∧ .

317

All things were *considered.* [w̶e̶r̶e̶ + ,]
The prognosis was good. [that]
The patient would follow instructions. [if]

———————————————————————————————————

———————————————————————————————————

4.   ∧ The pirate looked ∧ at the spot ∧ .
        The map was *spread out in front of him.* [w̶a̶s̶ + ,]
        He looked *greedily.*
        The treasure was buried at the spot. [where]

———————————————————————————————————

———————————————————————————————————

5.   ∧ She still refused to come into the house ∧ .
        Her face ∧ was *wet with rain.* [w̶a̶s̶, w̶e̶r̶e̶ + ,]
           Her *clothes* were wet with rain. [and]
        This was *until her aunt had left.*

———————————————————————————————————

———————————————————————————————————

6.   We had our party outdoors ∧∧ .
        This was *after all.*
        The rain had *stopped* ∧ . [h̶a̶d̶ + having + ,]
           This was *shortly before five.*

———————————————————————————————————

———————————————————————————————————

7.   ∧ The monk sat on the bench ∧∧ .
        His eyes were *closed* ∧ . [w̶e̶r̶e̶ + ,]
           His hands were *folded.* [and]
        He sat *for over an hour.*
        He sat *without saying a word.*

———————————————————————————————————

———————————————————————————————————

8. ∧ The house was no longer habitable.
    The roof was *destroyed by fire.* [w̶a̶s̶ + having been + ,]
   [, and]
   The squatters had to go elsewhere.

   _____

   _____

9. ∧ The bird soared into the sky ∧ .
    His wings were *flapping.* [w̶e̶r̶e̶ + ,]
    He *disappeared from view.* [and]

   _____

   _____

10. ∧ The woman decided _____ ∧ .
    Her work had *become boring.* [h̶a̶d̶ + having + ,]
    She decided *to change careers.*
    It meant taking a cut in salary. [, even if]

   _____

   _____

Write five sentences imitating pattern 15. Be sure to use the nominative   EXERCISE
absolute at the beginning, middle, and end of your sentences.

1. _____

   _____

2. _____

   _____

3. _____

   _____

4. _____

   _____

5. _____

   _____

PATTERN 16

This pattern will give you practice in combining two or more of the previous patterns. It also focuses on the use of the indefinite pronoun *it*, when it is used to emphasize some portion of a sentence.

Example:

1. It is questionable ∧ ∧ .

> *The members of the jury can decide the case.* [whether]
> *They haven't received the proper information.* [when]

It is questionable whether the members of the jury can decide the case when they haven't received the proper information.

In the previous sentence, the use of *it* puts special emphasis on the questionable nature of the jury's decision. Compare, for example, this version without the *it*.

> Whether the members of the jury can decide the case when they haven't received the proper information is questionable.

Please complete the following exercise.   EXERCISE

1. It is obvious ∧ ∧ .

> *I can give up smoking.* [that]
> *I make the effort.* [if only]

_____

_____

2. It can be difficult ∧ ∧ .

> This is *to make a decision.*
> *You are not ready to do so.* [when]

_____

_____

3. It is unlikely ∧ ∧ .

> *She will change her mind.* [that]
> *What he says.* [because of]

_____

_____

4.   It is true ∧ .

      She was in jail for most of her youth. [that]

[, but]

She is a different person now ∧ .

      She has a family. [that]

_____

_____

5.   It is not clear ∧ ∧ .

      He would do that. [why]

      He clearly has nothing to gain. [when]

_____

_____

6.   It can be said ∧ ∧ .

      She was a writer. [that]

      The writer *suffered for her art.* [who]

_____

_____

7.   It is apparent ∧ ∧ .

      The witness is lying. [that]

      She wants *to cover up her own guilt.*

_____

_____

8.   It is John ∧ ∧ .

      I want to see. [whom]

      The meeting is over. [whenever]

_____

_____

9.   It was for this reason ∧ ∧ .

      I objected to his statements. [that]

      The statements *were totally untrue.* [, which]

_____

_____

10.   It was in London $_\wedge$.

   I met my first wife. [that]

   My first wife *divorced me after only six months of marriage.*
   [, who]

   _____

   _____

  Write five sentences using the indefinite *it* as it was used in the previous **EXERCISE**
sentences.

1. _____

 _____

2. _____

 _____

3. _____

 _____

4. _____

 _____

5. _____

 _____

Pointers for
Final Editing

The following pages outline and illustrate some basic points of grammar that you should consider when you edit your final draft. Because the explanations in this section use grammatical terms that have not been introduced previously, you may want to refer to the glossary that begins on page 352.

Sentence
Fragments

Sentence fragments are parts or pieces of sentences punctuated as though they were whole sentences. Occasionally a writer may consciously use a sentence fragment for dramatic effect or emphasis, but most fragments are a result of haste rather than intent. When you are checking for fragments, you should always take the time to read your paper aloud, slowly. This will usually help you identify any fragments in your paper. Look, for example, at the following:

<blockquote>While he waited for the train.</blockquote>

This example is a dependent clause. Although it has a subject, "he," and a verb, "waited," it cannot stand alone and function as a sentence. Read it aloud and you will see that it does not provide the necessary sense of closure or completeness. You expect something to follow. That means you are dealing with a fragment rather than a complete sentence. To be revised, that fragment has to be joined to an independent clause. An independent clause can stand alone and function as a sentence.

> While he waited for the train, his briefcase was stolen.

Read the revised example aloud, and it is clear that you are dealing with a sentence, not a fragment. Unlike the dependent clause in the first example, it does *not* leave you with a sense of unfulfilled expectation and is therefore a complete sentence.

To edit for fragments with greatest efficiency, you should be aware of some typical grammatical constructions that are frequently taken for whole sentences but are, in fact, only partial ones.

1.   Watch out for dependent clauses beginning with any of the following pronouns: *who, what, which,* and *that.* Dependent clauses beginning with these pronouns sometimes appear to be complete sentences.

> The committee finished all the paperwork within the hour. *Which was not an easy thing to do.*

2.   Watch out for dependent clauses beginning with subordinate conjunctions such as *when, if, because, while* and *once.* They look like sentences, but they do not provide the necessary sense of closure. That is why reading aloud and reading slowly are important.

> He will probably run for re-election. *When the time is right.*

3.   Participles and gerunds at the beginning or in the middle of a group of words can be misleading, making a fragment look like a complete sentence. Gerunds are particularly deceptive when they are preceded by a preposition. Again, reading aloud can help you avoid mistaking a participial phrase for a complete sentence.

> She decided to plead innocent. *All the while knowing her chances were slim.*
> She got her diploma all right. *By paying for it.*

Read each of the following sentences aloud and decide whether it is a fragment or a complete sentence. If it is a fragment, turn it into a complete sentence.   EXERCISE   1

1. They decided to get married. After having known one another for over ten years.

   _____

   _____

2. My best friend, who spent five years in Viet Nam, has never been the same since his return. Largely because of his horrible experiences in the war.

   _____

   _____

3. The point is this: The book contains pornographic passages. With no redeeming value whatsoever.

   _____

   _____

4. His argument is simple ignorance of the law. Which is just plain silly. That argument will not stand up in court.

   _____

   _____

5. All over the world it's the same thing. People killing themselves to get ahead and finding out it's not worth it.

   _____

   _____

6. Certain side effects are bound to occur. Whenever you take a drug. In some way, the drug has to alter your normal body chemistry.

   _____

   _____

7. Children must be encouraged to speak out if they feel threatened by sexual abuse. The old adage "Children should be seen and not heard" can have dangerous consequences.

   _____

   _____

8. His health has never been good. He suffers from migraines and dizzy spells. Ever since he had that accident.

   _____

   _____

9. The Shah of Iran was forced to abdicate. Once he knew the army would no longer support him.

   _____

   _____

10. In winter it is easy to give in to depression. Especially if you do not have the support of friends and family.

    _____

    _____

Fused or Run-On Sentences

   Fused sentences or *run-on sentences* occur when you join together two independent clauses without using the appropriate punctuation or conjunction.

   They think the volcano will erupt this year all the signs are there.

Although they are harder to identify than fragments, you can usually discover them by reading your paper aloud, slowly and carefully, before you hand it in. Most of the time you will be able to hear where one independent clause runs into or fuses with another. Although you can usually rewrite such sentences by adding a period at the point where they fuse, you should also consider some other possibilities:

1. Make one of the clauses dependent.
2. If one clause restates the other, add a colon or a semicolon.
3. Add a coordinate conjunction.

   When you are revising a run-on sentence, you should "play with the possibilities," for all will not be equally effective. For example, item 1 in the following list would be a good choice only if it were not preceded or followed by other short sentences. If it were, it would not be a good replacement for a run-on sentence.

RUN-ON:

> The fire in Philadelphia was a disaster it destroyed over fifty homes.

POSSIBLE REVISIONS:

1. The fire in Philadelphia was a disaster. It destroyed over fifty homes.
2. The fire in Philadelphia was a disaster, for it destroyed over fifty homes.
3. The fire in Philadelphia was a disaster; it destroyed over fifty homes.
4. The fire in Philadelphia was a disaster that destroyed over fifty homes.
5. The fire in Philadelphia was a disaster: It destroyed over fifty homes.

Read through the following exercise and identify any run-on or fused sentences. Correct the ones you discover.

EXERCISE 2

1. You asked me to testify I do not think that is my responsibility.

   _____

   _____

2. Parents are becoming alarmed about the level of violence in music videos they fear the effects it may have on their children.

   _____

   _____

3. Children no longer know what it means to be young at fifteen they are already thinking and acting like adults.

   _____

   _____

4. It is hard to understand how any adult can abuse a helpless child.

   _____

   _____

5. *The Breakfast Club*, featuring Molly Ringwald, was a big hit she was clearly one of the reasons for the film's success.

   _____

   _____

6. If you wait long enough, yesterday's fad is bound to become tomorrow's fashion.

   _____

   _____

7. For years the singer Karen Carpenter was a victim of anorexia nervosa eventually the disease took her life.

   _____

   _____

8. It is hard to believe that people with a lot of money have any problems when you are rich you seem to have everything.

   _____

   _____

9. After the spectacular success of *An Officer and a Gentleman*, Richard Gere was the hottest actor in Hollywood unfortunately he did not follow that success with another. After that film, he was in a string of box office flops.

   _____

   _____

10. In 1932 Amelia Earhart flew the Atlantic solo, a flight that made her famous what made her even more famous was her mysterious disappearance and no one knows what happened to her.

    _____

    _____

COMMA SPLICES

A *comma splice* is a particular kind of run-on sentence, where the writer has joined two independent clauses with a comma.

> The dog was devoted to the little girl, he followed her wherever she went.

For the most part, that is not one of the functions of a comma. Particularly in academic writing, the comma should not be used to join independent clauses, and you should rewrite any sentence that contains a comma splice. You can correct a comma splice in the same way you correct any other run-on sentence.

Read through the following sentences and correct any comma splices.   EXERCISE   3

1. During the terrible years of military rule, Argentina was a horrible place without any semblance of law and order, thousands of people disappeared never to be heard from again.

   _____

   _____

2. Even though doctors warn against tanning because it causes skin cancer, every year millions of people bake themselves in the sun's hot rays.

   _____

   _____

3. *Some Like It Hot* was a movie starring Marilyn Monroe, many people say it was her best film.

   _____

   _____

4. Although no one in the administration really wants the proposed tax reforms, government officials know that they must act as though they do or suffer the public's fury.

   _____

   _____

5. I eliminated salt from my diet, that made a big difference in my health.

   _____

   _____

6. High blood pressure is a silent killer, many people suffer from it without knowing they do.

   _____

   _____

7. Although research confirming the link between cigarette smoking and cancer continues to grow, the tobacco industry steadfastly maintains that there is no evidence for claims that smoking cigarettes causes cancer.

_____

_____

8. Without a high school diploma, you are practically condemned to jobs with long hours and low pay.

_____

_____

9. Athletes who use steroids are asking for trouble, nevertheless the practice continues in almost every sport.

_____

_____

10. Why is it that boxers never realize when it is time to quit, just how much punishment do they think the human body can take without permanent damage?

_____

_____

Pronoun
Case Forms

Pronouns have three different case forms: the nominative, the objective, and the possessive.

NOMINATIVE	OBJECTIVE	POSSESSIVE
I	me	my, mine
we	us	our, ours
who	whom	whose
you	you	your, yours
he/she	him/her	his
it	it	its
they	them	theirs

For the most part, your knowledge of the language will automatically lead you to choose the correct case of a pronoun. But there are a few times when you will have to know some rules.

1. If the pronoun functions as the subject of a clause, it must be in the nominative case.

> INCORRECT:
>
> The class president and *him* decided to attend the party.
>
> CORRECT:
>
> The class president and *he* decided to attend the party.

2. Pronouns following prepositions should be in the objective case.

> INCORRECT:
>
> Just between you and *I*, he is a fool.
>
> CORRECT:
>
> Just between you and *me*, he is a fool.

3. Comparative constructions using words such as *than* and *as* can use both nominative and objective forms of the pronoun. It all depends on what you want to express. You can test for the correct form by completing the sentence you have in mind.

> My teacher praised my friend more than _____. [*I* or *me?*].
>> My teacher praised my friend more than he praised *me*.
>> My teacher praised my friend more than *I* did.

4. A pronoun preceding and modifying a gerund should be in the possessive case.

> INCORRECT:
>
> I cannot tolerate *him* snoring for one more night.
>
> CORRECT:
>
> I cannot tolerate *his* snoring for one more night.

5. For purposes of conversation, very few people distinguish between the pronoun forms *who* (nominative case) and *whom* (objective case). But

in formal writing, the distinction between the two is still maintained, and more than one writer has puzzled over sentences like the following:

> The senator, (*who* or *whom?*) the council had decided to censure, quit before they could do it.
> The man (*who* or *whom?*) is most qualified will get the job.

To make the correct decision, you should remove the relative clause and rework it to see whether *he* (nominative case) or *him* (objective case) would sound appropriate.

> The council had decided to censure *he*.
> The council had decided to censure *him*.

Here *him* sounds correct, whereas *he* sounds more than a bit odd. This tells you that *whom*, rather than *who*, is the correct pronoun:

> The senator, whom the council had decided to censure, quit before they could do it.

You can use the same test for the second sentence as well.

> *He* is most qualified.
> *Him* is most qualified.

Here *he* sounds correct, whereas *him* does not. That tells you to use the pronoun *who*:

> The man *who* is most qualified will get the job.

Select the correct form of the pronoun.   EXERCISE 4

1. The player (*who* or *whom?*) they are all talking about has decided to quit the circuit.
2. I cannot stand (*him* or *his?*) lying one more minute.
3. The decision is between you and (*he* or *him?*), no one else.
4. The chairman and (*we* or *us?*) members have to take that chance.
5. The woman (*who* or *whom?*) won the money almost lost her mind with joy.

6. She is so much more qualified than (*he* or *him?*).
7. That wrestler is almost a foot taller than (*I* or *me?*).
8. The man to (*who* or *whom?*) they gave the award refused to accept it.
9. From (*who* or *whom?*) did you receive that letter?
10. How can you stand (*him* or *his?*) constant smoking?

Pronoun Reference

The pronouns you use should clearly refer to one antecedent. An *ambiguous or divided reference* occurs when a pronoun can refer to two or more possible antecedents. For example:

> After the trial was over, there was an argument in the outer office, where the judge accused the lawyer of wasting *his* time. But after ten minutes of shouting, the two were friends and colleagues again.

Here *his* can refer to either the judge or the lawyer. It is not absolutely clear which one is meant. Therefore the sentence should be rewritten to eliminate the ambiguous reference.

> After the trial was over, there was an argument in the outer office, where the judge told the lawyer *he* never should have wasted *his* time defending a man who was so obviously guilty. But after ten minutes of shouting, the two were friends and colleagues again.

Indefinite reference occurs when you do not provide a clear antecedent for your pronoun. For example:

INDEFINITE REFERENCE:
In that part of the world, the inhabitants eat large quantities of fatty food, and *it* causes not just weight gain but heart disease as well.

REVISED:
In that part of the world, the inhabitants eat large quantities of fatty food. Unfortunately, the *heavy consumption of fat* causes both weight gain and heart disease.

Pronouns such as *which, this, it,* and *that* are often used to refer not just to one noun but to the idea of an entire sentence or clause. This is called *broad reference.* There is nothing wrong with this kind of reference as long as the antecedent is completely clear.

CORRECT BROAD REFERENCE:

Every time the judge pronounced a life sentence, he seemed to take pleasure in *it.*

FAULTY BROAD REFERENCE:

Students at the local university have decided to evaluate their teachers. But more than that, they intend to publish the evaluations in the school newspaper. *This* has caused a lot of controversy in the community.

REVISED:

Students at the local university have decided to evaluate their teachers. But even more important, they intend to publish the evaluations in the school newspaper. Although everyone agrees that the evaluations are a good idea, most teachers believe that the evaluations should not be published, and the question of publication has caused an enormous controversy in the community.

Rewrite any sentences where the pronouns do not clearly refer to one antecedent.   EXERCISE 5

1. They told us that the film was based on actual events recorded in eyewitness testimony. But it was not accurate.

   _____

   _____

2. When I went to Hawaii, I could not believe their hostility toward American tourists.

   _____

   _____

3. I met my husband through a computerized dating service, and it was a disaster.

   _____

   _____

4. The paper reported that a prominent senator favored the lowering of the legal drinking age to sixteen. This is ridiculous.

_____

_____

5. When the lawyer interrogated the witness, he appeared nervous.

_____

_____

6. Many people like to read about criminals and crime. They are always on the best seller list.

_____

_____

7. In Los Angeles, they don't know the meaning of snow.

_____

_____

8. Chances are that he will work for an entire lifetime at that firm and then be fired before he can be given a pension. They are known for such practices, which have earned them the public's contempt.

_____

_____

9. My father was a good policeman, and he wants me to be one too. But their life is too difficult for me.

_____

_____

10. Impulse buying is a real problem because it drastically reduces your savings.

_____

_____

Pronoun Agreement

Pronouns must agree with their antecedents in gender, number, and person. For the most part, this presents no problem, and your knowledge of the language will prevent your writing a sentence like "The girls picked up his boots." However, there are three or four constructions where you may not automatically know which pronoun to choose.

1.   Although many writers outside the academic setting have begun to use a plural pronoun with such words as *everybody, each, everyone, no one, nobody,* and *either,* student writers are generally expected to use the singular pronoun: "Everybody has to make his or her own decision in this matter."

2.   The impersonal *one* takes the third person unless the style is extremely formal: "In a case like this, one simply has to follow his or her instincts." However, if your instructor prefers a very formal style, use the following form: "In a case like this, one has to follow one's instincts."

3.   Even if they are followed by a plural modifier, such words as *each, either,* and *neither* still take a singular pronoun. "Each of the men has decided to quit his job." "Either of the contestants could lose her chance simply by making one very small mistake."

4.   For years masculine pronouns were used to refer to groups wherein both men and women were included. Now, however, many writers are trying to avoid this practice by considering some other alternatives. Some writers alternate masculine and feminine pronouns, using the masculine in one paragraph, the feminine in another. Some use both together: "Nobody ever really forgets his or her first love." And sometimes it is possible to recast the sentence: "It is hard to forget your first love."

Rewrite any of the following sentences that do not show the correct agreement between pronoun and antecedent.

EXERCISE   6

1. Everyone has to make their own decision in this matter.

_____

_____

2. Neither of the men will give up his chance to win the lottery.

_____

_____

3. One has to put yourself in the author's place.

_____

_____

4. Everyone was doing their best to keep the ship afloat.

_____

_____

5. Either one may lose her job in the economic crunch.

_____

_____

6. As a visitor in a foreign country, it is important that one abide by the local customs. You shouldn't assume that the American way is the only way.

_____

_____

7. Everybody has to make their own decision in this matter.

_____

_____

8. Each employee demanded a 20 percent increase in their salary.

_____

_____

9. No one has the right to impose their views on the lives of other people.

_____

_____

10. Each student is expected to hand in a final project or else they will receive a failing grade.

_____

_____

Dangling and Misplaced Modifiers

Used correctly, modifiers can enrich and enlarge your sentences, providing both vividness and specificity. But used incorrectly, they can muddle your thoughts and confuse your reader.

To use modifiers effectively, you should be aware that where you place your modifiers is important. Placement affects meaning. For example:

> I hate incompetents *like my boss.*
> *Like my boss,* I hate incompetents.

Shifting the modifier "like my boss" makes a big difference in the meaning of the sentence. In the first sentence the writer openly insults his superior. In the second he curries favor.

Unlike misplaced modifiers, *dangling modifiers* have no subject to modify:

> *Giving the matter some thought,* it's clearly a problem for the experts, not the amateurs.

If you ask yourself *who* in this sentence is giving the matter some thought, the answer is no one. That phrase does not modify anything in the sentence. That is why it is said to be "dangling." It should be rewritten so that the phrase has a subject to modify:

> *After giving the matter some thought,* I think it is clearly a matter for the experts, not the amateurs.

Read through the following sentences and rewrite any of them that contain dangling or misplaced modifiers.   **EXERCISE 7**

1. Thinking about it for a time, it seems clear that the matter cannot be put off for more than twenty-four hours. We are, in fact, entering a crisis.

   _____

   _____

2. In this anthology the women I have selected were important contributors to early American realism like Rose Terry Cooke, Mary Wilkins Freeman, and Sarah Orne Jewett.

   _____

   _____

3. While he was playing in the street, the motorcycle hit the child.

   _____

   _____

4. Wounding the bear, my nerve failed me completely.

   _____

   _____

5. Having bought a paper, the newsboy directed the reporter to his hotel.

   _____

   _____

6. In the late afternoon, I saw birds of every size and color walking happily though the park and enjoying the first spring day.

   _____

   _____

7. Having serious financial problems, the author's novel had to be a best seller.

   _____

   _____

8. After taking the wrong turn in the road, the hotel was nowhere to be found.

   _____

   _____

9. Sitting on the rotted branch, I watched the beautiful red bird.

   _____

   _____

10. After taking our seats, the game was canceled because of rain.

   _____

   _____

Essential and Nonessential Adjective Clauses

In the sentence combining exercises, you were introduced to a variety of clauses used as adjectives — for example, "The man *who came to dinner* never left" and "Michael Jackson, whom I met at a party, is much shorter than I expected." Within those exercises, directions for adding commas were provided for you. You did not have to decide for yourself. However, adjective clauses can be divided into two categories, essential and nonessential, and which category they fall into determines whether a comma or commas are required.

An adjective clause is called *essential* when it is used to specify particular members of a larger group. (You may also have heard the term *restrictive* applied to such a clause.) The following sentence is a good example: "All students who receive an A on their final paper will be exempt from the final exam." Within this sentence, the writer is not referring to all students but only to those who receive an A on their final paper. In this case, the clause "who receive an A on their final paper" is essential. That means it requires no commas.

An adjective clause is called *nonessential* when it is not necessary for specific identification. (The term *nonrestrictive* is also used.) The following sentence is a good example: "Students, who are never happy about taking finals, can at least think about the vacation that follows." Here the writer is referring to all students in general, and the clause "who are never happy about taking finals" is not used to specify a particular group. It is not essential, so commas are required.

For the most part, you can distinguish between an essential and a nonessential adjective clause simply by removing the clause from the sentence. If the meaning of the sentence changes dramatically, you are dealing with an essential clause. If it does not, the clause is nonessential. Compare the following pairs of sentences.

All the students in school *who cheated on the exam* will be suspended.

All the students in school will be suspended. (Eliminating the clause radically changes the meaning of the sentence. Therefore the clause is essential.)

Water, *which is essential for all living things,* has to be conserved like any other important resource.

Water has to be conserved like any other important resource. (Eliminating the clause does not radically change the meaning of the sentence. Therefore the clause is nonessential.)

In addition to the above rules, you should know two other things as well: (1) Adjective clauses beginning with *that* are always considered essential. (2) Some clauses are essential or nonessential, depending on your intention. Either one of the following, for example, is correct. It all depends on your point of view.

> Children *who don't like sitting still for a long time* would hate that movie.
>
> Children, *who don't like sitting still for a long time*, would hate that movie.

Read through the following sentences and decide whether the adjective clauses require commas.

EXERCISE 8

1. My grandfather who is an octogenarian is as lively and frisky as a 30-year-old.
2. The first speaker who was very amusing managed to keep the audience from leaving.
3. In the movie *Mrs. Soffel*, Diane Keaton who gives a spectacular performance plays a woman who runs off with a convicted murderer.
4. Any woman who wants to play on the soccer team should apply at the next meeting.
5. The decision that made him so angry was made shortly after the committee met on Monday.
6. When the police who don't take kindly to wisecracks stop you for speeding, it is a good idea to be respectful.
7. Any couple who wants to buy the house should contact Mr. Edwards.
8. The crop that they planted last year was completely eaten by slugs.
9. That clinic which was almost destroyed by a fire will reopen within the year.
10. Dagwood Bread which has almost no nutritional value still tastes absolutely delicious.

Appositives

To punctuate appositives correctly, you need to distinguish between those that are essential and those that are not. In the following sentence, the appositive is essential because it identifies one particular novel among several. Because it is essential, no commas are necessary.

> Stephen King's novel *The Shining* was made into a movie.

However, in the following example, the author wrote only one novel, and the appositive is nonessential. Therefore commas are necessary.

> For years Henry Roth's novel, *Call It Sleep*, was a forgotten classic.

Add commas wherever necessary.   EXERCISE   9

1. James Joyce Ireland's greatest writer loved and hated his country.
2. The novel *Lucky Jim* is a wonderful tale of life in academia.
3. Paul's friend Ernest is a world-class body builder.
4. Zorah Neale Hurston perhaps the finest writer to emerge from the Harlem Renaissance is still relatively unknown.
5. Nathaniel Hawthorne's novel *The Scarlet Letter* is too complicated to be read by high school students.
6. Bill Cosby one of the funniest men in Hollywood is also one of the richest.
7. John McEnroe the best player in tennis today is also the most temperamental.
8. Nutrasweet an artificial sweetener similar to saccharine may not have been adequately tested before being put on the market.
9. Erica Jong's first novel *Fear of Flying* was an immediate best seller.
10. The sixties an era of extraordinary turmoil and experimentation produced little real change.

The Apostrophe

The apostrophe has three basic functions:

1. It indicates possession: "That is Paul's problem."
2. It signals an omission or deletion: "He just won't go."[1]

---

[1] Some teachers do not consider contractions appropriate for formal writing, and they will insist that you rewrite sentences like "They won't allow that action to be taken" to read "They will not allow that action to be taken."

3. It indicates the plural of letters or numbers: "You spell that word with two *s*'s."

For the most part, it is only the apostrophe indicating possession that gives writers any difficulty. But this function of the apostrophe will become clearer if you learn some basic rules.

1. To make singular forms of a noun possessive, add *'s*, unless they already have two *s*'s and two syllables: "the boss's desk" but "Moses' law."
2. If the plural form of a word ends in *s*, you need only add an apostrophe: "the workers' union" and "the travelers' society."
3. Plural forms that do not end in *s* or *z* require an *'s* to show possession: "children's stories" and "men's clothing."
4. Hyphenated words show possession only in the last word: "I lost my brother-in-law's coat."
5. Never use an apostrophe with the possessive pronouns *his, hers, its, ours, yours, theirs,* and *whose*.

Revise the following phrases to make correct use of the apostrophe. The first one has already been revised as an example.   EXERCISE   10

1. The surface of the grass
   The grass's surface

2. The cackling of the geese

   _____

3. The welcome of the heroes

   _____

4. The edge of the razor

   _____

5. The house of my brother-in-law

   _____

6. The works of Dickens

———————————————————————————

7. The preference of the gentlemen

———————————————————————————

8. The poetry of Yeats

———————————————————————————

9. The novels of Kingsley Amis

———————————————————————————

10. The lair of the foxes

———————————————————————————

Subject–Verb Agreement

Although most students know and apply the general rule governing subjects and verbs ("A verb should always agree in number and person with its subject"), certain grammatical constructions create persistent problems.

1. Prepositional phrases following a subject do not affect a singular subject; the subject still requires a singular verb.

CORRECT:

The *President* together with his advisors *was* at the meeting.

INCORRECT:

The *President* together with his advisors *were* at the meeting.

CORRECT:

One of the bats *has* been shot.

INCORRECT:

One of the bats *have* been shot.

2. When two singular subjects are joined by *or* or *nor*, the subject is still considered singular.

CORRECT:
Either the *dog* or the *cat has* to go.

INCORRECT:
Either the *dog* or the *cat have* to go.

3. When the word *or* or *nor* joins a singular and a plural subject, the verb agrees with the subject that is closest to it.

CORRECT:
Neither the *manager* nor his *assistants know* how to check the stock.

INCORRECT:
Neither the *manager* nor his *assistants knows* how to check the stock.

4. When the subject is a relative pronoun, the verb should agree with the antecedent of that pronoun.

CORRECT:
She is one of the *managers* who *refuse* to eat with their employees.

INCORRECT:
She is one of the *managers* who *refuses* to eat with her employees.

5. Collective nouns such as *jury, audience,* and *family* take a singular verb when individual members are considered as a unit. They take a plural verb when the members are considered individually.

The audience *was* delighted with the play.

The audience *were* at odds with one another about the merits of the play.

Correct any sentences in which the subject and verb do not agree.   EXERCISE   11

1. The captain as well as the team members were penalized by the commission.
2. One of the players who were asked about the use of drugs in sports got very angry at the question.
3. Either the President or his assistant are going to attend the funeral.
4. The jury have found him guilty.
5. My mother along with all her friends have been invited to join the soccer league.
6. Either the manager or his employees has to take responsibility.
7. The proud father with his daughters by his side were the center of attention.
8. The photos in the album reminds me of that pleasant time.
9. Neither David nor his brother were going to call her for a date.
10. A list of groceries were found in the parking lot.

Wordiness

Wordiness is a common problem in student writing. Worried about making their papers long enough, many students consciously or unconsciously "pad" their papers by using words or phrases that increase the length of their essays without increasing the level of information. One way to eliminate wordiness is to look for words or phrases that provide nothing more than needless repetition. The following sentence, for example, needs to be edited: "The plant had been built by the cooperative effort of many different people working together." In this sentence, *working together* does nothing more than repeat what was already said in the phrase *cooperative effort*. The sentence should be revised to read "The plant had been built by the cooperative effort of many different people."

You can also eliminate wordiness by being careful not to overuse verbs in the passive voice. If you find yourself relying too heavily on the passive, you should revise some of your sentences.

PASSIVE:
The winning touchdown *was thrown* by the second-string quarterback.

REVISED TO ACTIVE:
The second-string quarterback *threw* the winning touchdown.

Whenever possible, eliminate unnecessary prepositional phrases.

Wordy:

The arm *of the man* had been wrenched from its socket.

Revised:

The *man's* arm had been wrenched from its socket.

Wordy:

At *an early stage in his development*, he learned the value of hard work and self-discipline.

Revised:

Early in his development, he learned the value of hard work and self-discipline.

Rewrite the following sentences to eliminate unnecessary words.   EXERCISE   12

1. The author was asked to rewrite the essay over again.

   _____

   _____

2. The need for love is a universal longing felt by all people.

   _____

   _____

3. The play was in such bad shape that they decided to have a daily rehearsal every day for the next two weeks.

   _____

   _____

4. Jumping from the top of the bridge, the man landed on his two feet, brushed himself off, and jogged away from the scene of the crime.

   _____

   _____

5. The tiny, scared, little rabbit ran from the child, who was trying to catch him in a net.

   _____

   _____

6. He is really a unique individual; there are few people in the world like him.

_____

_____

7. The final examination was failed by the entire graduating class.

_____

_____

8. The wheel of the truck had been punctured by the glass in the road.

_____

_____

9. The condition of the man could not be commented upon by the hospital staff.

_____

_____

10. An immediate decision has to be made by us at this point in time.

_____

_____

Word Choice

Word choice is not something you should think about when you first begin drafting. However, the closer you come to a final paper, the more you should think about the words you choose to express your ideas. At this point, the following guidelines can be of help.

1. Do not try and impress your readers with inflated language that you think sounds important. This is a common mistake of many inexperienced writers, and it results in sentences like this one:

> The seal balanced the *spherical object* on his nose.
>
> REVISED:
> The seal balanced the *ball* on his nose.

2.   Remember that some words are appropriate for informal conversation but not for academic prose. The following sentence, for example, would not be appropriate for the essays described in this text:

> He is a writer who just keeps *cranking out* best sellers, one
> right after the other.

To be considered appropriate, this sentence would have to be revised to eliminate the phrase "cranking out":

> He is a writer who continuously produces best sellers, one
> right after the other.

3.   Be wary of using expressions that you have heard many times before. They may be considered "trite"; that means they are overused. Trite expressions should be avoided because they suggest that the person using them has not really bothered to discover the right or the appropriate words but has instead grasped the most obvious ones available. The following sentences contain trite expressions that detract from the ideas they convey:

> As Vice President, he was known for being *brutally honest.*
>
> As a young boy, the convicted murderer Wayne Williams
> was considered *a shining example* of industry and obedience.

Sentences like these should be revised to eliminate the overused words or phrases:

> As Vice-President he was known for his extreme honesty.
>
> As a young boy, the convicted murderer Wayne Williams
> was considered industrious and obedient.

4.   Pay attention to the connotations of the words you use. Connotations are the emotional or attitudinal associations words acquire through use, and they can contradict the dictionary or denotational meaning of words. Certain words can mean the same thing according to the dictionary, but their connotations can still be very different, and you have to be aware of the associations they carry with them. Compare, for example, the following sentences:

In the Greek tragedy *Antigone*, the heroine's *disobedience* leads to her death.

In the Greek Tragedy *Antigone*, the heroine's *naughtiness* leads to her death.

According to the dictionary, *naughtiness* and *disobedience* are synonyms for one another and can be used interchangeably. But in this case, they cannot. The word "naughtiness" does not fit the context of the sentence, where death is the result of misbehavior. Although naughty once meant "wicked" or "evil," over the years it has been consistently applied to the behavior of mischievous children. As a result it is associated with behavior that is silly or annoying but hardly tragic.

Read through the following sentences and revise any that do not reflect appropriate word choice.   EXERCISE   13

1. When the police entered the house where the murder had been committed, they were appalled by the scene they found. There was blood everywhere, and the house was a real mess.

   _____

   _____

2. Because he had bounced several checks in one month, bank officials were no longer willing to maintain his account.

   _____

   _____

3. It must be lamented that the consumption of alcoholic beverages accounts for so many fatal accidents.

   _____

   _____

4. After training of a month's duration, I hope to be able to utilize the computer with some skill.

   _____

   _____

5. Because he had been a real chubbette as a child, he still believed he was fat, despite the evidence of his scale.

   _____

   _____

6. Because he was so photogenic, they thought he might have a career on the silver screen.

   _____

   _____

7. The consumption of fresh fruits and vegetables is important for the maintenance of good health.

   _____

   _____

8. The drugs he was taking for his heart were affecting him mentally and his behavior was becoming increasingly goofy.

   _____

   _____

9. Looking as proud as a peacock, the returning veteran marched in the parade.

   _____

   _____

10. At the age of four, it was already clear that Mary Ann Evans was a budding genius.

    _____

    _____

Glossary of
Grammatical Terms

This is a glossary of terms you may encounter in your composition classes. Most of the terms are part of the explanation in this text. However, those that are not could well appear in comments on your papers, so you should learn all of the terms that have been defined.

active voice   A verb is said to be in the active voice when its subject performs the action described in a sentence: "The police *chased* the thief."

adjective   An adjective restricts, limits, or in some way changes the meaning of the noun or pronoun it modifies. It can appear before or after the word it modifies: "the *strong* wind" or "The bull is *strong*." Adjectives answer such questions as "Which one?" "What kind?" and "How many?"

adverb   An adverb modifies words other than nouns and pronouns; it provides information about time, place, manner, degree, or means. Adverbs can modify adjectives ("She was *very* tall), verbs ("She ran *quickly*"), other adverbs ("That was done *very* carefully"), and whole sentences ("*Luckily* the party was over when we arrived").

antecedent   The antecedent is the word or words to which a pronoun refers.

There is the *man* who was arrested for murder.

The *boy* wanted a job for the summer, but he just couldn't get one.

clause   A clause is a group of words containing a subject and a verb. There are two kinds of clauses, dependent or subordinate and independent or main. By itself, a dependent clause does not constitute a sentence: "Because he wanted to escape." An independent clause, however, can stand alone and function as a sentence: "The dog hated the postman."

collective noun   A collective noun is a noun naming a collection or group of individuals: *crowd, audience, majority, generation.*

conjunctions   Conjunctions make connections. *Coordinate* conjunctions (*and, but, or, nor, for, so,* and *yet*) connect elements of equal rank, as do the *correlative* conjunctions (*either . . . or, neither . . . nor,* and *not only . . . but also*). By contrast, the *subordinate* conjunctions such as *if, because, when,* and *where* connect dependent clauses to a main clause.

conjunctive adverbs   When preceded by a semicolon, conjunctive adverbs such as *however, moreover,* and *likewise* can link sentences together: "The movie is exciting; *however,* you should be prepared to be very scared while you watch it."

gerund   A gerund is a verb form ending in *-ing* and used as a noun: "*Jogging* on concrete is more dangerous than it is beneficial."

infinitive   The infinitive is the base form of a verb. In many cases the infinitive form of a verb follows the word *to:* "I hope *to go* to the moon one day." The infinitive form of a verb can be used as a noun, as it is in the previous sentence. It can also be used as an adjective ("Here are the questions *to consider* before the conference") or as an adverb ("She was anxious *to thank* him").

modifier   A modifier can consist of one word or of several. Its function is to further restrict or describe a word or group of words.

passive voice   A verb is said to be in the passive voice when its subject receives rather than initiates the action: "The child *was hit* by the truck."

participle   A participle is a verb form used as an adjective; "the *laughing* hyena," "*broken* blossoms," and "*faded* charms."

phrase   A phrase is a group of two or more related words lacking both subject and verb. There are several kinds of phrases.

☐ Prepositional: He went *through the woods.*
☐ Participial: The woman *leaving the room* is my wife.
☐ Gerund: *Washing dishes* is not my favorite activity.
☐ Infinitive: *To see Europe* was his dream.
☐ Verb: He *has been married* for over a year.

predicate   The predicate is the part of a sentence that makes a statement about the subject. The predicate consists of the verb and its modifiers.

principal parts   All verbs have three principal parts, or forms, from which the tenses are derived. The three principal parts are the present infinitive, the past tense, and the past participle.

pronoun   A pronoun is a word that stands for a noun. There are several categories of pronouns: personal (*I, you, he, she, it, we*); demonstrative (*this, that, these, those*); indefinite (*anyone, one, anybody*); interrogative (*who, whom*); reflexive (*himself, herself, themselves*); and relative (*who, whom, that*).

strong verb   A strong verb does not form its past tense and past participle by adding *-d* or *-ed* to the infinitive stem. The final pages of this glossary (pp. 355–358) list the three principal parts of some troublesome strong verbs (also called "irregular" verbs).

subject   The subject is the topic of a sentence; it is the person, place, or thing that the sentence discusses or describes.

tense   Tense refers to the system of form changes in verbs used to indicate sequence in time. Although linguists have identified over thirty different tenses in English, the following six tenses are considered the essential ones for formal prose.

THE SIX ESSENTIAL TENSES IN ENGLISH

1. Present   I drive a car.   The verb indicates
                                                       something done on
                                                       a recurring basis.

THE SIX ESSENTIAL TENSES IN ENGLISH

2. Past	I drove a car.	The verb indicates a completed action.
3. Future	I will drive a car.	The verb indicates an action that has not yet taken place.
4. Present perfect	I have driven a car.	(1) The verb indicates an action that took place at some indefinite point in the past. (2) The verb indicates an action beginning in the past but continuing into the present.
5. Past perfect	I had driven the car only two weeks before it broke down.	The verb describes an action completed prior to a second action.
6. Future perfect	By the time you finish reading this, I shall have driven to Boston and back.	The verb describes an action that will be completed before some definite point in the future.

weak verb   A weak verb (also called a "regular" verb) forms its past tense and its past participle by adding -d, -ed, or -t to the infinitive stem.

THE PRINCIPAL PARTS OF SOME TROUBLESOME STRONG VERBS

PRESENT	PAST	PAST PARTICIPLE
awake	awoke, awaked	awoke, awaked
become	became	become
begin	began	begun
bend	bent	bent
bite	bit	bitten
bleed	bled	bled
blow	blown	blown

THE PRINCIPAL PARTS OF SOME TROUBLESOME STRONG VERBS

PRESENT	PAST	PAST PARTICIPLE
break	broke	broken
bring	brought	brought
build	built	built
burn	burnt, burned	burned
burst	burst	burst
buy	bought	bought
catch	caught	caught
choose	chose	chosen
come	came	come
cost	cost	cost
cut	cut	cut
dig	dug	dug
dive	dove, dived	dived
do	did	done
draw	drew	drawn
dream	dreamt, dreamed	dreamt
drink	drank	drunk
drive	drove	driven
eat	ate	eaten
fall	fell	fallen
feed	fed	fed
feel	felt	felt
fight	fought	fought
find	found	found
fly	flew	flown
forget	forgot	forgotten
forgive	forgave	forgiven
freeze	froze	frozen
get	got	gotten
give	gave	given
go	went	gone
grow	grew	grown
have	had	had
hide	hid	hidden
hit	hit	hit
hold	held	held

THE PRINCIPAL PARTS OF SOME TROUBLESOME STRONG VERBS

PRESENT	PAST	PAST PARTICIPLE
hurt	hurt	hurt
keep	kept	kept
know	knew	known
lay	laid	laid
leave	left	left
lend	lent	lent
let	let	let
lie	lay	lain
light	lit, lighted	lit, lighted
load	loaded	loaded
lose	lost	lost
make	made	made
meant	meant	meant
meet	met	met
mistake	mistook	mistaken
pay	paid	paid
put	put	put
quit	quit	quit
read	read	read
ride	rode	ridden
ring	rang	rung
rise	rose	risen
run	ran	run
say	said	said
see	saw	seen
sell	sold	sold
send	sent	sent
shake	shook	shaken
shine	shone	shone
shoot	shot	shot
shrink	shrank	shrunk
shut	shut	shut
sing	sang	sung
sink	sank	sunk
sit	sat	sat
sleep	slept	slept

The Principal Parts of Some Troublesome Strong Verbs

Present	Past	Past Participle
slide	slid	slid
speak	spoke	spoken
spend	spent	spent
split	split	split
spread	spread	spread
spring	sprang	sprung
stand	stood	stood
steal	stole	stolen
stick	stuck	stuck
sting	stung	stung
strike	struck	struck
swim	swam	swum
sweep	swept	swept
swing	swung	swung
take	took	taken
teach	taught	taught
tear	tore	torn
tell	told	told
think	thought	thought
throw	threw	thrown
understand	understood	understood
wake	woke	waked
wear	wore	worn
win	won	won
withdraw	withdrew	withdrawn
withhold	withheld	withheld
write	wrote	written

COPYRIGHT PAGE CONTINUED

INDEX

Academic voice, 220–224
Active voice, 352
Addition, conjunctive adverbs expressing, 83
Adjective clauses
  essential, 339–341
  nonessential, 339–341
Adjectives, 352
  increasing the number of in single sentence, 40
  infinitives as, 265
  participle as, 235
  relative clauses as, 117–118
Adverbs, 352
  conjunctive, 79, 82–83, 353
  increasing the number of in single sentence, 40
  infinitives as, 265
Agreement
  pronouns and, 335–336
  subject-verb, 344–346
Ambiguous reference, pronouns and, 333
Andrews, Lori B., "Exhibit A: Language—Our
  Trials Are a Labyrinth of Words: How You
  Talk Is Often More Important Than What
  You Say," 190–191
Annotated bibliographies, for research paper, 276
Antecedent, 352–353
  pronouns agreeing with, 335–336
Anxiety about writing, writer's notebook relieving,
  7
Apostrophe, 342–343
  before gerund, 238
Appositives, 155–156, 341–342
  emphasis created by, 203
Argument
  analyzing, 246–248
  building, 244–246
  conclusions of, 245–248, 252
  overgeneralization and, 246–247
  premise of, 245–248, 252, 253–254, 256
  see also Persuasive essay

Associations
  brainstorming eliciting, 55
  jotting down in writer's notebook, 5–6
  words having, 263
Audience
  final draft considering, 65–66
  thesis paragraph considering, 50–51
  voice indicating respect for, 221
Authorial voice, 211–216

Background information, thesis paragraph for, 49
Bettelheim, Bruno, 113
Bibliography
  annotated, 276
  book-length, 276
  in books, 276
  note cards for, 277–278
  for research paper, 276
  sources for, *see* Library
  in specialized encyclopedias, 276
  working, 273, 278, *see also* Library
  "Works Cited," 297–298
Biography, writing a, 312–314
Biography Index, 312
Block method of comparison, 98, 100
Brainstorming
  for illustrations, 90
  for supporting paragraph, 53–55
Broad reference, pronouns and, 334
Brooke, Rupert, "The Great Lover," 38
Buffon, George, 148

Call number, 278
"Can Psychologists Tip the Scales of Justice?"
  (Gobert), 188–190
"Can Stress Be Good for You?" (Seliger), 129–
  130
Card catalog, 275–277
  on-line, 285–286

Cases of pronoun, *see* Pronouns

Causation, conjunctive adverbs expressing, 83
  see also Cause and effect

Cause and effect, as pattern of development, 94–97

"Challenging Darwin" (Ingber), 147

"Chocolate: Food of the Gods" (Young), 109–111

Chronological order
  as pattern of development, 90–93
  tracing historical development using, 108–111
  transitional markers signaling, 178

Clarification
  of academic voice, 222
  thesis paragraph for, 48–49, 50

Classification, as pattern of development, 101–106

Clauses, 353
  adjective, 339–341
  noun, 120, 268–269
  relative, 117–118
  subordinate, 152–153
  see also Dependent clauses; Independent clauses

Coherence, between sentences and paragraphs, 67
  see also Inferences; Parallelism; Repetition and reference; Transitional markers and sentences

Collecting ideas, in writer's notebook, 4–6

Collections of articles, in "Works Cited," 311

Collective noun, 353
  verb agreeing with, 345

Colloquial diction, academic voice avoiding, 222–223

Combining sentences, 40
  see also Sentence patterns

Commas
  adjective clauses and, 339–341
  with appositive, 156, 342
  nominative absolutes separated by, 317

Comma splices, 328–329

Common knowledge, documentation and, 299, 310

Comparative constructions, pronoun case for, 331

Comparing and contrasting, as pattern of development, 97–100

"Computer at the Wedding, The" (Sweetham), 196–197

Computer-Readable Databases—A Directory and Data Source Book, 286

"Computers" (Van Gelder), 195–196

Computers, libraries using, 285–286

Conclusion, of argument, 245–248, 252
  premise as relevant to, 247
  premise not restating, 248
  see also Final paragraph

Conjunctions, 353
  coordinate, 43–44, 353
  correlative, 206–207
  subordinate, 152, 324, 353

Conjunctive adverbs, 79, 82–83, 353

Connotations, word choice considering, 349–350

Consistency, voice maintaining, 223–224

Context, function of a transitional marker and, 179–180

Controlling idea, *see* Thesis

Conversations
  inventing, 200–202
  language studied by analyzing, 200

Coordinate conjunctions, 43–44, 353
  parts and whole sentences combined with, 43–44

Correlative conjunctions, 206–207

Cousins, Norman, *Taking Charge of Your Health*, 163, 164

Current Biography, 312

Current events, tracing for writer's notebook, 315

Dangling modifiers, 338

Debatable thesis, in persuasive essay, 242–243

Decentering, 22

Definitions, for chronological order, 92–93

Deletion, apostrophe for, 342

Demonstrative pronouns, 354

Dependent clause, 353
  as sentence fragment, 323–324

Description, discovery questions about, 24

Development, *see* Patterns of development

Diagramming
  for cause and effect, 96
  for chronological order, 91–92

Directness, of academic voice, 222

Direct objects, infinitives as, 265

Directory of Online Databases, 286

Direct quotations, *see* Quotations

Discovery questions, 23–25, 29–30

Discovery strategies, exploring, 32

Divided method of comparison, 98, 100

Division, *see* Classification

Documentation, in research paper, 297–300. 306, 309–111

Drafts
  for cause and effect, 96–97
  for chronological order, 91–92
  for classification, 105–106
  for comparing and contrasting, 100
  final, 65–71
  for illustration method, 88–89

rest between, 57–58, 62, 63
revising, 34
topic sentence considered in, 131
voice as a creation of, 221
writer's notebook analyzing, 6–12
see also Final draft; First draft; Second draft

Editing, *see* Final editing
Effect, discovery questions about, 24
see also Cause and effect
Emphasis
conjunctive adverbs expressing, 83
transitional markers signaling, 178
withholding appositive creating, 203
Encyclopaedia Britannica, 313
Encyclopedias, specialized, 276
Endnotes, 298–299, 310
Essential adjective clause, 339–341
Euphemisms, writer's notebook and, 13
Evaluation, composing, 228–231
Examples, *see* Illustrations
"Exhibit A: Language—Our Trials Are a Labyrinth of Words: How You Talk Is Often More Important Than What You Say" (Andrews), 190–191
Experiences, generalizations from, 28, 30
Explicit responses, language analyzed in terms of, 200
Exploratory essay, 273–275
for drafting research paper, 289–291, 305, 308
Expository essay, 16
Extended metaphors and similes, 198
"Eyewitnesses: Essential But Unreliable—Their Evidence Is Often Vital and Sometimes Unique, But It Can Also Be Misleading and Dangerous" (Loftus), 191–192

Fairy tales, writer's notebook and, 112–114
Final draft, 65–71
of persuasive essay, 257–258
Final editing, 68, 323–351
for apostrophe, 342–343
for appositives, 341–342
for comma splices, 328–329
for dangling and misplaced modifiers, 337–338
for essential and nonessential adjective clauses, 339–341
for pronoun agreement, 335–336
for pronoun case forms, 330–332
for pronoun reference, 333–334
for run-on sentences, 326–327
for sentence fragments, 323–324

for subject-verb agreement, 344–346
for word choice, 348–350
for wordiness, 346–347
see also Revising; Sentence patterns
Final paragraph (conclusion), 67–68
transitional markers signaling, 178–179
First draft, 56–58
analyzing, 58–62
of persuasive essay, 250–254
Focused free writing, tentative thesis statement formed by, 21–23, 28–30
Footnotes, 104
Formal voice, 212–213
Free writing
focused form, 21–23
section for in writer's notebook, 2–4
tentative thesis statement formed by, 21–23, 28–30
Fused sentences, 326–327
Future perfect tense, 355
Future tense, 355

Gardner, John, *Grendel*, 114
Generalizations, from experiences, 28, 30
Gerund, 238, 353
pronoun case used with, 331
Gerund phrase, 354
Gobert, James L., "Can Psychologists Tip the Scales of Justice?" 188–190
Grammar, *see* Final editing; Sentence patterns
"Great Lover, The" (Brooke), 38
Grendel (Gardner), 114
Grimm, Jakob and Wilhelm, 113–114
Guide to Microforms in Print, 285

Historical development, essay tracing, 108–111
Humor, voice achieving, 214–216

Ideas
collecting in writer's notebook, 4–6
controlling, *see* Thesis
transitional markers signaling addition of, 177–178
Identification, discovery questions about, 24
Illustrations
as pattern of development, 86–89
transitional markers signaling addition of, 177–178
Imitating other writers, in writer's notebook, 6, 232–233
Implicit responses, language analyzed in terms of, 200

Indefinite reference, pronouns and, 333
Indentation for a paragraph, 66–67
Independent clauses, 324, 353
  run-on sentence from, 326–327
  semicolon connecting, 76
Index cards, for notes, 286
Indexes, in library
  computerized, 286
  to newspapers, 283–284
  to periodicals, 279–283
I Never Told Anybody (Koch), 14
Inference, coherence achieved through limiting,
  167–172
  between paragraphs, 170–172
  information added for, 167–168
  proper placement of information for, 168–170
Infinitive, 265–266, 353
Infinitive phrase, 354
Informal voice, 211, 215–216
Ingber, Dina, "Challenging Darwin," 147
Instructor, thesis paragraph considering, 50–51
Instructor's comments
  analyzing, 51
  in writer's notebook, 7
Interrogative pronoun, 354
Introductory paragraph, 33
Irrelevant sentences, paragraph unity avoiding,
  138–141
It, to emphasize some portion of sentence, 320

Kipling, Rudyard, 316
Koch, Kenneth
  I Never Told Anybody, 14
  Sleeping on the Wing, 264
Koromvokis, Lygeri, "Mummy Autopsies," 245

Lanham, Richard, 116
Letters, practice in writing, 315
Library
  call number, 278
  card catalog in, 275–277, 285–286
  computers in, 285–286
  indexes to newspapers in, 283–284
  indexes to periodicals in, 279–283
  microform material in, 285
  on-line card catalog in, 285–286
Library of Congress List of Subject Headings, 275
Lists, in writer's notebook, 148–149
Literary montage, 35–37
Location, discovery questions about, 24
Loftus, Elizabeth F., "Eyewitnesses: Essential But
  Unreliable—Their Evidence Is Often Vital

and Sometimes Unique, But It Can Also Be
  Misleading and Dangerous," 191–192

*McGraw-Hill Encyclopedia of World Biography,
  The*, 313
Major supporting paragraphs, in research paper,
  309
Major supporting sentences, 138
  parallel form signaling relationship between,
  180–181
Maxims, writer's notebook and, 73
Metaphors, writer's notebook and, 115–116
  extended, 198
  verbs expressing, 150
Microform, library sources on, 285
Minor supporting paragraphs, in research paper,
  309
Minor supporting sentences, 138
  parallel form signaling relationship between,
  180
Misplaced modifiers, 337–338
MLA Handbook for Writers of Research Papers,
  297, 298
Modification, transitional markers signaling, 178
Modifiers, 353
  dangling and misplaced, 337–338
  see also Adjectives
Montage, literary, 35–37
Moss, Howard, 115
"Mummy Autopsies" (Koromvokis), 145
Music, writing inspired by, 264

New Diary, The (Rainer), 264
Newspapers, indexes to, 283–284
New York Times Index, 283–284
Nominative absolutes, 317
Nominative pronoun case, 330–332
Nonessential adjective clause, 339–341
Nonrestrictive adjective clause, *see* Nonessential
  adjective clause
Nor, subject-verb agreement and, 345
Note cards, for bibliography, 277–278
Notes, for revising first draft, 62, 63
Note taking, for research paper, 286–288
Noun clauses
  that linking, 120
  wh words introducing, 268–269
Nouns
  gerund as, 238
  infinitives as, 265
Nursery rhymes, writer's notebook and, 112–
  113

Objective pronoun case, 330–332
"Old Mother Hubbard," 112–113
Omission, apostrophe for, 342
One, third person with, 336
Or, subject-verb agreement and, 345
Organization, for writing process, 33–34
Origin, discovery questions about, 24
Outlining
   for chronological order, 91–92
   for summary, 144
   unity of essay determined by, 66
   for writing process, 33
Overgeneralization, argument and, 246–247

Paragraphs, 67, 124–141
   as effective guide to meaning, 66–67
   importance of, 124–128
   question beginning, 133
   as summary, 144
   supporting sentences in, 135–138, 180–181
   thesis developed in, 126, 128
   unity of, 128, 138–141
   see also Supporting paragraphs; Thesis paragraph; Topic sentence
Parallelism, coherence achieved through, 180–183
   between supporting sentences, 180–181
   within paragraphs, 181–183
Paraphrasing
   documentation and, 299
   in research paper, 293–295, 307
Parenthetical references, 297, 298, 299
   for research paper, 306
Participial phrase, 235, 354
   as sentence fragment, 324
Participles, 235, 353
Passive voice, 346, 353
Past, discovery questions about, 24
Past participle, 235
   of irregular verbs, 355–358
Past perfect tense, 355
Past tense, 355
   of irregular verbs, 355–358
Patterns of development, 86–111
   cause and effect, 94–97
   chronological order, 90–93
   classification, 101–106
   comparing and contrasting, 97–100
   illustrations, 86–89
Periodicals
   indexes to, 279–283, 286
   in "Works Cited," 310–311

Personal pronouns, confident tone of voice achieved with, 224, 354
Persuasive essay, 242–262
   anticipating opposition to, 249–250, 252, 254, 256–257
   argument analyzed for, 246–248
   argument built for, 244–246
   debatable thesis developed for, 242–243
   final draft of, 257–259
   first draft of, 250–254
   revising, 251–259
   second draft of, 255–257
   thesis statement of, 251–252, 252–253
   voice of, 252, 252–253, 255
   writing, 260–262
Phrases, 354
   gerund, 354
   infinitive, 354
   participial, 235, 324, 354
   prepositional, 344–345, 347, 354
   verb, 354
Place, discovery questions about, 24
Plural, apostrophe for, 342
Point-by-point method of comparison, 98, 100
Possession, apostrophe for, 342–343
Possessive pronoun case, 330, 331
Pound, Ezra, 263
Predicate, 354
Premise of an argument, 245–248, 252, 253–254, 256
   accurate information as basis for, 247–248
   conclusion not restating, 248
   as relevant to the conclusion, 247
Prepositional phrases, 354
   following a subject, 344–345
   wordiness and, 347
Present, discovery questions about, 24
Present infinitive, *see* Infinitive
Present perfect participle, 235
Present perfect tense, 355
Present tense, 354
   of irregular verbs, 355–358
Principal parts of verbs, 354, 355–358
   see also Infinitive; Past participle; Past tense
Principle of division, *see* Classification
Problem, exploring topic by defining, 26–27
Pronouns
   ambiguous or divided reference, 333
   antecedent agreement and, 335–336
   antecedent of, 352–353
   broad reference, 334
   demonstrative, 354

Pronouns continued
  indefinite reference, 333
  interrogative, 354
  masculine and feminine, 336
  nominative case, 330–332
  objective case, 330–332
  personal, 224, 354
  possessive case, 330, 331
  reference and, 333–334
  reflexive, 354
  relative, 345, 354
Psychological Abstracts, 286
Purpose, discovery questions about, 24

Qualifying statements, 221–222
Question
  discovery, 23–25, 29–30
  paragraph begun with, 133
Quotations
  documentation and, 299
  for note taking, 287–288
  in research paper, 295, 300–301, 303–304,
    306–307

Rainer, Tristine, *The New Diary*, 264
Reader, *see* Audience
Reader's Guide to Periodical Literature, 279–281
  for supporting paragraphs, 55
Readex Microprint Publications, 285
Reasons, transitional markers signaling addition of,
    177–178
Reference, pronouns and, 333–334
  see also Repetition and reference, coherence
    achieved through
References, for research paper, 306
  see also Documentation
Reflexive pronouns, 354
Relationships, transitional markers signaling, 178
Relative clauses, modification within a single sen-
    tence by, 117–118
Relative pronoun, 354
  subject as, 345
Repetition
  conjunctive adverbs expressing, 83
  transitional markers signaling, 178
Repetition and reference, coherence achieved
    through, 160–165
  between paragraphs, 162–165
  in subject position, 162
  of word in controlling idea, 161–162
Research paper, 272–315
  biography as, 312–314

documentation for, 297–300, 306, 309–311
endnotes for, 298–299, 310
exploratory essay for drafting, 289–291, 305
exploratory essay as starting point for, 273–275
model, 301–311
note taking for, 286–288
paraphrasing in, 293–295, 307
parenthetical references for, 297, 298, 299, 306
quotations in, 295, 300–301, 303–304, 306–
    307
revising, 300–301
supporting paragraphs in, 309
surveying sources for, 278–279
texts and authors essential to topic of, 276
thesis in, 307
thesis statement of, 302
title of, 302
transitional phrases in, 304–305
voice of, 301
"Works Cited" or "Works Consulted" in, 298,
    310–311
  see also Documentation; Library
Resources in Education, 286
Restrictive adjective clause, *see* Essential adjective
    clause
Results, transitional markers signaling, 178–179
Reversal
  conjunctive adverbs expressing, 83
  transitional markers signaling, 178
Revising
  for cause and effect, 96–97
  for chronological order, 91–92
  for classification, 105–106
  for comparing and contrasting, 100
  evaluation, 231
  first draft, 58–62
  for illustration method, 88–89
  infinitives considered in, 265–266
  paragraphing considered in, 125, 126–128,
    135
  persuasive essay, 251–259
  repetition and reference considered in, 164–
    165
  research paper, 300–301
  sentences combined with subordinate clause
    noted in, 153
  summary, 144
  supporting sentences considered in, 138
  synthesis, 188
  topic sentences noted in, 131–132
  unity of paragraphs considered in, 141
  see also Final editing

Role-playing, for anticipating opposition to persuasive essay, 249–250
Rough draft, *see* Drafts
Run-on sentence, 326–327
  comma splice as, 328–329

Sears List of Subject Headings, 275
Second draft, 62–65
  analyzing, 65–68
  of persuasive essay, 255–257
  see also Drafts
Self, writer's notebook describing, 233–234
Seliger, Susan, "Can Stress Be Good for You?" 129–130
Semicolon
  with conjunctive adverbs, 79, 82–83
  sentences combined with, 76
Sentence fragments, 323–324
Sentence patterns, 40–46
  adverbs and adverbs increased in single sentence, 40
  appositives, 155–156, 203, 341–342
  coordinate conjunctions combining parts and whole sentences, 43–44
  correlative conjunctions, 206–207
  gerunds, 238, 331, 353
  infinitives, 265–266, 353
  it for emphasis, 320
  nominative absolutes, 317
  noun clauses linked by *that*, 120
  participles, 235, 353
  relative clauses, 117–118
  semicolon combining sentences, 76
  semicolon with conjunctive adverbs, 79, 82–83
  with subordinate clauses, 152–153
Sentences, 140
  combining, 40, *see also* Sentence patterns
  comma splices, 328–329
  imitating favorite, 150–151
  irrelevent, 138–141
  major supporting, 138, 180–181
  minor supporting, 138, 180
  run-on, 326–327
  supporting, 135–138
  transitional, 138
  see also Paragraphs; Topic sentence
Similes, in writer's notebook, 115
  extended, 198
Simplicity, of academic voice, 222
Sleeping on the Wing (Koch), 264
Social Science Index, 281–282
Source, discovery questions about, 24

Specialized encyclopedias, for research paper, 276
Specialized indexes, 281–283
  computerized, 286
Strong verbs, 354
  irregular, 355–358
Subject, 354
  infinitives as, 265
Subject Guide to Books in Print, 276, 313
Subject heading
  of card catalog, 275
  on note cards, 287, 289
Subject Index of the Christian Science Monitor, 283
Subject-verb agreement, 344–346
Subordinate clauses, 152–153
Subordinate conjunctions, 152, 353
  dependent clauses beginning with, 324
Summary
  for note taking, 287
  one-paragraph, 144
  transitional markers signaling, 178–179
Supporting paragraphs, 53, 86
  brainstorming for, 53–55
  final draft considering, 66
  in research paper, 309
  see also Patterns of development
Supporting sentences, 135–138
  major and minor, 138, 180–181
Sweetham, George, "The Computer at the Wedding," 196–197
Synthesis, writing a, 187–193

Taking Charge of Your Health (Cousins), 163, 164
"Technology Alone Is Not Enough—People Provide the Missing Link Between the Disabled and Computers" (Tyre), 194–195
Tense of verbs, 354–358
Tentative thesis, sources for research paper chosen based on, 277
Tentative thesis statement, 16, 22–23
  argument from, 245–246
  choosing, 30–31
  combining methods forming, 27–30
  defining a problem forming, 26–27
  discovery questions forming, 23–25, 29–30
  focused free writing forming, 21–23, 28–30
  for persuasive essay, 243
Tentative topic, 17–19
That
  noun clauses linked by, 120
  relative clauses introduced with, 117

Thesis
  debatable, 242–243
  major and minor paragraph developing, 128
  of paragraph, *see* Topic sentence
  paragraph developing one, 126, 128
  repetition of word mentioned in, 161–162
  in research paper, 305
  research paper repeating mention of, 300, 307
  topic sentences expressing, 131
  see also Tentative thesis statement
Thesis paragraph
  becoming your own reader of, 51–53
  dividing in two, 127–128
  drafting, 48–53
  final draft considering, 66
  role of the reader considered in drafting, 50–51
  second draft changing, 63–64
Thesis statement, 87
  brainstorming evaluated with, 55
  final draft considering, 66
  first draft analyzed regarding, 58–62
  of persuasive essay, 251–252, 253
  in research paper, 302
  thesis paragraph clarifying, 48–49
  thesis paragraph providing background for, 49
  see also Patterns of development
Third draft, *see* Final draft
Time relationship, conjunctive adverbs expressing, 83
  see also Chronological order
Time words, for chronological order, 92
Tone, *see* Voice
Topic
  defining a problem exploring, 26–27
  discovery questions exploring, 23–25, 29–30
  free writing on discovering thesis, 21–23, 28–30
  narrowing, 17–19
  tentative, 17–19
Topic sentence, 130–135
  answer to question as, 133–134
  function of, 131–132
  as last sentence, 132–133
  placement, 132–135
  restating in first and last sentences, 134–135
  as second sentence, 133
  summary noting, 144
Traditional viewpoint, challenging, 72
Transitional markers and sentences, coherence achieved through, 138, 173–179
  between paragraphs, 176–177
  context and, 179–180

  definition, 173
  limitations of, 174–175
  list of, 173, 177–179
  in research paper, 304–305
  within paragraphs, 173–176
Trite expressions, avoiding, 349
Trivia questions, in writer's notebook, 315
Twain, Mark, 35
Tyre, Terian, "Technology Alone Is Not Enough—People Provide Missing Link Between the Disabled and Computers," 194–195

Unity
  outlining indicating, 66
  of paragraphs, 128, 138–141

Van Gelder, Lindsy, "Computers," 195–196
Verb phrase, 354
Verbs
  active voice, 352
  collecting those expressing metaphorical relationship, 150
  future perfect tense, 355
  future tense, 355
  gerund, 238, 353
  infinitive, 265–266, 353
  irregular, 355–358
  participle, 353
  passive voice, 346, 353
  past perfect tense, 355
  past tense, 355
  predicate and, 354
  present perfect tense, 355
  present tense, 354
  principal parts of, 354, 355–358, *see also* Infinitive; Past participle; Past tense
  strong, 354, 355–358
  subject agreement with, 344–346
  weak, 355
Viewpoint, challenging traditional, 72
Visualization, for writing process, 33
Voice, 211–232
  academic, 220–224
  active, 352
  authorial, 211–216
  balance between formal and informal, 213–214
  consistency in, 67
  distant and formal, 212–213
  of first draft, 57
  humor in, 214–215
  passive, 346, 353

personal and familiar, 211, 215–216
of persuasive essay, 252, 253, 255
of research paper, 301
of second draft, 65

Wall Street Journal Index, 283
We, use of, 224
Weak verb, 355
Which, relative clauses introduced with, 117
Who
   relative clauses introduced with, 117
   whom distinct from, 331–332
Whom
   relative clauses introduced with, 117–118
   who distinct from, 331–332
wh words, noun clauses introducing, 268–269
Word choice, 348–350
Wordiness, 346–347

Words, associations for, 263
Working bibliography, 273–278
   see also Library
"Works Cited," 298
"Works Consulted," 298, 310–311
Writer's notebook, 1–15
   collecting ideas in, 4–6
   free writing section in, 2–4
   writing habits analyzed in, 6–12
Writer's questionnaire, awareness of writing process by, 7–12
Writer's voice, *see* Voice
Writing process
   writer's notebook analyzing personal, 6–12
   writer's questionnaire analyzing, 7–12

Young, Gordon, "Chocolate: Food of the Gods," 109–111